# New Essays

## IN

# Ethics and Public Policy

**Edited by**
**Kai Nielsen and Steven C. Patten**

©CANADIAN ASSOCIATION FOR PUBLISHING IN PHILOSOPHY
GUELPH, ONTARIO
1982

ISSN 0045-5091                    ISBN 0-919491-08-1

# Table of Contents

# Table of Contents

## EDITORS' PREFACE

The select bibliographies at the end of each section have been put together by the authors. They represent a limited set of readings that the authors judge to be of particular value on the topics of the essays.

The editors of this volume gratefully acknowledge the advice and assistance of Lila Spencer, Barry Allen and Lana Cooke.

K.N.
S.C.P.

CANADIAN JOURNAL OF PHILOSOPHY
Supplementary Volume VIII, 1982

# Mechanics on Duty: The Limitations of a Technical Definition of Moral Expertise for Work in Applied Ethics

ARTHUR L. CAPLAN, The Hastings Center

## I. Applied Ethics Comes of Age

A former Prime Minister of Israel is alleged to have said that her country would never ascend to the status of authentic statehood until it possessed certain well-known social attributes — organized crime, prostitution, and corruption. These features, while obviously undesirable, were she felt, reliable indices of societal maturation. This anecdote is suggestive in understanding current events pertaining to the field of applied ethics.

Philosophers have produced a massive body of opinion and argument on a diverse range of subjects under the rubric of applied (or practical) ethics. Moreover, they have assumed positions on various panels, commissions, governmental bodies and committees in the hope of making an informed contribution to the formulation of institutional and public policy. These accomplishments have begun to elicit the kinds of attributes commonly associated with philosophical maturation — exposées, debunkings, refutations, and ideologically informed critiques. These activities are no more welcome in philosophy than are crime and vice in modern societies but they do indicate that a certain level of development has been attained.

In its infancy roughly fifteen years ago applied ethics was a field concerned mainly with establishing its existence. Various individuals and groups went about the business of creating both the internal and external signposts of philosophical birth — speciality journals, professional society interest groups, centers and institutes, proper sub-speciality designations — e.g., bioethics, environmental ethics, etc. — and appropriate courses in academic departments. Many scholars within philosophy dismissed these initial efforts as faddish, pecuniary or both. Many of these critics were involved in the field of ethics *proper,* meaning metaethics. It seemed intellectually fraudulent to these philosophers to offer ethical expertise about issues of public policy in lieu of any philosophical consensus concerning the validity of any particular normative theory. Without agreement on such a theory social prescription would be both premature and groundless.

Despite these worries concerning the lack of a consensual base for applied work in ethics the field flourished. The degree of its success within both ethics and political philosophy can easily be seen by examining the content of anthologies and textbooks in these areas. A comparison between books dating from the mid-nineteen-sixties and those in widest use today reveals that normative policy concerns have replaced the metaethical focus that characterized books from the earlier period.[1]

Beyond the confines of academic philosophy a large and eager audience appeared to receive the findings of those doing work in applied ethics. Policy makers in diverse fields such as medicine, government, the military, nursing, law, business, engineering and foreign affairs began to turn more and more to those doing applied work for inspiration, advice and even, in some cases, concrete answers.

Applied ethics has surely 'arrived' as an active and vibrant area of philosophical endeavor. Indeed, a number of laudatory assessments of the health and prospects of the field have recently appeared in the literature.[2] One report even goes so far as to claim that applied ethics

---

1 See chapter one of Bernard Rosen and Arthur L. Caplan, *Ethics in the Undergraduate Curriculum* (Hastings-on-Hudson, NY: The Hastings Center 1981).

2 For example, M.G. Singer, 'Recent Trends and Future Prospects in Ethics,' *Metaphilosophy,* **12** (1981) 207-23

deserves credit for rescuing the field of ethics as it teetered on the brink of total and utter irrelevancy during the nineteen-sixties.[3]

Other less effusive status reports have, however, also recently appeared. These criticisms do not issue from the sort of metaethical anxiety that fueled an earlier generation of critical responses. Rather, the present crop of worries is rooted in both political and pragmatic concerns. Those with resolute beliefs on both ends of the political spectrum have begun to fret over the status accorded applied ethics in many circles.[4] Not a few of the doctors, lawyers, businessmen, and public officials whose initial hopes for moral enlightenment had been so high have begun to despair over the fruits of philosophical labors in applied ethics. Their disappointment has been particularly acute over the inability of philosophers and others to provide answers to moral problems of the sort that arise in the course of day-to-day work in hospitals, corporations and government.[5]

## II. The 'Poverty' of Applied Ethics

Cheryl Noble in a recent article in the journal *Working Papers*[6] mounts a sustained critique of applied ethics as it is currently practiced. She argues that the efforts of its philosophical practioners have had the infelicitous but unavoidable end-result of bolstering or reinforcing existing social institutions, practices and, most inexcusably, injustices. Applied ethics, on Noble's view, is doomed to fail primarily as a result of the fact that, despite philosophical wishes to the contrary, moral questions cannot be understood simply and purely in technical moral terms. She contends:

---

3   S. Toulmin, 'How Medicine Saved the Life of Ethics,' *Perspectives in Biology and Medicine,* **25** (1982) 736-50

4   M. Lilla, 'Ethos, "Ethics" and Public Service,' *The Public Interest,* **63** (1981) 3-17; P. Drucker, 'Ethical Chic,' *Forbes,* September 14, 1981, 159-63; J. Peter Euben, 'Philosophy and the Professions,' *Democracy,* (1981) 112-27

5   R. Morison, 'Bioethics After Two Decades,' *Hastings Center Report,* **11** (1981) 8-12

6   C. Noble, 'Ethics and Experts,' *Working Papers,* July/August 1980, 57-60

*Arthur L. Caplan*

> Because philosophers separate the task of moral criticism from that of social analysis, their conception of the kind of knowledge and insight needed to shed light on moral issues is unavoidably inadequate. Starting from a position of political and historical naïveté they inevitably arrive at conventional and tame conclusions drawn from a preexisting range of alternatives.[7]

What applied ethicists to in her view is act as hired pens, admittedly erudite ones, but, nonetheless, pens bought and beholden to the powerful and well ensconced. Furthermore, despite their capacity for technical reasoning philosophers simply do not have the knowledge necessary for solving practical moral problems. At best those in the field succeed in transforming complicated moral issues into the kind of simple-minded technicalities that philosophers delight in but that no one else deserves or needs.

Tacking in from an opposite political direction in another recent article is William J. Bennett, the current head of the National Endowment for the Humanities, who warns the unwary that

> one of the most serious ethical problems of our time has become the fad of the new ethics and its defenders.[8]

By the 'new ethics' Bennett is referring to the current efforts of philosophers to help formulate public policy.

What Bennett finds dangerous about applied ethics is, interestingly, not all that different in a way from what disturbs Noble about the enterprise. He believes that applied ethics has become so enamored of analytical technique, logical skill and conceptual agility that no content can be discerned for all the intellectual fireworks. Bennett sees applied ethics as steering away from any pretense of character formulation or behavioral guidance with skepticism or relativism as the only outcomes likely to result:

> The sheer emptiness of this vision of ethics, its unwillingness to assert that some things are right and others wrong, thus becomes an unwitting ally of moral indifference, and worse.[9]

Noble views applied ethics as a professionalized effort to usurp moral authority by abstracting moral issues from social reality. Bennett

---

7  Noble, 59

8  W.J. Bennett, 'Getting Ethics,' *Commentary,* December 1980, 65

9  Bennett, 64

sees in this area of philosophy nothing but an emphasis on technique — the mastery of argument, concepts, and theories — in the expertise claims of those who are doing some form of applied ethics. He fears that only sophisticated moral wrangling can eventuate from such an insubstantial enterprise.

Not all of the current audience for the musings of those in applied ethics seems satisfied with the philosophical fruits they now receive. Aside from the sour-grapes mutterings of those few individuals whose particular ox has been gored as a result of a morally inspired policy change about 'self appointed Ayatollahs of ethics,' many of those in policy or professional settings seem apprehensive about what it is that applied ethicists have to offer them. One physician has argued for a rather concrete standard of achievement for applied ethics in his profession:

> If clinical ethics ... can be shown to improve medical care, the resistance to medical ethics will be effectively stifled ... medical ethics will become an integrated aspect of professional life ... when it is no longer artificially divorced from the practice of medicine itself.[10]

However this physician seems unconvinced that the requisite improvements have as yet come about.

Other physicians seem less than eager to have the sage counsel of those in applied ethics in practicing their profession. In his most recent annual letter to the members of the British Medical Association, the secretary of that organization, Dr. J.D.J. Havard, has assured his fellow physicians that the BMA is ready to do battle with meddlesome ethicists:

> The BMA will be preparing for renewed attacks on the profession by pressure groups ... they have little real understanding of the clinical and ethical dilemmas which face practicing doctors ... or of the daily decisions which have to be taken. What is certain is that the law in its present state is wholly inappropriate to determine such issues as are the sociologists, philosophers, theologians and worst of all the politicians who seem suddenly so anxious to pronounce on medicine albeit at a distance ... a major task of the BMA will be to protect the profession and patients from the ill-advised attempts by outside groups to regulate and restrict the decisions which doctors have to take daily in the course of their professional work.[11]

---

10  M. Siegler, 'A Legacy of Osler: Teaching Clinical Ethics at the Bedside,' *Journal of the American Medical Association,* **239** (1981) 953

11  J.D.J. Havard, 'Letter from the Secretary,' *British Medical Journal,* **283** (1981) 1071

Even if applied ethics set itself the goal of reforming policy and practice in practical contexts such as medicine as Noble and Bennett demand, it is not evident that all of the intended target audience would by sympathetic to their efforts.

The common thread running through the comments of the two medical doctors is that the moral life of medicine only emerges in the daily actions and activities of this profession. Dr. Siegler thinks that applied ethics had better aim directly at the reform of clinical practice. Dr. Havard seems to believe that the gulf between clinical practice and moral talk is too broad to ever be bridged. Both physicians cite the complexities of actual professional practice as phenomena that must be reckoned with in analyzing moral issues in medicine. Similar claims about the epistemological importance of practice and activity have been made for a wide variety of other fields, crafts and professions many of which have formed the subject matters of contemporary applied ethics.

There seem to be a large number of doubts and reservations surfacing in various publications as to the legitimacy and feasibility of doing work in applied ethics. Most of these worries seem to have their roots in skepticism concerning the nature of the expertise possessed by those doing applied ethics. Many of the current critics of applied work believe that philosophers lack the kinds of knowledge requisite for attaining the goals they believe should be attained. Philosophers and others in the field of applied ethics do not seem to have been either clear or persuasive about exactly what goals they believe are appropriate for their endeavors. More importantly, they do not seem to have articulated the nature of the skills and knowledge that they possess such that the likelihood of attaining any goals could be ascertained. Since the goals that are likely to be attained are contingent upon the expertise that is available to those doing applied work it will be impossible to fairly evaluate the various sorts of criticisms that have been made of this kind of work without some analysis of the notion of expertise as it pertains to morality.

## III. What Is Moral Expertise?

Philosophers, perhaps surprisingly, have not written a great deal about the notion of moral expertise. However, what they have written displays a remarkable unanimity of opinion concerning what constitutes expertise in morality. Peter Singer in a discussion of the concept in the journal *Analysis* unpacks the notion by describing the skills of a moral expert:

> Someone familiar with moral concepts and with moral arguments, who has ample time to gather information and to think about it, may reasonably be expected to reach a soundly based conclusion more often than someone who is unfamiliar with moral concepts and moral arguments and has little time.[12]

Expertise in ethics consists for Singer in having the following skills: (a) familiarity with moral concepts, (b) training in the logic of moral argument, and (c) the luxury of time to gather information and think about moral questions.

Tom Beauchamp[13] and Richard Eggerman[14] in recent discussions of the nature of applied ethics appear to agree with Singer's analysis. Eggerman states that moral philosophers are 'masters of concepts, principles, and models that provide a fundamental rationale for the various phenomena of the moral life.'[15] Beauchamp adds an additional element to Singer's noting that philosophers trained in ethics are often able to deductively trace out the consequences of particular actions or policies better than other persons can. Other recent discussions of applied ethics also pinpoint the mastery of moral theories and analytical skills as the basis of expertise claims by those in applied ethics.[16]

Given these analyses of moral expertise it is easy to see where critics such as Noble and Bennett find fuel for their complaints about applied ethics. The definitions of expertise proposed by Singer and others are grounded solely in theoretical mastery and analytical skills. On this interpretation of expertise philosophers doing applied ethics are qualified to make contributions to the moral discourse of practical affairs only by dint of their capacity to serve as conceptual policemen. Their skills in argument and their familiarity with moral theory will allow them to pinpoint logical confusions in the views of others, to subsume information

---

12  P. Singer, 'Moral Experts,' *Analysis,* **32** (1972) 117

13  T.L. Beauchamp, 'What Philosophers Can Offer,' *Hastings Center Report,* **12** (1982) 13-14

14  R.W. Eggerman, 'Moral Philosophers and Moral Advisors,' *Metaphilosophy,* **10** (1979) 159-71

15  Eggerman, 168

16  K. Danner Clouser, 'Bioethics,' in W. Reich, ed., *Encylopedia of Bioethics* (New York: Free Press 1978) Volume 1, 115-27; R. Munson, *Intervention and Reflection: Basic Issues in Medical Ethics* (Belmont, CA: Wadsworth 1979); T.L. Beauchamp and J. Childress, *Principles of Biomedical Ethics* (New York: Oxford University Press 1979); P. Singer, *Practical Ethics* (New York: Cambridge University Press 1980); M.D. Bayles, 'Moral Theory and Application,' Leys Memorial Lecture, Southern Illinois University, April, 1982

under relevant moral theories which are for the most part unknown to laymen, and, to carefully work through the moral implications of various policies and practices in light of these theories.

There is nothing in this conception of moral expertise that would even remotely suggest that moral philosophers know better than others what behavioral or policy ends are suitable for guiding human conduct. Nor is there any hint that expertise thus defined will demand a knowledge of any particular type of information practical, social or otherwise. On the view outlined by Singer and other writers moral expertise is a matter of analytical skills enlightened by moral theories and nothing more.

## IV. Applied Ethics As Moral Engineering

The analysis of moral expertise summarized above is closely wedded to a model of application which might best be termed the 'engineering model' of applied ethics.[17] It presumes that application in ethical contexts is akin to application in such scientific contexts as engineering, medicine, and other technical arts. This model presumes that:

(a) There is a body of knowledge that persons can be more or less knowledgeable about;

(b) This knowledge becomes applied by mechanically deducing conclusions from theories in light of relevant empirical facts;

(c) The deduction can and must be carried out in an impartial, disinterested and value-free manner.

The model reflects a popular view of the nature of expertise in the sciences. In those fields which aim at practical goals, such as engineering or medicine, good practioners are in possession of a body of theoretically based knowledge and a set of laws produced over the eons by more theoretically inclined (and clever) natural scientists. When fac-

---

17 A.L. Caplan, 'Ethical Engineers Need Not Apply: The State of Applied Ethics Today,' *Science, Technology and Human Values*, **6** (1980) 27-33, and, 'Can Applied Ethics Be Effective in Health Care and Should It Strive To Be?', *Ethics* (forthcoming 1983)

ed with practical problems such as building a bridge or ameliorating a disease, practioners, on this model, simply gather information and feed it into their existing store of theories, laws, and models. They do not engage in the setting of goals or aims, but rather through the process of deduction determine the optimal means for attaining the goal or aim that is requested of them.

For the purposes of this paper it is irrelevant whether this popular conception accurately describes what practioners in scientific fields actually do in the course of their work. What is important is the belief current in many quarters of philosophy that the engineering model is the appropriate one for describing what those in applied ethics can and should do. The applied ethicist on the engineering model serves as a go-between for theoreticians of normative ethics and denizens of the everyday world. Having mastered the extant range of normative theories and moral traditions and armed with an understanding of deductive logic the applied ethicist is able to combine theory with empirical data to provide solutions to various moral quandaries which are raised by those persons concerned with practical affairs or public policy formulation. The metaphor that seems most apt for describing the functions of the philosopher engaged in applied work on the engineering model is that of a computer. Properly programmed with moral theory, the applied ethicist can be fed various bits of data, and, after a series of rather complicated logical operations, will disgorge definitive moral conclusions.

## V. Moral Problems Cannot Be Dissected with Blunt Instruments.

The picture of applied work in ethics conveyed by the engineering model and by the technical interpretation of ethical expertise which is so widespread in the philosophical literature is simply wrong. The model does not explain which normative theories ought be included in the applied ethicist's quiver. Nor is it at all obvious what weightings and orderings ought be given to these theories when they come into conflict as they inevitably will. Most importantly, as Noble, Bennett and many hands-on practioners have argued, the resolution of moral issues demands more than the ability to marry moral theory with the facts.

There is something quite peculiar about the idea that the basic skill requisite for success in applied ethics is competency in argument and logic. If this were true it would suggest that practical ethics is really a matter for logicians not moral philosophers. Logicians are far more likely to be able to detect bad arguments and catch logical fallacies than are those trained in ethics.

Additionally, the focus on analytical skill puts the person doing applied ethics into the bizarre position of remaining ethically neutral and personally disengaged from the entire business of ethical analysis. Kierkegaard's comment about an acquaintance who wished to remain indifferent in considering moral issues is telling against this claim:

> There is something treacherous in wishing to be merely an observor.[18]

The exclusive emphasis on technical skills evident in the engineering model places the philosopher in a totally passive stance with respect to the moral problems he or she is being asked to consider. The applied ethicist has no role except that of shaping and crafting the raw factual materials supplied by others with the tools of moral theory.

The charges of cooptation levelled by critics from both ends of the political spectrum derives directly from the value-neutrality implicit in a view of application which emphasizes only mechanical deduction from theory. The disdain for applied ethics evident in the writings of many practioners and policy makers arises from the peripheral role accorded all forms of expertise except facility with moral theories. In both cases the critics seem correct. The views of expertise and application current in applied ethics do seem to severely constrain the kinds of contributions that can be made to the formulation of professional and public policy.

## VI. The Lure of Technical Expertise

How has it happened that those in applied ethics have come to define themselves into as confining a space as the engineering model permits? In part this has come about because the demands for concrete answers and policy recommendations have come from those involved in extremely complicated areas of policy formulation. Many professions have grown increasingly specialized over the years, and as a result have developed traditions of farming out problems to groups of sub-specialists. In such a climate it is all too easy to view ethics as just one more area of technical sub-specialization. In medicine, for example, a large variety of specialists are involved in the care of patients. It is all too

---

18  S. Kierkegaard, *Either/Or*, Volume II, trans., W. Lowrie (Oxford: Oxford University Press 1946) 14

easy to succumb to the view that the person doing applied ethics represents one more consultant that will sometimes have to be brought into patient care.

Similarly, at the level of public policy participants have grown used to the idea that massive problems can best be handled by dividing them into smaller problems which can then be assigned to a particular group of experts. For example, if the officials in a particular city want to build a public park they know they must call upon the skills of engineers, economists, urban planners, architects, psychologists and demographers. If these officials are contemplating closing a municipal hospital they will call upon the services of physicians, public health officials, economists and, perhaps, those in medical ethics. If they do call upon those in medical ethics their expectation is that these persons will discharge their tasks in a manner akin to that utilized by these other types of experts. Given these expectations, it is quite tempting for those in applied ethics to cast their expertise into an established framework for carrying out policy formulation rather than to try and specify other models that might better describe their skills.

The engineering model has also flourished as a result of the emphasis, or even obsession, still evident in ethics with the justification of normative theories. Meta-ethical worries about the legitimacy of moral discourse may have receded into the philosophical past but arguments over the adequacy of the underpinnings of various normative theories have taken their place.[19] It is only natural that those persons who were trained in ethics in the post-sixties period would be caught up in the frenzied hunt for the Holy Grail of the a priori defensible normative theory. Justification has become for ethics what explanation has been for many years in the philosophy of science — both literally and figuratively. Most moral philosophers believe that only mechanical deduction from a hierarchical set of ordered axiomatic principles will suffice to justify a particular moral view. This view of justification obviously apes an older view in the philosophy of science that explanation consists only in the deduction of statements from a hierarchical set of ordered nomological principles. In their efforts to make ethics respectable, moral philosophers adopted a scientistic view of morality that emphasizes the role of theory and deduction in moral analysis. The engineering model of applied ethics is a logical spin-off from this scientistic conception of ethics.

The paucity of the goals deemed attainable by those in applied ethics and excoriated by its various critics is a direct consequence of the in-

---

19  K. Nielsen, 'On Needing a Moral Theory,' *Metaphilosophy,* **13** (1982) 97-116

ability of those in the field to look beyond the confines of the engineering model. The siren song of technical expertise has lured many philosophers working in both professional and policy settings into the fallacious belief that it is their role and their role alone to settle moral questions and give moral advice. The easy way in which those who have attempted to analyze the nature of moral expertise have slipped into discussions of the attributes and skills of experts illustrates this point.

The fact that a person is in possession of moral expertise, technically defined sensu Singer, does not thereby render such a person 'expert' at moral matters. As Gilbert Ryle insisted there is a sharp difference between 'knowing that' and 'knowing how.' A person may possess all sorts of expertise concerning a wide variety of subjects but such knowledge in itself does not guarantee that the person will be skilled in its application.[20]

The risk of the abuse of expertise in the name of engineering solutions to moral problems is made even greater when one remembers the power and authority that surround ethics in most cultures. While the citizens of the Western democracies may not view the discipline of ethics as something deserving of very much economic support, morality is still seen as the discourse of ultimate appeal in political and policy affairs. Moral experts could easily trump the ethical, social, and political views of the laity by baptizing a decision or policy as moral or immoral. Thus, arguments for the existence of various forms of expertise with regard to ethics should not be taken as simultaneously justifying the creation of moral mandarins. The fact that expertise concerning ethics may be possible does not in itself provide sufficient rationale for endowing some individuals with authority over moral matters. Pace Plato, expertise alone is not enough for legitimating authority. The question of what societies should do with those who possess expertise in ethics is a political one that appears to be no different from political decisions about the kinds of rewards, status and powers that ought be granted individuals in possession of any form of expertise.

The fact that a conceptual gulf exists between expertise and socially sanctioned experts suggests that the examination of the properties of experts is a poor way to go about discerning the nature of expertise in any domain. If the title of 'expert' is as likely to be conferred for political reasons as it is for reasons of special expertise then efforts to tease out the nature of expertise by examining the properties and activities of experts are not likely to succeed. At best what might be discovered are the kinds of roles, tasks, and powers various societies or groups have deem-

---

20  B. Szabados, 'On "Moral Expertise" ', *Canadian Journal of Philosophy*, **8** (1978) 117-29

ed useful to assign to particular persons at a particular time. What Singer, Beauchamp and others have discovered about moral expertise in their investigation of moral experts are the kinds of skills that have allowed the engineering model to flourish in contemporary liberal societies and professions. Moral 'experts' are restricted to the possession of technical skills in argumentation and logic, value neutrality, and tolerant passivity. These are the only traits contemporary Western societies will allow of their moral 'experts.' There is no reason, however, to think that these traits give an accurate portrait of either the nature of moral expertise, or, the kinds of skills someone doing applied ethics ought to possess.

## VII. Moral Diagnosis and Moral Judgment

The major failing of the engineering model is that it emphasizes technical abilities and skills which those actually working in the field rarely use in the manner suggested by the model. While it is possible to deduce an unanticipated conclusion from a factually supplemented normative theory this is so unusual an event that its occurrence is more likely to result in a publication in a philosophical journal than in an announcement to policy makers in a hospital, board room or legislature. There are at least two other skills which those in applied ethics find as useful as logical analysis which are key components of ethical expertise – diagnostic skill and moral judgment.

Applied moral philosophers will often sheepishly admit to each other in private conversation that their greatest contribution to practical affairs seems to be not the provision of answers but the discovery of problems where none were previously thought to exist. While the engineering model makes this contribution a vice rather than a virtue it would seem to be precisely what applied ethics does best in facilitating the creation of sound public policies.

Because of their training in ethics, moral philosophers are, as Singer and others correctly note, familiar with moral theories and concepts. This knowledge often permits them to see moral issues that other persons do not. For example, someone sensitive to the various senses of paternalism, consent and voluntariness articulated in moral philosophy is likely to be able to raise intelligent questions about the consensual transactions operative in medicine, nursing, law or social work. While such persons may be uncertain or skeptical about the validity of any particular normative theory or principles, such reservations do not prevent them from raising questions about prevailing practices and customs in the light of normative considerations. Indeed, in some ways agnostics have a distinct advantage over advocates of particular normative theories in raising questions about ordinary moral beliefs in that they are able to utilize a wider set of normative theories in constructing critiques.

Moral diagnosis, the skills of discerning moral issues and classifying moral problems, would seem to be just as important a component of moral expertise as the ability to solve obvious moral problems. This skill accurately describes what those in applied ethics often in fact do upon entering into the realm of public affairs. The good applied ethicist is a careful student of the customs, mores and practices current in the particular area of public life that is being examined. Only by having a solid footing in descriptive ethics can a useful contribution be made to practical matters. Physicians, lawyers, military officers and government officials do not need to be told that acts such as lying, cheating or stealing are morally wrong and make for bad public policy as revealed by deduction from the latest normative theory of a Rawls, Nozick, Brandt, Singer or Gewirth. What they do need to know and what moral philosophers are well-qualified to tell them in virtue of their expertise is whether particular actions or policies might, unbeknownst to them, fall into one of these suspect moral categories.

The moral philosopher doing applied ethics is not so much a moral engineer as a moral diagnostician. Non-philosophers almost always come to those in applied ethics seeking advice or solutions for the moral problems that they recognize as such. But the applied ethicist is no more bound to accept the legitimacy of any moral problem as it is given than is the diagnostician in medicine bound to accept the patient's complaints or symptoms as definitive of a medical problem. Just as the physician can oftentimes discern the underlying cause of a symptom, or can detect the presence of medical problems long before they become apparent to the layman, the philosopher doing applied ethics should be able to (a) see moral issues others have missed, (b) anticipate issues before they actually occur, and (c) properly classify the moral problems which arise in the ordinary ebb and flow of events in public and professional life. A knowledge of moral theories, traditions and concepts allows the moral philosopher to see the normative aspects of ordinary events in ways that those more directly involved do not and sometimes will not.

The person doing applied ethics rarely tries to lead the practitioner or the public to the promised land of right conduct or sound policy. Rather, the applied ethicist attempts to show persons that problems and pitfalls may exist where none were previously discerned. Admittedly this can be an anxiety producing activity for those individuals whose behavior or policies are under critical examination. However, the fact that it is hardly fun to visit other diagnosticians such as a doctor, dentist or automobile mechanic does not mean that it would imprudent to do so. Fears about the relativistic consequences of subjecting public policy and professional practices to the cold light of moral examination as expressed by Bennett and Havard are not borne out by the diagnostic and prophylactic practices enganged in by experts in many other fields.

If it is granted that diagnostic acumen constitutes a large part of the expertise possessed by those trained in ethics then the question naturally arises as to whether there exists a logic underlying this skill. Is there an algorithm that can be mastered and taught such that diagnosis in moral matters could be understood as a skill rather than as a mysterious art?

The question is not easily answered. But it certainly is deserving of careful examination. By focusing solely on the process of deductive problem-solving and the attendent issue of what consitutes proper justification of normative claims applied ethicists have missed an opportunity to understand a process that is critical for their own work as well as for ethics as a whole. The ways in which moral phenomena are identified and individuated are surely worthy of careful consideration since the answers given to moral questions depend entirely on the nature of the questions that are asked.

Skill in identifying and framing moral problems is not the only element of ethical expertise missing from the engineering model's conception of work in applied ethics. Those trained in ethics have a set of traditions and theories which allow them to deliberate about and judge moral issues in ways not available to the layman. Moral judgment is a skill that forms a key part of ethical expertise.

Good judgment in ethics consists in part of being able to use moral knowledge to see moral issues from different points of view. Moral theory and principles are the tools by which moral issues can be examined from a wide variety of perspectives. John Dewey offered an excellent antidote to the neutrality and passivity characteristic of the engineering approach to applied work:

> I cannot resolve this practical situation which faces me merely by looking at it. I must attack it with such instruments of analysis as I have at hand. What we call moral rules are precisely such instruments of analysis.[21]

Good judgment in ethics is not merely a function of the rapidity with which a principle can be applied to a case. It consists in the sensitivity and thoughfulness which are brought to bear on the history and circumstances pertaining to any given situation, action or policy. Good judgment about moral matters demands the ability to know how and

---

21   J. Ratner, ed., *The Philosophy of John Dewey* (New York: Holt 1928) 314

whether various kinds of relationships alter the duties and rights of various individuals. Different principles may be relevant in thinking through a case depending upon the presence or absence of such relationships as friendship, kinship, leadership, etc. Some professions and social roles may in certain situations admit of exemptions from ordinary moral rules — e.g., truth-telling in medicine — while other moral rules may pertain only to special social and professional roles — e.g., the principle of confidentialty for attorneys and psychiatrists.[22] The more knowledge one has about the various kinds of relationships and roles that exist among individuals in everyday life the better skilled one will be in the exercise of practical judgment with regard to normative matters.

The social sciences, law, history and literature would seem to have far more to contribute to the cultivation of moral judgment than the study of either ethics or philosophy. Without some sensitivity to the effect on morality of the various and constantly shifting nature of human relationships and some acquaintance with the moral values associated with, to borrow Bradley's famous phrase, a station and its duties, the application of theory based principles to the complexities of practical affairs is likely to be extremely heavy-handed. While there is no doubt a certain ineffable dimension to the skill of sound moral judgment,[23] those persons who are trained or skilled in the social sciences and its cognate fields are more likely to employ abstract universal principles in an intelligent manner. Since moral principles are only useful when they are supplemented with empirical information, the richer the information that is available to the applied ethicist, the better the quality of analysis that is likely to result.

## VIII. What Aims Should Guide Work in Applied Ethics?

Moral diagnosis and moral judgment are two of the most important factors missing from the current analysis of what constitutes expertise in applied ethics. The engineering model with its dogged focus upon the

---

22  These role-specific rules illustrate what Alan Goldman has termed 'strong differentiation' in professional ethics. See his *The Moral Foundations of Professional Ethics* (Totowa, NJ: Rowman and Littlefield 1980) chapter one.

23  The ineffability of moral judgment is defended in S. Toulmin, 'The Tyranny of Principles,' *Hastings Center Report,* **11** (1981) 4-10, and in C. Larmore, 'Moral Judgment,' *Review of Metaphysics,* **35** (1981-2) 275-96.

problem-solving skills of moral philosophers degrades and distorts the contribution that those in applied ethics can make to public policy and practical affairs. The model relegates the applied ethicist to the role of a mindless and impersonal calculator constantly brokering between high-powered moral theoreticians and needy practitioners. It oversimplifies the task of ethical analysis by equating the process with the mechanical application of theory-based axiomatic principles to pre-packaged cases. It encourages a suspect view of ethics as consisting solely of a method for producing after-the-fact justifications for prevailing normative beliefs by stressing the technical nature of the moral philosopher's expertise. The model presents a highly distorted picture of those who do applied ethics as philosophical hacks who will supply the requisite principle, platitude, or palaver to those in a position to pay for them.

From a purely philosophical point of view the most regrettable consequence of the fallacious conception of expertise contained in the engineering model is that it prevents those in ethics from seeing what a truly mature field of applied ethics could offer to those interested in normative ethical theory. Applied ethics, properly understood, can provide a better understanding of individuation, identification and classification with respect to moral beliefs and moral acts. It can give a clearer picture than that usually available in ethics of the relationship that exists between descriptive ethics and normative ethics. A fully-developed applied ethics would afford the moral philosopher an opportunity to examine the delicate interplay that occurs among facts, social roles, and prescriptive principles in reaching moral decisions. And it would allow moral philosophers to better explicate the murky concepts of moral judgment, professional authority and political authority. Freed from the distorting influence of the engineering model, applied ethics can be seen for what it really is — a source of enrichment for moral discouse in professional and public affairs, and, an important resource for those interested in ethical theory.[24]

---

24 I would like to acknowledge the support of the National Endowment for the Humanities in the preparation of this manuscript.

*Arthur L. Caplan*

## Select Bibliography

Cheryl Noble, 'Ethics and Experts,' *Working Papers,* July 1980, 57-60

Peter Singer, 'Moral Experts,' *Analysis,* **32** (1972) 115-17

Peter Singer, *Practical Ethics* (New York: Cambridge University Press 1980)

Béla Szabados, 'On "Moral Expertise",' *Canadian Journal of Philosophy,* **8** (1978) 117-29

Alan Goldman, *The Moral Foundations of Professional Ethics* (Totowa, NJ: Rowman and Littlefield 1980)

Charles Larmore, 'Moral Judgment,' *Review of Metaphysics,* **35** (1981-2) 275-96

R.W. Eggerman, 'Moral Philosophers as Moral Advisors,' *Metaphilosophy,* **10** (1979) 159-71

A.L. Caplan, 'Can Applied Ethics Be Effective in Health Care and Should It Strive to Be?', *Ethics* (January, 1983; forthcoming)

CANADIAN JOURNAL OF PHILOSOPHY
Supplementary Volume VIII, 1982

# The Moral Equivalence of Action
# and Omission

JUDITH LICHTENBERG, University of Maryland

Is doing nothing sometimes as bad as doing something bad? In this or some less naive form the question I address in this paper is an old one that has been asked not only by philosophers and religious thinkers but also by ordinary people in their more reflective moments. We have recently seen its relevance to such issues as abortion, euthanasia, and the legitimate conduct of war. Active euthanasia is distinguished from passive, aiming to kill from killing as an unintended effect of one's aims, bringing about harm from letting it happen. The Catholic doctrine of the double effect endorses the moral distinction between what one positively does and what one allows to occur.

   The significance of the action/omission distinction also has crucial implications for central political issues, though this has not been adequately recognized. Libertarian views like Nozick's, according to which political coercion is limited to the classical nightwatchman functions of protection from force, fraud, theft and enforcement of contract, depend on the assumption of a necessary moral difference between action and omission. This is expressed in terms of individuals' rights and obligations: people have uncontracted negative rights and obligations but not uncontracted positive ones, and it is such fundmental rights and obliga-

19

tions that legitimize coercion.[1] The action/omission distinction is also at the heart of the controversy over negative and positive freedom.

Here I maintain that the fact of a strand of behavior's involving an action or an omission is per se morally irrelevant. In the first part I distinguish the various ways action and omission might be or are different — conceptually and morally, necessarily and practically — and consider some problems that result when these are confused. In II two ideal cases are presented which I believe reveal the equivalence of action and omission. In III-V I consider objections to this view, apparent counterexamples and their supporting arguments. Looking closely at the examples offered by both sides brings into focus the considerations proper to an agent deciding what to do. Morally relevant features fall under two general headings: (1) certainty or probability of the connection between an act or omission and the harm to be avoided; and (2) sacrifice or cost to the agent in having to forbear or to act. The idea that there is a moral difference between action and omission comes from comparing cases that are asymmetrical with respect to these features; when comparable cases are compared, the gulf disappears. This becomes especially clear as we break away from the paradigm of harmful behavior which has come to obscure our thinking — actions which result directly and immediately in harm — and attend to behaior along the continuum whose harmful effects are increasingly less direct and immediate, both in space and in time.[2]

## I

It is often said that a person's behavior can't be neatly divided into what he does and does not do. Yet unless action and omission can be distinguished, the question of their moral equivalence or difference isn't intelligible: there aren't two distinguishable things to be compared. Doubt about their distinctness arises from the realization that one has access to a strand of behavior only via some description of it, and that

---

1   Robert Nozick, *Anarchy, State, and Utopia* (New York: Basic Books 1974); e.g. pp. ix, 7, 32. For an extended argument for the claims made in this paragraph, see my *On Being Obligated to Give Aid: Moral and Political Arguments,* unpublished doctoral dissertation (City University of New York 1978) ch. 3.

2   For such a treatment, see *ibid.,* ch. 5.

the same strand can often be described alternatively in terms of something the agent did, or in terms of something he didn't do. So, e.g., if a parent doesn't feed his child and the child dies, one might say any of the following: he didn't feed his child; he starved his child; he let his child die; he caused his child's death. It would seem, then, that strands of behavior are not per se actions or omissions.

The puzzle here can on further reflection be dispelled. In the first place, it is clear that not every active verb corresponds to a positive action.[3] In saying the parent starved his child one does not say or imply that the parent performed physical actions that resulted in the child's death — on the contrary. The use of 'starve' emphasizes the significance of the parent's omission, as perceived by the speaker.

But the description of the parent as starving his child is not just an injection of the speaker's moral beliefs into his description. Compare the parent's behavior with another case. If a stranger doesn't give food to a beggar and the beggar dies, we will say that the stranger didn't feed the beggar, but not that he starved the beggar.[4] Yet the same strand of behavior — no physical actions relevant to the starving person's death — is involved in both cases. What warrants the different descriptions is that the parent has undertaken to care for his child, but the stranger has not undertaken to care for the beggar. Agreeing or undertaking to do something not only establishes a moral obligation; it also legitimizes certain otherwise inappropriate descriptions. Specifically, it legitimizes descriptions expanded in scope to include more than the bare omission. For the omission is, in light of the undertaking, no longer bare; it is not what I shall call a genuine or ex nihilo omission. The apparent similarity of the parent's and the stranger's behavior is illusory. Although both 'didn't feed,' the parent in addition *did certain things* (e.g. brought a child into the world) which warrant picking up the train of behavior at an earlier stage.

---

3   I.e. a physical occurrence. If actions are physical occurrences, then, contrary to the schoolbook view, verbs are not necessarily action words. But we may operate under the influence of the simpler picture: we may think that sacrificing a person, or treating him as a means, necessarily involves doing something rather than not doing. Nozick, e.g., assumes that one can satisfy the Kantian injunction not to treat a person as a means simply by forbearance. But whether one sacrifices someone or treats him as a means depends on the reasons for one's conduct See p. 34ff.

4   In other cases it would be odd to say of someone that he didn't *x*, even when he *didn't x*. One doesn't say 'He didn't feed *x*' unless there is some reason to think he would have, could have, should have, might have fed *x*. See Eric D'Arcy, *Human Acts* (Oxford: Clarendon Press 1963) 41ff.

For a large class of omissions — those that occur in the context of a prior agreement or undertaking of some kind — one has discretion to describe what happens either negatively or positively. Positive descriptions cover a longer strand of behavior of which the omission is only a part. By attending to such omissions one may be led to think there is no conceptual difference between action and omission.[5] For about a given segment of behavior it is not usually hard to distinguish physical movements from their absence. The question under consideration is whether one can be obligated to perform physical movements without having performed earlier physical movements — as, it is generally thought, one can be obligated *not* to perform physical movements without having performed earlier physical movements. (Nozick, for example, believes there is an uncontracted obligation not to commit aggression but no such obligation to give aid; and accordingly the state may coerce people not to commit aggression but not to aid others.)

Given the conceptual distinctness of action and omission, the question arises whether they are morally different or not. A person is committed to a moral difference between them if, given a pair of cases parallel in every respect except that one requires positive action and the other requires forbearance, he thinks the latter more morally binding than the former. Just what 'more morally binding' means will vary according to the particular moral theory and as the moral difference between action and omission is thought to be more or less significant. At the least one will have to say that given a pair of otherwise parallel cases, 'acting badly' is worse than 'omitting badly.'

It should be noted, however, that a moral difference of this kind will not do the work for which it is generally needed. To distinguish generically between, e.g., negative and positive rights, as Nozick does, action/omission must be not just one morally relevant feature among others but one which overrides others, which by itself generates a qualitative difference between cases requiring action and those requiring forbearance. It is not clear how one would argue for the stronger claim; since I deny even a weak difference, I leave this problem to those who need to solve it.

Necessary differences (both weak and strong) between action and omission are to be contrasted with practical differences. The latter might, in practice, be as significant as necessary ones: one might reach very different conclusions about cases because some morally relevant characteristic(s) were contingently connected — highly correlated — with the action/omission distinction. If, e.g., refraining ordinarily does

---

5  See Graham Hughes, 'Criminal Omissions,' *Yale Law Journal*, **67** (1958) 598; Orvill C. Snyder. 'Liability for Negative Conduct,' *Virginia Law Review*, **35** (1949).

not involve significant cost to the agent while positive action does, then this ought to be reflected in conclusions about most cases. But this question is different in kind from the question of a necessary difference; and the answers are not to be found in the same ways.

The distinction between a necessary difference between action and omission and a practical one would seem to be quite clear. Yet the claim that negative duties are more stringent than positive ones is sometimes ambiguous:

> It is an empirical fact that in most cases it is possible for a person not to inflict serious physical injury on any other person. It is also an empirical fact that in no case is it possible for a person to aid everyone who needs help ... In short, the negative duty of not killing can be discharged completely ... But the positive duty of saving can never be discharged completely.[6]

Since it isn't possible for a person to aid everyone who needs help, obviously one cannot be obligated to do so. But it in no way follows that one's obligations to aid some particular person in specific circumstances isn't as stringent as one's duty not to inflict physical injury. Trammell's general point about dischargeability depends on this confusion of the general and the particular. For a particular obligation to save this individual now *can* be discharged completely: save him and it is discharged. And since there is no obligation to save all who need saving, there is no obligation which can't be discharged. The concept of dischargeability doesn't apply to the particular case, because a particular obligation is always an obligation to do what can be done. With respect to the general, talk of dischargeability is a misleading way of asserting the universality or exceptionlessness of a right or obligation. The duty not to kill can be completely discharged in the sense that it is possible *never* to kill (but not in the sense that one 'finishes' not killing all those one is obligated not to kill). But though it is possible, few people believe the duty not to kill is exceptionless. And, furthermore, the extreme case of killing is misleading as exemplar of the general problem of harming. It is not clear that the duty not to cause harm is so much more easily discharged than the duty to prevent it. So Trammell's point shows at most a difference in degree between negative and positive duties, not a difference in kind.

---

6  Richard Trammell, 'Saving Life and Taking Life,' *Journal of Philosophy*, **72** (1975) 133. For further evidence of Trammell's confusion of the general and the particular and of practical and necessary differences, see below, pp. 27-29

## II

Imagine the following situation. A person is stranded on a desert island, far from other land and human life. The island provides no source of sustenance, and provisions are almost gone. Just as he is about to give up hope, the stranded man sights a vessel. It lands, and a sailor comes ashore. The ship contains plenty of supplies, as well as providing a way back to the human world.

Now consider two possible scenarios that follow. In the first, the sailor won't share his provisions with the stranded man, and won't take him aboard the ship. He is ready to leave as he has come. In the second, the sailor attempts to kill the man he finds on the island.

I believe that in these circumstances, the sailor's failure to share his provisions or his ship with the stranded man is morally equivalent to his killing him.[7] Is this a judgment of the sailor's conduct or of his character, or both? So far no mention has been made of any motives, intentions or the like. But although it is important to distinguish the evaluation of conduct from that of agents, here we want to ensure that no differences but action/omission operate, even if only implicity, to affect our judgment. Harmful actions and omissions resulting in harm are often asymmetrical in terms of motives and intentions. This is because a sane person doesn't ordinarily attack someone unless he has some sort of a reason; but a reason isn't needed to explain why someone doesn't act except in certain circumstances.[8] But the present case provides such circumstances. Intuitively, the sailor's refusal to take the stranded man aboard cries out for an explanation as much as his killing him does. It is no less plausible that he wants him dead if he leaves him alone than if he kills him. Looked at the other way, the idea that the sailor kills for no reason seems no more absurd than that he leaves for no reason. So the assumption of parallel internal states isn't artificial here.

---

7 Certain features of this case are worth noting. The sailor's failure to aid doesn't make the stranded man worse off than he would have been had the sailor not appeared at all; the sailor has had no causal role in bringing about the plight of the other. So this situation is unlike that where someone owns the only waterhole in the desert. It is comparable to Nozick's case of the medical researcher who 'synthesizes a new substance that effectively treats a certain disease and who refuses to sell except on his terms.' The substance is easily available, and so the researcher's appropriation of it doesn't make others worse off than they would have been had he not appropriated it. On Nozick's view, the researcher is within his rights in refusing to sell (Nozick, 179-81).

8 This doesn't mean that a reason couldn't be given why someone doesn't do something, should the question arise. But clearly one doesn't *have* a reason for not doing all the many things one isn't doing at any given time.

What is it about these circumstances that makes the sailor's failure to aid as wrong as killing? One condition is that no significant sacrifice of any kind is required for him to help, just as none is required for him to refrain from killing. But what is most important is that there is a probability bordering on certainty that if he leaves the stranded man he will die. It is not just that he can save him, but that no one else can. (So the case is unlike many of the examples that come up in discussions of these issues: only the solitary bystander can be so sure that his omission is sufficient for death to occur.)

This morally crucial factor − the certainty of the connection between conduct and harmful consequence − explains the prohibition against physical aggression. For physical aggression greatly increases the chances that harm will ensue. Of course, if what a person does is described as killing someone − a description incorporating both physical movements and their consequences − then the connection between action and consequence is not just morally certain but logically necessary. But a description of what someone does not do can also be given which connects the omission necessarily with a certain upshot.[9] Here it is enough to say that, given descriptions that do not incorporate the death, the (contingent) connection between certain physical movements of the sailor and the other's death is not more probable than the connection between his leaving the stranded man alone without provisions and the latter's death. We can be quite certain that he will die in either case.

A pair of cases whose description is entirely upshot-free reveals the equivalence of action and omission more clearly. Suppose a person finds himself in a room before a set of controls. In the first scenario, he is told that if he pushes a certain button, someone in another room will die. In the second, he is told that if he does not push a certain button, that person will die.[10] Here it seems incontrovertible that the agent's duty to refrain from pushing the button in the first case is equal to his duty to push it in the second. Why? As far as the agent has any reason to believe, the probability that acting will result in death in the first case is

---

9 E.g. the description 'letting die.' One could specify more or less stringent conditions under which it was legitimate to describe someone as letting another person die. See Jonathan Bennett, 'Whatever the Consequences,' *Analysis,* **26** (1966); Bruce Russell, 'On the Relative Strictness of Negative and Positive Duties,' *American Philosophical Quarterly,* **14** (1977) 87.

10 Michael Tooley gives a similar example, but in his two people's lives are involved. This introduces obscuring factors having to do with sacrificing one person to save another. See below, p. 34ff. (Tooley, 'Abortion and Infanticide Revisited,' quoted in Trammell, 136n.)

equal to the probability that not acting will result in death in the second. (And it is clear that no other variables distinguish the cases: e.g. the 'effort' required to push the button is no greater than the 'effort' required to refrain.)

A way of further testing one's judgment is to ask what follows upon aggression or failure to aid in terms of the rights and obligations of the involved parties. To return to the desert island example, it is clear that if the sailor tries to kill the stranded man, the latter has the right to defend himself. But it seems also that if the sailor refuses to share what he has (when he can, with no loss to himself), the stranded man may do what he must to preserve himself. If he must steal, then he may steal; if he must kill, then he may kill. But this right of the stranded man is not sufficient to show that the sailor is obligated to save him. A Hobbesian, e.g., would acknowledge an absolute right of self-preservation without positing a corresponding obligation on the part of another. (Non-Hobbesians can test their judgment of the stranded man's right by comparing it to their judgment of the right of a murderer to preserve himself.) More telling is one's judgment of the sailor who has tried to kill or failed to aid, and has suffered the consequences. If the stranded man kills him in self-defense, no moral imbalance has been created; no injustice has been done. Similarly, if in the struggle to get what he needs to survive the stranded man can't avoid killing the sailor, no injustice has been done either, and for the same reason: the sailor has brought his troubles on himself. This situation can be contrasted with one where a person kills someone who threatens his life through no fault of his own (what Nozick calls an 'innocent threat'); i.e. the agent kills in self-defense. Even though we may justify the killing, such situations are morally problematic precisely because the innocent threat does not choose to endanger others' lives, and could not avoid it. But the case of the sailor poses no such moral dilemma, because the sailor is not innocent. He has chosen to act the way he does, when he could easily have acted otherwise. So our attitude toward his death is the same whether he actually tries to kill or just fails to aid.

## III

There are, I think, two main lines of argument that underlie opposition to the equivalence thesis. One has to do with the extent to which sacrifice or difficulty is involved in fulfilling negative and positive duties; the other concerns the attribution of responsibility for the plight of those harmed or left unaided. I shall take these up in turn.

The sacrifice question has been touched on above, in the discussion of dischargeability and the confusion of necessary and practical differences between action and omission. It is raised by this example of Trammell's:

> If someone threatened to steal $ 1000 from a person if he did not take a gun and shoot a stranger between the eyes, it would be very wrong for him to kill the stranger to save his $ 1000. But if someone asked from that person $ 1000 to save a stranger, it would seem that his obligation to grant this request would not be as great as his obligation to refuse the first demand — even if he had good reason for believing that without his $ 1000 the stranger would certainly die.[11]

In general, Trammell argues that negative duties are stricter than positive ones (in part) because they are easier to fulfil and don't involve great sacrifices.[12] This is perfectly consistent with the equivalence of action and omission; and indeed it would seem to follow that when a negative duty did involve great sacrifice, this would diminish its stringency. But now Trammell says that morally we require people to make greater sacrifices to fulfil negative duties than positive ones, implying that their greater stringency is independent of how much sacrifice is involved. One may suspect that insensitivity to the distinctions between what is true in general and what is true of any particular case, and between necessary and practical differences, has led Trammell to impose his view of what is true in general on the case which is supposed to test

---

11  Trammell, 131. A hazard of such complicated and artificial examples is that irrelevant factors intrude to influence our judgment. Notice here, e.g., that the person in the first case is being threatened. For it is not just that one is expected not to kill under such threats; it is questionable whether one ought to alter any of one's behavior in response to threats. Certainly if I wouldn't kill to avoid the threatened loss of my money, I wouldn't fail to save someone for that reason either. But there is no threat in Trammell's second case, and so the two cases are not parallel.
    Part of the reason we oppose giving in to threats is that it is hard to be sure the threat will be carried out if one doesn't comply. As I am less sure, I am less inclined to cooperate, especially if what is demanded is irrevocable. On the other hand, how disposed I am to give up a lot to save someone depends on how certainly the death will follow upon my failure to act and on how immediate the need is. If I thought 'Unless I hand over the money right now, he'll die on the spot,' I would be more inclined to do it than if there were time to make up my mind, time in which something or someone else might intervene. Depending on how we fill in these particulars or how our imaginations complete the story Trammell leaves untold, our assessment of the relative moral status of the cases changes or becomes explainable on grounds other than action/omission.

12  Trammell, 133-5; see also above, p. 23

for what is necessarily true. This kind of 'spillover effect' is no doubt common in ordinary thinking and partly accounts for the prevalence of the view that negative duties are stricter than positive.

To test the hypothesis that morally we require greater sacrifices in the fulfilment of negative than positive duties, we need two cases in which the sacrifice involved in fulfilling the duty is approximately equivalent *and* significant (since similar assessment for cases where the sacrifice is equivalent but minimal is, Trammell thinks, inconclusive), and where other morally relevant factors are parallel. But the problem is that it is very difficult to construct such cases. For what is needed is a case to compare with the one where I am required to give up something very significant − say, my life's savings − to save someone, and where only I can save him. For it is Trammell's feeling that one would not be morally bound to do *this* that leads him to say that greater sacrifices are required in the fulfilment of negative than positive duties.

It's easy to think of cases where significant sacrifices have to be made to avoid harming or even killing people, where those harmed or killed are unspecified, and the harm is indirect. Such situations form the substance of many legal and political problems, involving such issues as pollution and civil liberties. Here it seems clear that the question of how much sacrifice is involved for people to refrain from doing something operates in a straightforward way to determine judgments about whether the actions ought to be permitted. This tells in favor of the view that the cost involved in acting or not acting is a determinant of obligation, rather than being determined by it.

But in the special cases needed to compare with those direct omissions where great sacrifice is involved to aid someone, it is hard to imagine the appropriate circumstances. For why, after all, when one is about to pull the trigger or plunge the knife into his heart, can't one simply refrain, just like that? How *could* a great sacrifice be involved? That it is so hard to imagine a comparable situation is in itself reason to be suspicious, for the sense that action and omission aren't equivalent is strongest where parallel cases are not available. Where they are it is often easier to see how other factors intrude.

One conclusion we may draw is that direct physical violence is the paradigm of prohibited behavior precisely because it exemplifies the extreme of the two morally relevant factors: certainty that one's action will result in harm, and minimal sacrifice needed to refrain. If it happened that people had to give up something significant to avoid directly harming or killing people, this would be relevant, just as it is in the less extreme cases. Thus, in the only comparable instances of the extreme case that are plausible, where one might have to risk life or limb to avoid harming someone − situations of extreme scarcity, or freak occurrences (having to drive over a cliff to avoid running someone over) − having to make such a sacrifice crucially enters into our judgment. Many would say that the usual duties are in such circumstances inapplicable.[13] So all the ways we reason about these questions support the view that if, or rather when, negative duties are more stringent than positive ones, it is because they involve less sacrifice and are therefore easier to fulfil.[14]

## IV

The question of responsibility is raised by another of Trammell's examples:

> (1) Jones sees that Smith will be killed [by a bomb] unless he warns him. But Jones is apathetic. So Smith is killed by the bomb even though Jones could have warned him. (2) Jones is practicing shooting his gun. Smith accidentally walks in the path and Jones sees Smith; but Jones's reaction is apathy. Jones pulls the trigger and Smith is killed.

This example supports the 'plausibility of the distinction between action and inaction,' Trammell thinks, because

> In Case 2, if Jones had not pulled the trigger, Smith would not have been killed. But in Case 1, Smith might still have been killed by the bomb even if Jones had never existed. The link between action and responsibility does not seem accidental, since the more directly and clearly a person is responsible for another person needing to be saved, the more likely we are to say that the first person is killing the second.[15]

---

13  See, e.g., Hobbes, *Leviathan*, pt. 1, ch. 14; Hume, *Enquiry Concerning the Principles of Morals*, sec. 3, pt. 1.

14  I have benefitted from discussion of these issues with Frances Myrna Kamm.
   A related argument sometimes made to support a necessary difference between action and omission is that action requires an output of energy or effort not involved when a person doesn't act. The argument presupposes a machine-like conception of human beings. For a machine, energy is required for the performance of operations, not for nonperformance: machines do not forbear. But if a person wants to do something, not acting may involve as much or more effort than is required to act when one does not want or wants not to act. (Think of trying to break a habit, or keeping to a diet.) To demand that a person not act is not to demand nothing.

15  Richard Trammell, 'Tooley's Moral Symmetry Principle,' *Philosophy and Public Affairs,* 5 (1975-76) 308. Trammell is obviously talking about some kind of non-moral (e.g. causal) responsibility, since it is moral responsibility we are trying to determine. But his manner of expression obscures the crucial issue. For the question is not whether we would describe a particular failure to save as a killing, but whether in a given set of circumstances these are morally equivalent.

What Trammell means to say is that there is a significant moral difference between killing (or, more generally, doing positive harm) and not saving (more generally, not aiding), because no matter how otherwise alike the circumstances, in the former case one has caused or brought into existence the harm, while in the latter case one has not. Whether morally significant or not, this difference is necessary in the sense that it distinguishes all actions from all (genuine, or ex nihilo) omissions. Instead of asking whether action and omission are morally equivalent, we could ask if (other things being equal) not preventing harm is as bad as causing it; or if making someone worse off is necessarily worse than not making him better off.

The idea that bringing a harm into existence (what I call being causally responsible for it) is morally of a different order than failing to prevent or alleviate it goes deep in our thinking about moral responsibility. This is odd, on reflection. For moral responsibility can be ascribed only (as far as we now know) to human beings, while causal responsibility can be ascribed to almost everything in nature. This ought to lead one to ask what it is about human beings that makes their causal agency morally significant.

What distinguishes the causal role of a human being from that of an object or nonhuman animal is that ordinarily, at least, the human being can choose to act in one way or another; and he can choose on the basis of his knowledge of various things. If this were not so, causal agency would be as morally irrelevant for humans as it is for everything else in nature. And, indeed, when a person could not have chosen not to be a causal agent in a process that results in someone's harm, he is absolved of moral responsibility. Morally his conduct is on a par with floods and earthquakes: unfortunate but not morally ascribable to anyone.

Normally, however, a person is *able to choose not to act in a way that he foresees will cause harm* to someone.[16] It is this that gives causal agency moral significance. But this condition equally warrants (other things being equal) holding a person morally responsible when he is *able to choose to act in a way that he foresees will prevent harm* to someone. For it is the ability to choose now to act, in light of knowledge, that distinguishes human beings from the rest of nature and legitimizes

---

16 Sometimes we hold people responsible for causing harm when they didn't foresee the consequences of their actions, because we think they ought to have foreseen them. But this is warranted only on the assumption that the person is responsible for his ignorance, i.e. that he could have chosen not to put himself in a position where he would be ignorant. As Aristotle says about drunkenness, 'the moving principle is in the man himself, since he had the power of not getting drunk and his getting drunk was the cause of his ignorance' (*Nicomachean Ethics*, 1113b30).

holding them (and nothing else) morally responsible — for what they do and for what they do not do. With respect to adult humans, causal responsibility is merely a sign, usually though not always reliable, of moral responsibility. That moral responsibility ultimately has nothing to do with causal responsibility is revealed in the case of one who knows that someone will die if he does/does not (in the alternative scenes) push a button. There it seems incontrovertible that one is equally obligated in both cases. And it is clear that the only difference between the cases (unlike the complicated examples given by Trammell and others which do not clearly isolate the feature under consideration) is that in the one case one must choose to perform a minimal physical movement to avoid someone's death and in the other one must choose not to perform it.

If still it seems somehow unfair or wrong that we can be held morally responsible in situations we do not create, the defect would seem to be in the nature of things — something, therefore, that must be taken for granted. We can be held morally responsible because within certain constraints we can choose how to act; but it is just a fact that we can't, beyond a certain point, choose the circumstances from which we must choose. But this applies equally to acting and refraining. It's true that if someone falls into the water and starts to drown, it's not the passerby's fault. But likewise if a person finds himself inclined to kill someone, it may not be his fault that he is so inclined. Just as we think the latter is morally required to refrain if he can, so also the passerby may be required to act if he can. Confronted with circumstances, we have to choose and can't choose not to choose.

If there is no moral difference between causing harm and failing to prevent it, then, if Trammell's cases are indeed parallel in every other respect, Jones's failure to warn Smith of the bomb is morally equivalent to his shooting him. The inclination to think otherwise comes from the natural assumption that other asymmetries are embedded in the cases. Simply avowing that they are parallel is not enough to ensure that such assumptions won't intrude, though not necessarily explicitly or consciously. So, e.g., in the first case it is natural to imagine that someone else might be able to warn Smith of the bomb; that Jones might be in some danger himself if he warned Smith; that the urgency of the situation might cause Jones to lose his head, thereby making his inaction partially excusable.[17]

---

17 The cases then resemble the desert island example. But the test used there to confirm the equivalent evaluations won't work here. The sailor's refusal to aid warrants the stranded man in doing what he must to preserve himself; and the sailor, having chosen not to cooperate, can't claim an injustice. But in this case

One might be reluctant to accept the equivalence thesis because it is thought to imply that a person causally responsible for a harm is no more obligated to alleviate it than one not causally responsible for it. But what follows is just that one who is *merely* causally responsible is no more obligated than one who is not; and this is not difficult to accept. When the person who has caused harm could have *not* caused it (had he chosen to), then his causal agency implies moral responsibility. However obligated to give aid a person with no causal responsibility might be, one who has non-accidentally or negligently caused harm is bound by that obligation plus the duty arising from having caused the harm.

If, e.g., a person accidentally and non-negligently trips a non-swimmer who then falls into the lake, the former is causally responsible for the latter's predicament. This agent is as obligated (no more and no less) to try to save the nonswimmer as anyone else similarly situated. For

> To call the act accidental and non-negligent is to imply that the relevant person is completely absolved of moral responsibility for the resulting situation. If the person has no moral responsibility for the situation, there would seem to be no grounds for assigning him a greater duty for changing it than others similarly situated.[18]

But the situation is very different when someone deliberately pushes a non-swimmer into the lake. Such a person is morally responsible for the resulting predicament because he could have chosen not to do what he did. His action is morally comparable to that of someone who willingly allows a non-swimmer to fall into the lake when he could easily prevent his falling in – e.g., by holding out his hand. This action and this omission are related in the same way to the non-swimmer's trouble: he wouldn't be in trouble if the first person hadn't pushed him, or if the second had held out his hand.

The question then arises what a person's obligation is given the existence of the harm – when the non-swimmer is flailing about in the water. On the view I have argued for, if for some reason everyone else (including any guilty parties) has disappeared from the scene, the failure

---

what Smith needs (the information that there is a bomb) is something he doesn't know he needs; and of course if he did know he needed it, he wouldn't need it – he would have it. There is nothing for Smith to wrest from Jones, and nothing for Jones to lose to Smith.

18  Russell, 92. Any inclination to think otherwise can probably be explained by a kind of spillover of guilt from the typical case of causal responsibility that is not accidental or non-negligent, as well as doubt (implanted by Freud, among others) as to the accidentalness of so-called accidents.

to save of the sole remaining individual (where no sacrifice is required, etc.) is morally equivalent to his killing the drowning man; for his omission is sufficient for the death to occur. But if we are asking which of a number of individuals is obligated (or how obligated) to remedy the situation, someone's having non-accidentally or negligently caused the harm is morally relevant, for it is his action that has vastly increased the probability of harm in the first place. (Similarly, other things being equal, for one who at the critical moment chose not to hold out his hand.) Of course, in the situation described, *any* person's failure to try to save would be blameworthy, to say the least. But considering the whole episode, one who could have chosen to behave in such a way that the harm would not have occurred is morally responsible for not so choosing, as well as being bound in the way anyone finding himself able to save would be.

Thus, the equivalence of action and omission is consistent with the commonsense belief that (normally) one who has caused a person harm owes him more in the way of assistance than one who has not.


## V

Commonly taken as counterexamples to the equivalence thesis are those cases where one must choose, e.g., between killing a person in order to save others, and not killing him with the result that these others die. Though all agree that more deaths are worse than fewer, almost no one believes that it is permissible to kill people 'in the interests of cancer research or to obtain, let us say, spare parts for grafting on to those who need them.'[19]

A similiar problem is posed by this familiar example, described by Philippa Foot:

> Suppose that a judge or magistrate is faced with rioters demanding that a culprit be found for a certain crime and threatening otherwise to take their own bloody revenge on a particular section of the community. The real culprit being unknown, the judge sees himself as able to prevent the bloodshed only by framing some innocent person and having him executed.[20]

---

19  Philippa Foot, 'The Problem of Abortion and the Doctrine of the Double Effect,' *Oxford Review*, no. 5 (1967); reprinted in James Rachels, ed., *Moral Problems*, 2d ed. (New York: Harper & Row 1975) 64.

20  Foot, 63

Foot's explanation of the belief that it is not permissible for the judge to frame an innocent person, and that, more generally, one may not kill a person in order to save others, is that 'even where the strictest duty of positive aid exists, this still does not weigh as if a negative duty were involved.'[21]

One thing to be noticed about these cases, in contrast to those presented earlier, is that they all involve a choice between two evils and between the interests of different individuals. More than this, they all involve a decision about whether to sacrifice one person for another — something so repellent we are reluctant to allow it no matter what the cost. But whatever it is about sacrificing a person or his interests that is objectionable, it has no necessary connection with the action/omission distinction. This is demonstrated nicely by Russell's twist on the case described by Foot: here the judge's charge is a diabetic.[22] So to stop the rioters the judge needn't kill his charge; he need only refrain from giving him his insulin, and let him die. It is clear that if it is wrong for the judge to execute his prisoner, it is equally wrong for him to let him die in this way. For in either case he sacrifices the person, and it is this that is objectionable. Similar variations can be introduced in the medical cases to show that what is wrong with killing people for their parts has nothing per se to do with the greater stringency of negative duties. (Instead of killing the patient for his heart or liver, the nurse watches as he chokes on his dinner.)

What is common to these cases is that the death or injury of one person is needed for some purpose. The most common way to achieve someone's death is to kill him; and this makes it look as if it is the action of killing per se that is wrong. But cases where death can be achieved by refraining from performing a simple action that would prevent it reveals that it is achieving the death, and not achieving it through action, that is objectionable.[23] In both the negative and the positive case, one chooses to act in a way that one knows will result in someone's death; and one chooses to act in that way *because* one knows it will result in a death. This doesn't explain everything important about the issue of sacrificing people, nor does it follow that it is never permissible to do so. But it shows that the problem these cases present is not that of the significance

---

21   Foot, 67

22   Russell, 90

23   So Regina in Lillian Hellman's play *The Little Foxes,* who waits to get her husband's medicine until it is too late, is the moral equivalent of a murderer. See n. 3 above.

of the action/omission distinction. One can sacrifice a person by killing him, or by letting him die.

I conclude that there is no moral difference between action and omission. The tendency to think otherwise results from the commission of various errors and fallacies, which can be briefly summarized as follows: (a) Comparing cases that are asymmetrical with respect to features other than action/omission. (This is almost inevitable if one compares an omission with physical violence.) (b) Not distinguishing clearly between necessary and practical differences, so that what is at most a practical difference is generalized to operate as a necessary one. (c) Mistaking what is morally significant about a case or a class of cases. (E.g., taking causal agency per se to be morally significant; or thinking that what is wrong with sacrificing a person is that it involves killing.) (d) Mistakenly thinking that the equivalence of action and omission has unacceptable consequences. (E.g., that one who causes harm is under no greater obligation to alleviate it than one who does not; or that nothing short of total devotion to the well-being of others is morally possible.[24])

The moral equivalence of action and omission is supported at one level by its consistency with a coherent and persuasive view of what an agent deciding how to act ought to take into account: the connection between his conduct and a certain consequence, and the amount of sacrifice required of him to fulfill a would-be obligation. At a deeper level, the idea that action and omission are equivalent is strengthened by its connection with the very condition of moral responsibility: the possibility of choosing, given a set of circumstances, how to act.[25]

---

24 Concerning the latter question, nothing at all follows from the equivalence thesis. If changes need to be made in our way of life (as I believe they do), these will follow from practical differences.

25 I am grateful to Bernard Baumrin, Gertrude Ezorsky. Virginia Held and J.B. Schneewind for helpful conversations and criticisms of an earlier version of this paper.

*Judith Lichtenberg*

## Select Bibliography

Bennett, Jonathan, 'Whatever the Consequences,' *Analysis,* **26** (1966); reprinted in Steinbock.

D'Arcy, Eric, *Human Acts: An Essay in Their Moral Evaluation* (Oxford: Clarendon Press 1963).

Fitzgerald, P.J., 'Acting and Refraining,' *Analysis,* **27** (1967).

Foot, Philippa, 'The Problem of Abortion and the Doctrine of the Double Effect,' *Oxford Review,* 5 (1967); reprinted in Steinbock.

Glover, Jonathan, *Causing Death and Saving Lives* (Harmondsworth: Penguin 1977).

Hart, H.L.A., and A.M. Honoré, *Causation in the Law* (Oxford: Clarendon Press 1959).

Hughes, Graham, 'Criminal Omissions,' *Yale Law Journal,* **67** (1958).

Kleining, John, 'Good Samaritanism,' *Philosophy and Public Affairs,* **5** (1975-7).

Nozick, Robert, *Anarchy, State, and Utopia* (New York: Basic Books 1974).

Russell, Bruce, 'On the Relative Strictness of Negative and Positive Duties,' *American Philosophical Quarterly,* **14** (1977); reprinted in Steinbock.

Shue, Henry, *Basic Rights: Subsistence, Affluence, and U.S. Foreign Policy* (Princeton, N.J.: Princeton University Press 1980).

Steinbock, Bonnie (editor), *Killing and Letting Die* (Englewood Cliffs, N.J.: Prentice-Hall, 1980); includes essays by Bennett, Foot, Russell, Trammell, and others.

Tooley, Michael, 'Abortion and Infanticide,' *Philosophy and Public Affairs,* **2** (1972).

Trammell, Richard, 'Saving Life and Taking Life,' *Journal of Philosophy,* **72** (1975).

Trammell, Richard, 'Tooley's Moral Symmetry Principle,' *Philosophy and Public Affairs,* **5** (1976).

CANADIAN JOURNAL OF PHILOSOPHY
Supplementary Volume VIII, 1982

# Acts, Omissions, and Common Sense Morality

LAURENCE THOMAS, University of North Carolina
at Chapel Hill

*I*

Common Sense Morality condemns us for being indifferent to the suffering of others.[1] Even so, it sharply distinguishes between this and our knowingly and needlessly contributing to the suffering of others. (That we are talking about voluntary behavior throughout is to be understood.) And it holds that the latter constitutes the greater moral wrong. It would seem that common sense morality is not without a point. From the premise that a person knowingly and needlessly takes steps to cause others to suffer, it would certainly be correct for us to conclude that he desires to see others suffer and is sufficiently motivated by this desire that he brings about the suffering of others. For it is clear

---

1 The expression 'common sense morality' is obviously inspired by what Henry Sidgwick, in *The Method of Ethics*, 7th ed., called the morality of common sense. By this, I take Sidgwick to mean the moral views which reflect the moral judgements which people make in practice (cf. p. 361). Sidgwick attached enough importance to the morality of common sense that he endeavored to show that utilitarianism was not very much at odds with it (cf. Bk IV, chs. 2 & 3). Talk about common sense morality is not without its pitfalls, though. However, I prefer to proceed in this way rather than to talk about some particular non-consequentialist moral theory.

that such a person intentionally brings it about that others suffer; and one cannot intentionally bring about this or anything else in the absence of the desire for it.² By contrast, from the premise that a person knowingly and needlessly lets others suffer, we cannot *thereby* conclude that he desires to see others suffer. For a person who is indifferent to the suffering of others might knowingly and needlessly let others suffer, though it follows from his being just this sort of person that he does not desire their suffering and, therefore, that the desire for their suffering cannot figure into an explanation of his knowingly and needlessly letting them suffer.³

---

2  Writers who differ sharply on other aspects of the nature of human action share this view. Cf. Donald Davidson, *Essays on Actions and Events* (New York: Oxford University Press 1980) 22-3 and Alvin Goldman, *A Theory of Human Action* (Englewood Cliffs, N.J.: Prentice-Hall Inc. 1970) 50-6. To perform an action is to act intentionally under some description or the other, and so to act with a certain desire.

3  Of course, it may be that what one does intentionally, and so with the appropriate desire, is to let something happen. The point in the text, needless to say, is that not all instances of letting something happen are instances of doing something intentionally. This squares with what Roderick Chisolm says in 'The Agent as Cause,' in Myles Brand and Douglas Walton, eds., *Action Theory* (Boston, MA: D. Reidel Publishing Company 1976). He writes:

> We may characterize deliberate omission in this way:
> S deliberately omits undertaking *p* at *t* = Df. *S* considers at *t* undertaking *p* and *S* does not undertake *p* at *t*. (207)

The person who is indifferent to the suffering of others is not one who considers alleviating the suffering of another, but then drops the idea. This is not an idea which would have occurred to him in the first place. His not helping others is not a function of his deciding not to; rather, it is a function of his being the sort of person who is not moved by the suffering of others. The belief that he could prevent the needless suffering of another has no motivational content for him *at all*. Hence, his not doing so *cannot* be explained by reference to the desire to see others suffer.

I should note that the practice of bleeding, which was engaged in up until the early 1900s, does not count against any of the claims made in the text. It was engaged in because it was thought that diseases resulted from an imbalance in the body's life spirits and that this imbalance could be corrected by letting a person bleed. Since physicians then were mistaken about this, it follows, of course, that in bleeding patients they (the physicians) needlessly caused their patients to suffer. However, this they did not do knowingly. So, in the absence of any additional premises, it would be a mistake to infer that physicians who then engaged in the practice of bleeding desired to see their patients suffer. See R.H. Major, *A History of Medicine*, vols. 1 & 2 (Springfield, IL: Thomas Publishing Co. 1954). I am indebted to C. Arden Miller, M.D., for clarification here.

If the desire to see others suffer is precisely what motivates a person to let them suffer, then, according to common sense morality, his letting them do so is as heinous and morally objectionable as his knowingly and needlessly taking steps to cause them to suffer. So, in our moral evaluations of either acts or omissions, common sense morality makes relevant that they do or do not stem from certain motivations. An act and an omission which are known to have the same consequences are morally equivalent, then, if and only if they stem from the same motivational structure, as I shall say.

Now, to be sure, it is not always obvious when an act and an omission would stem from the same motivational structure. But, I take it that unless one is already committed to utilitarianism, or some other consequentialist moral theory,[4] there is all the difference in the world between a person who knowingly and needlessly contributes to the suffering of others and one who knowingly and needlessly lets others suffer. Though both fail to do what is morally right, it is the former who does the greater moral wrong.

All of this seems so very obvious that it is something of a puzzle to me that the moral equivalence of acts and omissions (MEAO) doctrine is becoming increasingly popular.[5] The doctrine reads thus: every act and omission which are known by the moral agent in question to have the same consequences are morally equivalent. No reference at all is made to motivational structure, which marks the difference between it and its common sense morality counterpart. I do not find it strange that a utilitarian should embrace the MEAO-doctrine, since this is what a consistent one must do, utilitarianism being a consequentialist moral theory.[6] However, no utilitarian should write as if the doctrine has the status of a pre-theoretical moral truth which any moral theory must embrace if it is to be a satisfactory one, but one which just so happens to be a consequence of utilitarianism. For the doctrine has not yet been shown to have this status. To show that it has this status one must show

---

4   The emphasis here is upon utilitarianism, since it is the one consequentialist moral theory which comes to mind in connection with regulating the basic structure of society.

5   Some of the most important essays which have been written on the topic have been collected in Bonnie Steinbock, ed., *Killing and Letting Die* (Englewood Cliffs, NJ: Prentice-Hall, Inc. 1980). See, especially, Jonathan Bennett, 'Whatever the Consequences'; Bruce Russel, 'On the Relative Strictness of Negative and Positive Duties'; and Michael Tooley, 'An Irrelevant Consideration: Killing Versus Letting Die'.

6   Cf. Peter Singer, *Practical Ethics* (New York: Cambridge University Press 1980).

that the case for indifference cannot be made.[7] And I do not know what to make of those who think this except that they have a deep misconception of the psychological make-up of persons. For the move from

    (a)  X let $\phi$ occur to Y

to

    (b)  X desired that $\phi$ should occur to Y

and, then,

    (c)  X's letting $\phi$ occur to Y stemmed from his being motivated by the desire to see $\phi$ occur to Y

is a fallacious one. To prevent any misunderstanding, I am not claiming that these three claims are logically incompatible with one another; rather, my point is simply that logic, alone, will not get us from (a) to (b) and on to (c). The move requires some additional premises. For just this reason it is quite a mystery to me why anyone would be inclined to think that the case for indifference can never be made when it comes to distinguishing between acts and omissions.

Those who advocate the MEOA-doctrine as something of a pre-theoretical moral truth often proceed as follows. They construct two or more examples. In one, it turns out that almost any sensitive person would be inclined to agree that the relevant act and omission are morally equivallent. This example is then used to get us to make the same concession in connection with a different, but supposedly morally parallel, example where we might be less inclined to say that the the relevant act and omission are morally equivalent. And it is supposed to be that it cannot be reasonable for a person to maintain that the relevant act and omission are morally equivalent in one example, but not in the other. But they are wrong. According to common sense morality, our willingness to regard an act and an omission, which the agent in question knows to have the same consequences, as morally equivalent should directly correspond to the extent to which we deem it implausible to suppose that the act and the omission might stem from different motivational structures. As we shall see, in what follows, the reason why

---

7  Many advocates of the MEAO-doctrine seem to think that it is a pre-theoretical moral truth. This is certainly true of James Rachels and Judith Lichtenberg, whose examples I later discuss in the text.

a person often differs in her or his assessment of these supposedly parallel examples is that they turn out not to be parallel with respect to motivational structure. Invariably, it turns out that with one example, it is implausible to suppose that the act and the omission could stem from different motivational structures, but that it is not implausible to suppose this in the purportedly parallel example.

Consider the following two examples from a recent essay by Judith Lichtenberg, 'The Moral Equivalence of Action and Omission':[8]

> *Example 1* A person is stranded on a desert island, far from other land and human life. The island provides no source of sustenance, and provisions are almost gone. Just as he is about to give up hope, the stranded man sights a vessel. It lands, and a sailor comes ashore. The ship contains plenty of supplies as well as providing a way back to the human world. The sailor either kills (the relevant act) the stranded man or leaves him (the relevant omission) just as he found him, in which case the man will surely die.

> *Example 2* Suppose a person finds himself in a room before a set of controls. In the first scenario, he is told that if he pushes a certain button (the relevant act), someone in another room will die. In the second, he is told that if he does not push a certain button (the relevant omission), that person will die.

If we are reluctant to say that in (E1) the act and the omission are morally equivalent, (E2) is meant to convince us that we should not be.

However, there is a perfectly good reason why a person might regard (E2) in this way, but not (E1). Because the only difference between the act and the omission, in (E2), is that the former consists in pushing a button and the latter in not doing so, it is hard to imagine how one could get a difference between them in motivational structure. It takes so little effort to push a button that one is inclined to think that no one would fail to save a person's life if this is all he had to do unless, in fact, he actually desired to see the person dead. Of course, it is possible to tell a story where this turns out not to be so. But, the point is that one does not imagine such a story being told. One thinks, instead, that the

---

8 This volume, pp. 19-36. The two examples of Lichtenberg's which appear in the text (pp. 24-6) almost persuaded me of the truth of the MEAO-doctrine. For, I certainly thought that she was right about the act and the omission in the second example being morally equivalent. I wanted to understand, then, why I was reluctant to say this about the act and the omission in the first one.

person's not pushing the button in the second instance is to be explained by reference to a strong desire on his part to see the person in the other room dead. And this, it must now be said, is exactly what one thinks of the person in the first scenario in (E2).

With (E1), by contrast, it is less implausible, though not very plausible, in fact, to suppose that we could have a difference in motivational structure between the act and the omission. This serves to explain the mixed feelings which a person might have regarding it. One certainly feels that the sailor should be moved to save the man's life. However, there is enough of a difference between the causal structure which killing him involves and the causal structure which saving his life involves that from the fact that a person is not moved to do the latter, it does not follow that he desires the outcome which would result were he to do the former. We can bring this point out by embellishing (E1) a bit:

> *Example 1\** The sailor is 10 or 30 or 90 miles away from the island on which the man is stranded. He spots the man's elaborate signal for help which informs him that the island provides no source of sustenance and that his provisions are almost gone. The ship contains plenty of supplies as well as providing a way back to the human world. The sailor either makes the 10 or 30 or 90 mile trip to the island and kills (the relevant act) the man or he continues (the relevant omission) on his merry way, in which case the man will surely die. Absolutely nothing turns upon the sailor's continuing on his merry way.

Observe that the further away the sailor is from the island the less implausible it becomes to suppose that a difference in motivational structure is possible between the omission and the act. (At least this is so up to a point. If we were talking about distances of 800, 900, or 1000 miles, it clearly would not matter.) If the sailor travels the distance of 30 miles in order to kill the stranded person, then he is quite obviously motivated by the desire to see him dead. But if, at this distance, the sailor merely continues on his way, it is quite plausible to suppose that he is simply indifferent to the fate of the man. While I do not have an account of the causal structure of acts to offer, what (E1), E2), and (E1\*) suggest is this: The less resemblance there is between the causal structure of the act of harming a person and the causal structure of the act of preventing him from being harmed, as is evidenced by the complexity of both acts and the ease with which each can be performed, the easier it will be to get a difference in motivational structure between an act and an omission. I shall return to this point below.

With the above examples, I have, by way of common sense morality, tried to show that a non-consequentialist who maintains that in (E2) the act and the omission are morally equivalent, while being reluctant to say this in connection with (E1), is not at all open to the charge of being unreasonable. So, if common sense morality is sound, then the needless killing of a person is worse than the needless letting of a person die (the relevant knowledge is assumed), *provided that one can attribute the latter to indifference.* This does not mean that one who does the latter does no wrong and, therefore, is not morally culpable for doing it. It only means that one who does the latter is not as morally culpable as one who does the former. It is certainly true that one may desire the death of a person and that this may be the very reason why one lets that person die. But why anyone should think that all lettings of a person die must stem from a desire such as this is hard to fathom. (It is understood that the desire here is inappropriate, since we are not talking about justified killings.)

I should like to underscore the arguments of this essay by looking at two examples from James Rachel's widely discussed essay 'Active and Passive Euthanasia.'[9] He takes the following two cases as evidence that the MEOA-doctrine is sound and, in particular, that there is no difference between killing and letting die:

> *Case 1* Smith stands to gain a large inheritance if anything should happen to his six-year old cousin. One evening while the child is taking his bath, Smith sneaks into the bathroom and drowns the child, and then arranges things so that it will look like an accident.

> *Case 2* Jones also stands to gain if anything should happen to his six-year old cousin. Like Smith, Jones sneaks in planning to drown the child in his bath. However, just as he enters the bathroom Jones sees the child slip and hit his head and fall face down in the water. Jones is delighted; he stands by, ready to push the child's head back under if it is necessary. With only a little thrashing about, the child drowns all by himself, 'accidentally,' as Jones watches and does nothing.

It is so very obvious that the act and the omission are equally wrong here. But that is not because the consequences, alone, are the same, though that the they are the same is relevant. Rather, they are equally wrong because the consequences are the same and the act and the

---

9  In Steinbock.

omission both stem from the same motivational structure. At least this is so from the standpoint of common sense morality.

I should remark parenthetically that at no point have I said that in order to get an equivalence between acts and omissions the motivational structure must stem from the same factors. Both Smith and Jones are motivated to act cruelly out of greed. It would not matter, though, if one were motivated out of greed and the other out of jealousy over the cousin's intelligence. For, in both cases, what we get is the motivation to be cruel to another. The motivational structure must be the same, although the factors which give rise to it may vary enormously.

Now, it will be observed that (C2) is like the second scenario in (E2). There is simply no room for indifference to be an explanation for the inaction, at least not without a very long and unobvious story. So, suppose that (A): Smith, Jones, and their respective cousins are on an otherwise empty beach. The two cousins are in the water. Smith swims out and drowns his; Jones lies on the beach while his drowns. Smith and Jones are both excellent swimmers, and each stands to gain equally and substantially from the death of his cousin. Next (B): keep the story on the beach, but leave out the part about each standing to gain from the death of his cousin. Finally (C): contrast the (B) scenario with parallel bathroom scenes, that is, Smith drowns his cousin in the bathtub and Jones watches his cousin drown in the bathtub; neither has anything to gain from the death of his cousin.

In (A) it is hardly plausible that indifference toward the death of his cousin can be the explanation for Jones' inaction, whereas in (B) this is not as implausible an explanation for Jones' inaction; though, to be sure, one does not want to stake a great deal on this. Notice, however, that with (C), it almost implausible that indifference could be an explanation for Jones' inaction. Why is this? Some of my earlier remarks point to an answer. Presumably holding the head of a six-year old under water until he drowns cannot be much more difficult or easier than lifting him out of the water to prevent him from drowning. The causal structure of the act of drowning the child and of the act of saving him sufficiently resemble one another that one is inclined to think that there is little room for a difference in motivational structure between them. And let me just conclude with the observation that our thinking about these two cases is no doubt colored somewhat by the fact that we are talking about the cousins of these two people. After all, it is much easier to imagine someone being indifferent to a stranger dying than to a member of his family dying. In any event, if I correctly assessed Cases 1 and 2, then they are not, contrary to what Rachels may believe, evidence of the truth of the MEAO-doctrine.

The case for indifference cannot always be made; and this I have not argued. But sometimes it can be. And when it can, I have tried to show that common sense morality provides us with a perfectly consistent and good reason for maintaining that we do not have a morally equivalent act and omission. For, according to it, any person who knowingly and needlessly contributes to the suffering of others is motivated to do what is evil, whereas this is not true of a person who is indifferent to the suffering of others. Thus, while an omission which stems from indifference is considered to be morally objectionable, that very same omission is considered to be more morally objectionable if it stems from the motivation to do evil. And only an omission which stems from the latter motivation is equivalent to its corresponding act. One might maintain that the case for indifference can never be made or, alternatively, that all moral wrongs are equally wrong. But I should think that all of this is just so much waving of the hands.

Of course, a utilitarian will not be moved by any of this, since utilitarian theory entails that a difference in motivational structure is irrelevant if the consequences of an act and an omission are exactly the same. By way of response, I can only say that this is perhaps further evidence of the fact that the theory fails to take the separateness of persons seriously.[10] For surely, a world in which people are indifferent to the suffering of others, and so do not aim to bring it about that others suffer, is, for all of its possible shortcomings, morally superior to one in which people have this as their aim.

---

10  Cf. John Rawls, *A Theory of Justice* (Cambridge, MA: Harvard University Press 1971) 187

## Select Bibliography

Ackerman, Bruce, *Social Justice and The Liberal State* (New Haven, Ct.: Yale University Press 1980).

Blumenfeld, Jean, 'Causing Harm and Bringing Aid,' *American Philosophical Quarterly,* **18** (1981) 323-9.

Lerner, Melvin J., 'The Justice Motive: Some Hypotheses as to its Origins and Forms,' *Journal of Personality,* **45** (1977).

Macaulay, J., and L. Berkowitz (editors), *Altruism and Helping Behavior* (New York: Academic Press 1970).

Rushton, J. Phillippe, *Altruism, Socialization and Society* (Englewood Cliffs, N.J.: Prentice-Hall 1980).

Singer, Peter, *Practical Ethics* (Cambridge: Cambridge University Press 1979).

Steinbock, Bonnie (editor), *Killing and Letting Die* (Englewood Cliffs, N.J.: Prentice-Hall, 1980).

Sumner, L.W., *Abortion and Moral Theory* (Princeton, N.J.: Princeton University Press 1980).

Thibaut, John, and Laurens Walker, *Procedural Justice: A Psychological Analysis* (Hillsdale, N.J.: Lawrence Erlbaum Associates, Publishers 1975).

Wispe, Lauren (editor), *Altruism, Sympathy, and Helping: Psychological and Sociological Principles* (New York: Academic Press 1978).

CANADIAN JOURNAL OF PHILOSOPHY
Supplementary Volume VIII, 1982

# Autonomy and Paternalism

ROBERT YOUNG, La Trobe University

Paternalism has generally been thought of as forcible or coercive interference with a person's liberty of action which is (believed to be) justified because it will prevent harm to that person's welfare interests or the like.[1] Opposition to paternalistic interference with adults, whether it involves the intervention of the state (legal paternalism) or another adult individual, has usually been based on a concern to preserve human autonomy or self-determination. More strictly it is opposition to so-called 'strong' paternalism — interventions to protect or benefit a person despite the person's informed voluntary consent to the contrary —

---

1 Despite the widespread acceptance of this sort of account it has been criticized for being too narrow. It would take us too far afield to consider these criticisms in detail but it may be as well to mention the efforts recently by Bernard Gert and Charles Culver to spell out a range of cases which they believe involve neither interference with liberty nor coercion. Cf. 'Paternalistic Behaviour,' *Philosophy and Public Affairs*, **6** (1976) 45-57, and 'The Justification of Paternalism,' *Ethics*, **87** (1979) 370-90. I do not accept the rather restrictive interpretation they place on the notion of *liberty* but this is not the place to substantiate my view. More importantly, the commonly accepted view (unlike theirs — see clause [iv] of their proposed formulation) does not beg the central question with which I shall be concerned since it does not restrict 'paternalism' to what I distinguish below as 'strong paternalism'.

which has been grounded on such a commitment to self-determination. 'Weak' paternalism involves interference where there is (or is believed to be) a defect in the decision-making capacities of the person interfered with (or to ascertain whether the person's behaviour is fully reflective). It is claimed to be justifiable insofar as *consent* to the interference would be forthcoming were these capacities restored.

There is an ambiguity here which is not always noticed. This consent requirement admits of two readings. First, we may construe it as a counterfactual which applies to the person at the time when his (or her) liberty is restricted. Thus we might ask: if *S* were not suffering from defects in his decision-making capacities at this time, would he nonetheless choose to perform the act now paternalistically being restricted? If the answer is 'no,' the weak paternalist on this interpretation would think the paternalistic intervention justified, but if the answer is 'yes' he (or she) would think it unjustified. Second, we could construe the consent requirement as restricting justifiable paternalistic interferences to those occasions where the person whose liberty we restrict is suffering from defects in his capacity to make decisions but would, if these defects were subsequently to be eradicated, *at that time* give retroactive approval to our paternalistic actions. The former reading, which gives precedence to the individual's state of mind at the time when he is paternalistically restrained (after making due allowance for his impaired capacities), is the one that perhaps best captures the intentions of weak paternalists. But the second reading has figured in the thinking of at least some weak paternalists. The fact that subsequent consent would be one sort of evidence to support the counterfactual judgment involved in the former reading may have helped obscure the differences between the two readings.

The nub of the weak paternalist's reasoning is that there is nothing improper about restricting people's self-determination to prevent them from acting in ways to which they neither can occurrently give genuine consent nor would give consent when fully competent. As well, though, some writers who are staunch opponents of strong paternalism have sought to justify weak paternalism on the ground that it may *enhance* autonomy. Mill, for instance, in discussing why autonomous adults should not be permitted freely to sell themselves into perpetual slavery offers as his reason that it is not freedom to be permitted to give up one's freedom (rather than suggesting e.g. that the person would subsequently consent to the intervention).[2] Later I shall register my disagreement with Mill's characterization of this case (in terms of weak paternalism)

---

2 *On Liberty* in *Collected Works of J.S. Mill*, ed. J.M. Robson (Toronto, 1963- ) vol. XVIII, 299-300.

but for the moment neither this nor his consistency concern me. I introduce him here because his manoeuvre conveniently brings into focus several of the chief concerns of this present paper.

I shall argue, first, that a policy only of weak paternalism lacks comprehensiveness in that it fails to do justice to certain widely shared and deeply entrenched moral convictions relevant to paternalistic intervention. Second, I shall argue that this deficiency can nonetheless be made good because these convictions do line up well with a policy of (selective) strong paternalism. Finally, I will try to turn the tables completely on those liberals who support weak paternalism but oppose strong paternalism by arguing that strong paternalism is sometimes needed to preserve autonomy. Or, to put the point another way, I shall argue that those who seriously value autonomy cannot remain content with weak paternalism.

# I

Weak paternalism, I have indicated, involves interferences where there is (or is believed to be) a defect in the decision-making capacities of the person interfered with and is claimed to be justifiable insofar as consent to the interference would be forthcoming were the capacities in question to be restored. Moreover, I have reported some advocates of weak paternalism as claiming that there is nothing improper about restricting people's self-determination to prevent them from acting in ways to which they cannot occurrently give genuine consent because their decision-making capacities are impaired. This is legitimate provided only that had they not been thus affected they would have chosen differently (or, alternatively that they would later ratify the intervention if given the opportunity). Mill, while holding that in self-regarding matters the individual's independence is 'of right, absolute' appeals to the former consideration in arguing that children and those 'in their nonage' fail to possess such an absolute right.[3] A similar justification would appear to be in his mind when he sanctions interferences with those who are 'delirious or in some state of excitement or absorption incompatible with the full use of the reflecting faculty.'[4] In *Principles of Political Economy (Collected Works,* Vol. III), however, Mill allows paternalistic

---

3  Mill, 224

4  Mill, 294

interferences where a person is a poor judge or guardian of his or her real interests, especially in matters of education and culture, or where an irrevocable decision has been taken which would have far-reaching consequences on the distant, and hence less vivid, interests of the decision-taker (p. 803, 938). These qualifications, in effect, pick out persons thought *incompetent* to give full-blooded consent in certain matters or make decisions of certain types.[5] Some weak paternalists have further extended the categories of incompetence to include others like the senile, the mentally inferior, the compulsive and the ignorant on the ground that these, too, are persons whose capacity to choose in ways that promote their welfare or satisfy their needs is defective.

Now that we are armed with a better understanding of the range of conditions under which weak paternalistic interventions are thought to be appropriate we must turn our attention to the idea of actual or anticipated consent since it is this consent which is claimed to nullify the otherwise objectionable features of paternalism.

Certainly actual consent mandates paternalism (as in Dworkin's[6] example of Odysseus who ordered his underlings to restrain him in the presence of the Sirens), at least until the consent is withdrawn. Most of the incompetents mentioned by weak paternalists are held to be justifiably restricted because the individuals would, it is held, have chosen differently had they been in more favourable circumstances as regards their decision-making capacities. Support for this claim is standardly offered in the form of a presumption that people who allow themselves to be injured or harmed are, in doing so, not consenting freely and informedly. Thus Mill suggests of the person (justifiably) restrained from crossing an unsafe bridge that he will come to appreciate the restraint because 'liberty consists in doing what one desires, and he does not desire to fall into the river' (p. 294).[7] In similar vein Dworkin sees the paternalistic treatment of adults in relation to health and life as a kind of insurance policy taken out against making decisions which are far-reaching, potentially dangerous and irreversible.[8]

---

5 The limitation to 'decisions of certain types' is because people are rarely, if ever, incompetent across the board. Cf. J. Murphy,' Incompetence and Paternalism,' *Archiv für Rechts- und Sozialphilosophie,* **60** (1974) 465-86 (esp. p. 467f).

6 G. Dworkin, 'Paternalism,' *The Monist,* **56** (1972) 64-84 (esp. p. 77)

7 Cf. C.L. Ten's claim in 'Paternalism and Morality,' *Ratio,* **13** (1971) 56-66 that there is 'a general presumption that men do not like to have severe physical injury inflicted on them' (p. 65). Ten believes there is no such general presumption concerning moral harm. The relation between paternalism and the 'enforcement of morality' will be considered later in the essay.

8 Cf., too, Murphy, 481, who, à la Rawls, sees limited paternalism as justifiable in the absence of a guarantee that individuals won't be reduced to incompetence that will compromise their access to primary goods.

But what of the notion of *anticipated* consent? There are various problems with this idea. I shall briefly mention one which has had some airing recently and then raise another more central to my purposes. The first is an especially serious consideration for those inclined to subscribe to the second of the readings of 'consent' which I outlined in my opening remarks. But given the somewhat confused position of weak paternalists on how consent is to be construed it would also have an impact on those supporting the first reading who consider retroactive approval for paternalism to be relevant evidence about the state of mind of a person at the time of paternalistic restriction. In her paper 'Justifying Paternalism,'[9] Rosemary Carter has pointed out that subsequent consent can be achieved by manipulation, especially with children. A child might, by dint of the successful distortion of his or her beliefs, desires and preferences, come to approve of the pressures used to develop precisely these beliefs and attitudes. Such consent hardly justifies the interference. Similar considerations would apply to an adult who is made the subject of manipulation (or, more extremely, who is 'brainwashed' into a new set of beliefs) and comes thereby to approve of the manipulation (or the brainwashing).[10]

Nonetheless, as John Kleinig remarked to me, in the absence of a theory of distortion Carter's principle is not as helpful as at first sight it appears. Whether we acknowledge the presence of distortion tends to turn on what we *value*. This threatens a dangerous circularity for it may lead to using our conception of the good for a person as a criterion for what a person can rationally or informedly consent to.[11] It becomes hard consequently to get agreement of a sort suitable as a foundation for a general policy on interventions.[12]

This, however, is a relatively minor problem for the weak paternalist resort to anticipated consent. The major problem concerns what follows when we have good reason to believe some individual would not subse-

---

9  *Canadian Journal of Philosophy,* **7** (1977) 133-45

10  Cf. John Rawls, *A Theory of Justice* (Cambridge, MA.: Harvard University Press 1971) 249-50.

11  Cf. Murphy, 482, note 29.

12  Carter's case of parents from a narrow religious sect who distort the development of their child's intellectual or artistic skills may strike responsive chords in her usual reader. What, though, of Kleinig's example of the man who has been brought up to see his future in industry and commerce, who finds his world an exciting, competitive one and who, moreover, actually sees himself indebted to his parents for the adequacy of his preparation to enter the world he relishes?

quently thank us for interfering (and so, other things being equal, would not have consented either at the time or afterwards to the intervention). The rebuttable presumption on which the anticipated consent model is built may, in other words, be rebutted and so fail to hold in particular cases since it relies on what is at best a strongly supported empirical generalization.

Suppose a child never comes to agree that the fluoride tablets administered by his or her parents were worth it. Suppose a person even after lengthy discussion of his or her intention does not appreciate our stopping him from jumping off a high bridge, or from swimming after dark on an unpatrolled beach known to have dangerous riptides. We cannot properly infer the irrationality of such people on these behavioural scores alone. Let us turn the screws a little harder against the alleged sufficiency of weak paternalism: suppose $S$ knows that heroin addiction causes severe physical harm and likely death before thirty years of age, but still chooses to take the drug because he wants the pleasure of the moment more than anything else. Assume, furthermore, that we independently have good grounds for believing $S$ is emotionally stable and of sound reason. A policy of weak paternalism cannot in such a case justify intervention to prevent $S$'s taking heroin. (As we shall see later a strong paternalist would argue for intervention where such a person would by his (or her) action undermine other valued but more dispositional commitments.)

It is instructive to see what weak paternalists have said of these problematic cases for their position. Carter to some degree bites the bullet and contends that if the motive for legislating against heroin usage is to prevent people harming themselves such legislation will be unjustified. But she nonetheless suggests (p. 145) that if a majority of citizens want the legislation as a safeguard against their own weakness of will (and at the same time require a *sacrifice* on the part of those who do not want such legislation) the legislation will be paternalistic and justified. The strong impression given is that this is an account of why in reality we do endorse such interventionalist policies on the taking of heroin. As such it is clearly beside the point, and in fact represents an *ad hoc* manoeuvre to save a theory. Moreover, Carter's reasoning is quite unconvincing when applied to the restrictions placed on participation in certain work and recreational activities without prescribed safety equipment, speedway racing by inadequately qualified drivers, professional boxing between grossly ill-matched boxers, contracting to become a wage-slave, ritual human sacrifice of consenting participants from weird cults, voluntary participation in unnecessary, risky experiments and so on. But, more importantly for present purposes, the weak paternalist position is at odds with widely held and deeply entrenched moral convictions to the effect that either the state or other adults are justified in intervening in just such cases.

In reply it is sometimes claimed that in cases like those mentioned there is real uncertainty about the extent to which the actions in question are informed and voluntary. If this were so all apparent cases of strong paternalism would collapse into cases of weak paternalism. But there seems no good reason to think it is so. Others contend that we should just jettison the convictions that underlie these contemporary examples of paternalism, but even in a period where the clamour for liberty rights is at a peak there appears to be little or no weakening in the support for (strong) paternalist interventions *in matters like those listed*. Rather than spurn these convictions we would do better to give up an exclusivist weak paternalism, especially since, as I shall argue below, the concern for autonomy reflected in support for weak paternalism is better safeguarded by a policy of (selective) strong paternalism under the guidelines which I shall later advance.

Let us turn to Dworkin. Just whether Dworkin is accurately to be regarded as a weak paternalist is open to dispute. At least two writers[13] take Dworkin to be defending a strong form of paternalism. Unfortunately what Dworkin says makes for conflicting evidence. He frequently emphasizes the importance of future-oriented consent and this, as we've seen, is characteristic of weak paternalists. But there is, as well, talk of restricting a person's voluntary actions whenever it can reasonably be claimed that *fully rational* persons would choose such restrictions, from which it may be inferred that the individual's actual choices need not prove decisive. The issue is not cleared up when we attend to the instances of justified paternalism he offers, for in the main they involve impaired choices (e.g. taking addicitive drugs which hinder reasoned choices or attempting suicide while under psychological pressure). The one apparently clear exception comes in the course of his exposition of Mill's views on slavery (p. 75f) where he appears to agree with Mill that paternalism is justifiable even when a decision to become a slave is voluntarily taken.

Nonetheless, I think Dworkin is appropriately to be thought of as a weak paternalist because that is the general drift of his essay (particularly in section VI), because of his talk of what fully rational individuals would agree to in the way of paternalistic restrictions, which is best read as evidence that he thinks it prudent sometimes to restrict our liberties in light of the fact that we do not always occurrently recognize what is in

---

13 M. Bayles, 'Criminal Paternalism,' in J.R. Pennock and J.W. Chapman, eds., *Nomos XV: The Limits of Law* (New York: Athlone 1974) 174-88; J. Hodson, 'The Principle of Paternalism,' *American Philosophical Quarterly*, **14** (1977) 61-9

our best interests (see p. 78), and because of the position he takes on a case to be outlined, which has significant parallels to that of contracting into slavery.

Dworkin offers as examples of distinct sorts of irrationality the Christian Scientist[14] who prefers to die rather than have a blood transfusion and the person who, while aware of the risks, refuses to wear a seat-belt in an automobile because of the inconvenience (p. 78f). The second person will, according to Dworkin, be shown just to have miscalculated if he is like most people other than in placing an enormously high negative value on inconvenience. The Jehovah's Witness, by contrast, attaches incorrect weights to certain of his values. Dworkin thinks that where evaluative differences are involved there should be greater reluctance to act paternalistically and hence would support intervention in the second, though not the first, of his cases. There are two points to be made about this claim. First, Dworkin relies on our accepting that the person who refuses to wear a seat-belt solely because of its inconvenience would be open to persuasion once the calculations of risks are laid before him. But it would only be 'irrational' of a person to refuse to be swayed by the calculations in the sense of *irrationality* which does duty for *incorrectness*. To say of a person in the case where he fails to do the calculations correctly that he is irrational is only to say that he is objectively wrong about the matter in question. This forces us beyond the sense of 'rationality' appealed to in the weak paternalist case. Perhaps Dworkin's mistake stems from neglecting cases where people aren't ignorant but instead fail properly to care for their interests. Secondly, those of us who would support intervention in the case of the Jehovah's Witness wish to do so because such a person, too, is wrong to think as he does. He is evaluatively deluded. There is a parallel evaluative delusion on which I shall later elaborate in the case of selling oneself into slavery. (Not for nothing is there a famous work, *Thirty Years a Watchtower Slave*, by a Jehovah's Witness who was liberated from the organization.) Yet Dworkin's judgment suggests otherwise. Hence if his earlier remarks on slavery are tantamount to an endorsement of strong paternalism he is here inconsistent. Better, I think, to see the weight of evidence on the side of his being a weak paternalist while in like manner with Mill adopting a position on voluntary slavery which sits uneasily with this.[15]

---

14 He should have said 'Jehovah's Witness.'

15 In 'Mill versus Paternalism,' *Ethics*, **90** (1980) 470-89, Richard Arneson urges that it is best to regard Mill's views on voluntary slavery as an aberration from his more libertarian views elsewhere. But, one might ask, why not regard Mill's

## II

The response is sometimes made to criticisms like those advanced in the previous section that they have plausibility only if we accept not just strong paternalism but the *enforcement of morality* as well. In advocating (legal or other) prohibitions on certain practices, like those on slavery,[16] or in lending support to laws designed to regulate and control the establishment of a 'Jonestown,' the taking of certain drugs, involvement in prostitution, or even requiring workers to contribute to superannuation schemes, the strong paternalist, it is claimed, is advocating that his (or her) own moral values be enforced, even on those who do not share them. In urging the priority of, for example, harm prevention over voluntary participation in harmful activities (like the taking of heroin), is the strong paternalist involved in seeking the translation of *his* value commitments into the law for *all*?[17]

One way that a strong paternalist might be tempted to take with this argument is to say that the weak paternalist's position is in no better plight because in advocating the priority in law of the standard of voluntariness he too is seeking legal enforcement of his moral position. Thus all laws that have a paternalistic character invoke moral values. Despite its tempting appearance this response won't do because it is too simple-minded. It turns on linking moral values and legal restrictions in a way different from the one urged by legal moralists. the legal moralist is concerned with the protection of persons from 'moral harm,' to use Devlin's[18] phrase, and the young from moral corruption. Since the

---

remarks, or Dworkin's or Feinberg's in 'Legal Paternalism,' *Canadian Journal of Philosophy,* **1** (1971-2) 105-24, where there is a similar recognition of the difficulties such cases pose for an exclusive weak paternalist policy, as evidence of the inherent unsatisfactoriness of such a policy?

16 Carole Pateman suggested to me that the parallels between marriage for women and slavery are so strong as to show that what is called for is not so much 'paternalism' as radical social change. While I certainly don't want to gainsay her point, there are weighty issues to do with paternalism which require attention and would do so even under better social orders.

17 Cf. C.E. Harris, 'Paternalism and the Enforcement of Morality,' *Southwestern Journal of Philosophy,* **8** (1977) 85-93. Christine Pierce in 'Hart on Paternalism,' *Analysis,* **35** (1975) 205-7 argues that obscurities in H.L.A. Hart's views on paternalism in *Law, Liberty and Morality* (London: Oxford University Press 1963), esp. p. 33, suggest that he has not kept paternalism separate from the enforcement of morality.

18 P. Devlin, *The Enforcement of Morals* (London: Oxford University Press 1965). It might be said that the position of the legal moralist is not as highminded as this

strong paternalist sometimes advocates interferences, like compelling a Jehovah's Witness to have a blood transfusion, which, even though they force the citizen to be involved in what he (or she) considers immoral, are aimed at protecting him from physical harm not from self-imposed moral harm, the reply is insufficiently broad. The interconnectedness of legal and moral matters is not the point at issue in talk of the enforcement of morality.

It might seem more promising for the strong paternalist simply to borrow from the weak paternalist account of the distinction between paternalism and legal moralism advanced by C.L. Ten in 'Paternalism and Morality.' Ten points out that (weak) paternalistic interventions are not aimed at preventing moral wickedness (or, if this should appear too strong, 'moral harm'). Second, he notes that the ground for paternalistic interventions is the protection or promotion of the interests of particular persons who are to be prevented from harming themselves. The interventions are thus anchored to specific interests. In contradistinction the enforcement of morality is justified typically by appeal to various general considerations, like the preservation intact of a particular form of social existence urged by Devlin. These considerations may have little or nothing to do with the interests of the persons (say, individual consenting adult homosexuals) whose moral behaviour is subject to legal proscription.

While this is a response with which a weak paternalist may be able to rest content it would be dishonest of me to suggest that it will do the whole job as far as a strong paternalist (at least of my ilk) is concerned. The distinction urged by Ten will be preserved with many of the interventions which a strong paternalist wishes to justify. There is one class of cases, however, where it becomes moot whether to talk of strong paternalism or of the enforcement of a moral position.

The objection before us seeks to associate strong paternalism with the odium that surrounds talk of the enforcement of morality. I shall argue that the sense in which the interventions at issue would constitute the enforcement of a moral position is suficiently removed from that given to the term by Devlin and others to take the sting out of the objection.

Consider one of the cases which we have seen proves troublesome to weak paternalism: permitting a person freely and informedly to contract into slavery. Mill, for instance, claims that giving due recognition to

---

way of putting things suggests. There is some truth in this claim since legal moralists have sometimes wanted to prohibit things simply because they are thought immoral or sinful. The position sketched in the text is nonetheless the one to which the more careful exponents of legal moralism lend their support.

the principle of individual freedom cannot require that a person should be free not to be free. It is, he says, not freedom to be allowed to alienate one's freedom. This is all, of course, utterly *a priori* since there are various considerations which might induce a person freely and informedly to contract into slavery: in return for a great benefit one has received or will receive; for reasons of religious devotion; as a means of advancing some cause of deep importance to oneself and so on. Despite the failure of this weak paternalistic line of Mill's, Mill himself gives the clue, if not a well-developed argument, as to how we might justify intervening to prevent people freely and informedly selling themselves into slavery.[19] He points out (*On Liberty,* p. 299) that to permit people such a liberty would prevent the preservation of their liberty *to make future choices.* As he puts it:

> ... But by selling himself for a slave, he abdicates his liberty; he forgoes any future use of it beyond that single act ...

To restrict a person's immediate freedom is sometimes to promote a wider range of future freedoms for the person. Here is the link with autonomy. To be autonomous is to be one's own man or woman; it is not merely to be free but to be free to order one's life in a unified way according to a plan or conception which fully expresses one's own individual preferences, interests and so on.[20] The autonomous person is then, to put it in popular terms, his own man or her own woman. This is, as far as it goes, an accurate enough picture. However, I suggest that we need to go further and distinguish the *occurrent* sense of autonomy that this popular picture usually represents from the dispositional or *global* sense of autonomy. When we talk of people acting autonomously in particular situations we are talking of their occurrent autonomy. But when we wish to make a more global judgment about the self-directedness of someone's life what is at issue is whether in the broad it is ordered according to a plan or conception which fully expresses his or her own will. By 'plan' I do not mean to suggest something too formal, but rather whatever it is that a person wants to do in and with his or her life, and, therefore, to cover career, life-style, dominant concerns, and so on. (It is obvious, of course, that people's preferences, interests and so on do not always coincide and as well that an individual's other values

---

19 Cf. Dworkin, p. 76, where, if my earlier argument was sound, a similar suggestion is made from within a weak paternalist framework.

20 A conception I have elaborated in 'Autonomy and the "Inner Self" ', *American Philosophical Quarterly,* **17** (1980) 35-43.

may come to assume at some time more importance for him (or her) than his autonomy, so the commitment we have to the valuableness of personal autonomy[21] can at best be a defeasible commitment.)

Since slavery, no matter how gladly the act of becoming a slave is entered into, renders one human the mere possession or property of another and thereby violates the individual's *global* autonomy, we are justified in intervening to prevent persons contracting into it. Whether or not such an intervening is to be characterized as 'strong paternalism' or as 'the enforcement of a moral position' (in the sense that I shall use this latter term) turns on whether the protection of an individual's liberty to make future choices is in his (or her) interest all things considered. If a person forgoes his global autonomy by contracting voluntarily into permanent slavery and is judged to be *harmed* in consequence (the loss of autonomy more than counterbalancing any gains from enslavement), intervention to stop the enforcement of the contract is strongly paternalistic.

However, if the gains derived from contracting voluntarily into permanent slavery outweigh the loss that stems from foregoing global autonomy, that if it is actually to the *benefit* of the individual to become a perpetual slave, to prohibit such a contract would not be strongly paternalistic. If such a prohibition is to be justified it would seem that it must be done on the grounds that it is *immoral* for one person to own another. So where the benefits anticipated by the would-be slave are significant, and not available without enslavement, to intervene to prevent enslavement would be to enforce a moral position. It seems to me, though, that the objector to whom I have been responding can take no real comfort from this admission since the immorality involved in one individual's 'owning' another bears no relation to the standards of sexual morality which Devlin and others urged should be enforced by the state in order to prevent 'moral harm' and even to maintain societal integrity.

My stance clearly places a high value on autonomy, especially in its global dimension. It is necessary to say that the commitment we have to autonomy is, nonetheless, defeasible. Suppose that the authorities in a certain country have indicated that they will not permit the members of a particular family to emigrate except in exchange for a key member of it who is in exile. Suppose further that while there is no threat of physical harm to the resident members of the family they would be

---

21 A commitment nicely brought out in e.g. Robert Nozick's discussion of the hoary philosophical example of an 'experience machine.' See *Anarchy, State, and Utopia* (New York: Basic Books 1974) 42ff. Feinberg's discussion of the value of autonomy in *Social Philosophy* (Englewood Cliffs, NJ: Prentice Hall 1973) 20f is also helpful.

freed from the serious and ongoing harassment to which they are subject if they could leave. Suppose finally that it is known that if the
wanted exile puts himself in the hands of the authorities he will become
a virtual slave to the regime. This is a case where intervention would
clearly be strongly paternalistic but despite the high value we place on
autonomy we may refuse to intervene because here consequentialist
considerations override (allowing that Anscombian scruples about deal-
ing with people corrupt enough to exact such bargains can be set aside).
This then seems to be one of those exceptional cases where consequentialist factors are sufficiently significant to take precedence over such
normally prior values as doing justice, protecting such human rights as
there may be or, as here, preserving autonomy. These consequentialist
considerations make a case for *not* intervening to protect people from
voluntarily entering into total enslavement.

Even if this is correct it does not gainsay my central point that for
those who place a high value on autonomy its preservation provides the
foundation for an important argument for strong paternalism which,
moreover, is generalizable to cover the range of circumstances mentioned earlier in the essay where I argued the limitations of weak paternalism.

## III

Are other objections to my strong paternalist stance also able to be over-
come? I believe so. Consider an objection mounted by Feinberg which
could be turned against my position.[22] He urges that if we take respect
for a person's voluntary choice as such as an ultimate principle then we
can consistently oppose strong paternalism in all its manifestations. Fortunately, we need not consider the issue of whether liberty or autonomy
for Feinberg is good for its own sake or merely as a means to other
goods; for when confronted with the all-crucial case of voluntarily contracting into slavery he hedges his bets by claiming that administrative
considerations, for instance the cumbersome and expensive legal
machinery that would be needed to test for voluntariness, justify
outlawing such slavery.

There are several comments to be made about this objection and its
subsequent hedging. First, it should be noticed that acceptance of

---

22 'Legal Paternalism,' 116ff.

Feinberg's ultimate principle would commit one to giving precedence to the worth (intrinsic or instrumental) of occurrent autonomy – the choice of the moment – rather than to global or dispositional autonomy since enslavement clearly impinges on the whole pattern of a person's choices. It is far from obvious that such a commitment is desirable. (If Feinberg were to construe his doctrine of the sovereignty of voluntary choice in global terms there would be no disagreement between us but his remarks [p. 120f] preclude such a construction.) Second, in defending his claims about the administrative complications that would be associated with *extreme* forfeitures of freedom, Feinberg points out that certain resignations of liberties are obviously permissible and cites such legally sanctioned practices as foregoing particular liberties in reasonable employment contracts or commercial ventures. I have two comments here. To begin with, it is not enough to cite such instances of limited, albeit extensive, forfeitures because one of the grounds on which we differentiate reasonable contracts involving forfeitures from unreasonable ones (amounting to perpetual slavery) is the extent and nature of the curtailed liberties. We can and do want to differentiate such matters – as Feinberg would agree – so it is no help to cite the reasonable forfeitures to underpin a doctrine, even a hedged one, of the sovereignty of the voluntary chooser. As well, though, Feinberg's contention that the legal machinery that would be needed to test voluntariness in such matters so as to warrant our outlawing slavery would be cumbersome and expensive, is hardly very persuasive. The reason is that we already find it needful and possible to test voluntariness in other important legal matters, and seem certain to be required to do so even more if anticipated legal changes occur in relation to e.g. voluntary euthanasia. And whether or not his claims on this score are persuasive they could hardly provide the whole ground for any *principled* policy that a society might develop on e.g. slavery contracts, voluntary taking of heroin or voluntary participation in seriously risky, unnecessary experiments.

Yet, it may still appear that there is something fishy about the claim that a policy of strong paternalism (even a selective one) can be justified on the grounds that it preserves autonomy. Isn't it true that in paternalistically preventing someone who wants to sell himself into perpetual slavery from becoming a slave that the strong paternalist is *thereby* violating that person's autonomy? Indeed isn't it tantamount to treating the person in question in precisely the way the master treats the slave? Undoubtedly it is from challenges like these that the greatest threat to strong paternalism comes. I shall try to answer these challenges by briefly recapping some of the points I have made earlier.

I indicated previously that in the global sense of autonomy a person's career, life-style, dominant concerns and the like will be central to his (or her) conception of his life. Autonomy as regards the important interests in a person's life must be of the global kind rather than the occurrent, because only in the former sense does the course of an individual's life enjoy a unified order and avoid self-defeating conflict in fundamentals. To maximize autonomy over the course of a lifetime it is global autonomy that must be preserved. Given that it is this conception of autonomy which we should seek to foster, strong paternalist interventions will sometimes be needed. The strong paternalist may thereby be required to violate occurrent autonomy but unlike the weak paternalist he will think such forfeitures worthwhile because of his commitment to global autonomy.

## IV

Even those who concede that a reasonable foundation can be found in my preceding argument to support strong paternalism *in theory* may nonetheless be reluctant to support it *in practice*. Some attention needs, therefore, to be given to the guidelines appropriate to the implementation of a policy involving strong paternalism, particularly as regards legal paternalism. I shall lead into a discussion of these guidelines by considering an argument of Mill's of a quite different character from that associated with the priority of liberty. Mill claims that even where (legal) paternalism is motivated by the best of intentions it is more often than not misguided.

In *On Liberty* he writes:

> But the strongest of all the arguments against the interference of the public with purely personal conduct is that, when it does interfere, the odds are that it interferes wrongly, and in the wrong place. On questions of social morality, of duty to others, the opinion of the public, that is, of an overruling majority, though often wrong, is likely to be still oftener right; because on such questions they are only required to judge of their own interests; of the manner in which some mode of conduct, if allowed to be practised, would effect (sic) themselves. But the opinion of a similar majority, imposed as a law on the minority, on questions of self-regarding conduct, is quite as likely to be wrong as right; for in these cases public opinion means, at the best, some people's opinion of what is good or bad for other people ... (283)[23]

---

23  Cf., too, R. Sartorius, *Individual Conduct and Social Norms* (Encino and Belmont, (CA: Dickenson 1975) 155f.

This is a curious argument though not chiefly for the reason offered by Hart in criticizing Mill, namely that we are now less inclined to believe that individuals know their own interests best. It is curious rather because it question-beggingly supposes judgments (by others) of harm to certain individuals to be matters of mere opinion. Moreover what we have come to call 'the enforcement of morality' is seemingly un-characteristically conflated by Mill with paternalism, which I have already argued in section II is indefensible. Indeed, compounding con-fusion, Mill gives his famous example of legislation by Muslims against the eating of pork and then concludes his argument by urging that

> The only tenable ground of condemnation would be, that with the personal tastes and self-regarding concerns of individuals the public has no business to interfere. (285)

This by his own admission is to do with a matter of morality as far as Muslims are concerned,[24] though he began by 'speaking of conduct which, while it does no wrong to others, is supposed to do great harm to the agent himself' (p. 283).

Mill's argument clearly does not provide an absolute barrier to pater-nalism. But its confusions militate even against his claim that pater-nalistic legislation would be misguided. Furthermore, I earlier gave il-lustrative cases of where we may without reference to mere 'opinion' *reliably* conclude that serious harm will ensue even to voluntary par-ticipants. Finally, one can distill from the writings of two recent defenders of weak paternalism several considerations relevant to the dismissal of Mill's fears and which serve to limit paternalism to the kinds of instances I previously argued were clearly justifiable.[25]

Dworkin (pp. 82-4) and Murphy (pp. 483-5) have each advanced criteria for limiting the scope of paternalism. Basically these criteria operate to specify the nature of the harm to be prevented more closely and more systematically than I have to date. A prominent consideration is whether the harm is of a serious or major sort and, associated with this, whether it is easily reversed. Grave harms such as loss of future liberty, loss of mental powers or serious physical impairment can be regarded as a direct obstacle either to autonomy or its enjoyment. Thus

---

24 But, significantly, it is diminished by Mill to a matter of personal *taste*.

25 *Pace* T. Beauchamp, 'Paternalism and Biobehavioral Control,' *The Monist*, **60** (1977) 62-80, where it is argued *inter alia* that all legal paternalism should be re-jected in part because it would not be possible accurately enough to restrict in-terventions.

where a drug has the effect of causing permanent brain damage the case for paternalism is radically unlike that for marijuana usage. Similarly, multiple ingredient analgesics causing renal damage to significant numbers of users will be in a different case to single ingredient ones. A second concern is the extent and character of the interventions to be countenanced. The intervention must clearly be linked to the harm-threatening behaviour; be, after due account has been taken of cost or convenience, the alternative least interruptive of liberty; be limited in duration; and, where the paternalism is legal in character, the procedures to be followed and the personnel who are to have the power of interference must be clearly specified. Thirdly, Dworkin argues that given 'the resources of ignorance, ill-will and stupidity available to the law-makers of a society' (p. 83), a heavy and clear burden of proof rests on the state to demonstrate the exact nature of the seriously harmful effects (or beneficial consequences) and their probability of occurrence. This would seem especially to be so where the activity at issue plays a determinative role in a person's life-plan. While there might be circumstances where the weather is such that even skilled mountain-climbers should be prevented for a time from climbing one could not normally urge the argument from autonomy as the basis for hindering a person in the pursuit of a life-plan that revolves around the conquest of mountain hazards.

It may be thought by some readers that the position I have defended is obviously faulty where *death* is the harm threatened by a person's behaviour or proposed behaviour. Surely, some may say, suicide and voluntary euthanasia should not be restricted even under the safeguards just outlined. Are we not in danger of returning to the oppressive mores of earlier generations on such matters if strong paternalism is endorsed? The argument from autonomy once again comes into its own here. Those who seek voluntary euthanasia do so because they have incurable conditions which involve intolerable pain and suffering or have in obtaining relief from such pain forfeited a recognizably human existence.[26] Such persons clearly have concluded quite reasonably that the fulfilment of further aspects of their life-plan is now out of the question. In acceding to their request for voluntary euthanasia we do not preclude significant future choices. So adoption of a policy of legal paternalism — whether of the strong or the weak variety — is not at all

---

26 Those who descend into such an existence can, of course, be candidates for *voluntary* euthanasia if they have made an advance declaration or 'living will' to the effect that under such circumstances they want euthanasia to be administered. For more on the topic see my 'Voluntary and Nonvoluntary Euthanasia,' *The Monist*, **59** (1976) 264-83.

incompatible with legalizing voluntary euthanasia. In relation to suicide similar points are in order. Where there is established a clear irrationality about the range and significance of autonomy open to a would-be suicide we could appeal to weak paternalist grounds in restraining the individual. Such an appeal would also be in order where it is at the time unclear whether the person's behaviour is fully reflective. Other justifications for preventing suicide would almost certainly not be paternalistic (e.g. in that harm to others will otherwise be occasioned). The strong paternalist is not, therefore, committed to a policy which threatens to undermine human freedom over such an important area as death or the manner of one's dying.

## V

We do have to consider as a community whether the *gain* in having legal scope for paternalistic interferences (as well as interpersonal scope) is sufficiently worthwhile to warrant the effort and trouble needed to establish guidelines that will minimize manipulation for the purposes of arbitrary or repressive interferences with liberty.[27] And we do have to consider whether there would be any *loss* if we failed to provide in law for strong paternalism. I have argued that there is a gain to be had which is worth the effort of establishing careful guidelines because failure to make this provision would for some people some of the time significantly diminish their autonomy as regards primary human goods.[28]

---

27  On this score I wholeheartedly support remarks especially of Murphy and Beauchamp about the treatment often meted out to the institutionalised and to 'problem' children.

28  I would like to thank John Campbell, Robert Fox, John Kleinig, H.J. McCloskey and Michael Stocker for their helpful criticisms of a previous draft.

## Select Bibliography

Arneson, R., 'Mill versus Paternalism,' *Ethics,* **90** (1980) 470-89.

Bayles, M., 'Criminal Paternalism,' in *The Limits of Law, Nomos* xv (New York: Athlone 1974) 174-88.

Beauchamp, T., 'On Justifications for Coercive Genetic Engineering,' in *Biomedical Ethics and the Law,* edited by R.F. Almeder and J.M. Humber (New York: Plenum Press 1976).

Beauchamp, T., 'Paternalism,' in *Encyclopedia of Bioethics,* edited by Warren T. Reich (New York: Free Press 1978).

Beauchamp, T., 'Paternalism and Biobehavioral Control,' *The Monist,* **60** (1977) 62-80.

Buchanan, A., 'Medical Paternalism,' *Philosophy and Public Affairs,* **7** (1977-78) 370-90

Carter, R., 'Justifying Paternalism,' *Canadian Journal of Philosophy,* **7** (1977-78) 133-45.

Crocker, L., *Positive Liberty* (The Hague: Nijhoff 1980).

Dworkin, G., 'Paternalism,' *The Monist,* **56** (1972) 64-84.

Feinberg, J., 'Legal Paternalism,' *Canadian Journal of Philosophy,* **1** (1971-72) 105-24. (See qualifying remarks in Feinberg's *Rights, Justice and the Bounds of Liberty* [Princeton, NJ: Princeton University Press 1980])

Feinberg, J., 'The Child's Right to an Open Future,' In *Whose Child?: Children's Rights, Parental Authority and State Power,* edited by W. Aiken and H. La Follette (Totowa, NJ: Littlefield Adams and Co. 1980).

Fotion, N., 'Paternalism,' *Ethics,* **89** (1979) 191-210.

Gert, B., and C. Culver, 'Paternalistic Behavior,' *Philosophy and Public Affairs,* **6** (1976-77) 45-57.

Gert, B., and C. Culver, 'The Justication of Paternalism,' *Ethics,* **89** (1979) 370-90.

Gutmann, A, 'Children, Paternalism and Education,' *Philosophy and Public Affairs,* **9** (1979-80) 338-58.

Harris, C., 'Paternalism and the Enforcement of Morality,' *Southwestern Journal of Philosophy,* **8** (1977) 85-93.

Hodson, J., 'The Principle of Paternalism,' *American PhilosophicalQuarterly,* **14** (1977) 61-9.

Hospers, J., 'Libertarianism and Legal Paternalism,' *Journal of Libertarian Studies,* **4** (1980) 255-65.

Husak, D., 'Paternalism and Autonomy,' *Philosophy and Public Affairs,* **10** (1980-81) 27-46.

65

May, L., 'Paternalism and Self-Interest,' *Journal of Value Inquiry,* **14** (1980) 195-216.

Mill, J.S., *On Liberty.*

Murphy, J., 'Incompetence and Paternalism,' *Archiv für Rechts- und Sozialphilosophie,* **60** (1974) 465-86.

Newton, L., 'Liberty and Laetrile: Implications of Right of Access,' *Journal of Value Inquiry,* **15** (1981) 55-67.

Regan, D., 'Justifications for Paternalism,' in *The Limits of Law, Nomos XV* (New York: Athlone 1974) 189-210.

Rawls, J., *A Theory of Justice* (Cambridge, MA: Haward University Press 1971).

Robison, W.L. and M.S. Pritchard (eds.), *Medical Responsibility* (Clifton, NJ: Humana Press 1979), [various papers].

Ten, C.L., *Mill On Liberty,* (Oxford: Clarendon Press 1980).

VanDeVeer, D., 'Paternalism and Subsequent Consent,' *Canadian Journal of Philosophy,* **9** (1979) 631-42.

VanDeVeer, D., 'Autonomy-Respecting Paternalism,' *Social Theory and Practice,* **6** (1980) 187-207.

VanDeVeer, D., 'The Contractual for Withholding Medical Information,' *Philosophy and Public Affairs,* **9** (1979-80) 198-205.

Wikler, D., 'Paternalism and the Mildly Retarded,' *Philosophy and Public Affairs,* **8** (1978-79) 377-92.

CANADIAN JOURNAL OF PHILOSOPHY
Supplementary Volume VIII, 1982

# Paternalism and Justification*

JAMES WOODWARD, Memphis State University

Much recent discussion in moral philosophy has focused on the contrast between those moral theories which are consequentialist in structure and those moral theories which admit independent side constraints on the means which can be used to achieve various ends. In this essay I shall attempt to show that this contrast provides an illuminating framework against which to understand two conflicting strategies for justifying paternalistic interference. The first, consequentialist strategy takes paternalistic interference to be justified when it will protect or perhaps enhance some valued goal or end state, such as an agent's welfare or future ability to choose. Gerald Dworkin's essay 'Paternalism'[1] contains what is perhaps the most compelling recent development of this sort of rationale for paternalistic interference and accordingly much of my subsequent discussion will focus on this essay. The second, non-consequentialist strategy holds that the consent of the person interfered

---

\* I would like to thank Phillip Devine, Norman Gillespie, Hardy Jones, Martin Perlmutter, and Ken Winkler for helpful comments on earlier versions of this essay.

1 Gerald Dworkin, 'Paternalism' in *Morality and the Law*, ed. Richard Wasserstrom (Belmont, CA: Wadsworth 1971) 107-26.

with functions as a side-constraint on the justification of paternalistic interference and that without such consent, paternalistic interference is not justified, no matter how much good it may do an agent. In this essay I shall develop the contrast between these two different ways of justifying paternalistic interference and attempt to show that the second, non-consequentialist kind of justification is to be preferred to the first.

By paternalistic interference we may understand interference with a person's liberty of action or ability or opportunity to acquire information for reasons having to do not with rights and welfare of others but rather with the good of the person so treated. It is true, of course, that when a person engages in self-damaging behavior, he often also imposes costs on others. These costs will sometimes yield very good reasons for restricting such conduct, but these reasons will not be paternalistic reasons and hence will be beyond the scope of this essay.

## I

One very plausible consequentialist rationale for paternalistic interference is suggested, if not fully endorsed, by Gerald Dworkin in his essay 'Paternalism.' Agreeing with Mill's contention that paternalistic interference is justified in order to prevent someone from selling himself into slavery, Dworkin writes

> The main consideration for not allowing such a contract [in which a person sells himself into slavery] is the need to preserve the liberty of the person to make some future choices. This gives a principle — a very narrow one — by which to justify some paternalistic interferences. Paternalism is justified only to preserve a wider range of freedom of the individual in question.[2]

Let us call this rationale the diminishment of freedom rationale (DFR). This rationale tells us that paternalistic interference is justified only when it is necessary to prevent an agent from engaging in a course of action which will significantly diminish his freedom to make future choices.

We can think of DFR as one instance of a general family of consequentialist rationales for paternalistic interference which share the same

---

2 Dworkin, 118. I think that the context makes it clear that Dworkin thinks of DFR as a condition which is sometimes sufficient as well as necessary for paternalistic interference. I might also remark that I follow Dworkin in using 'freedom to choose' and 'ability to choose' interchangeably.

general structure. Each such rationale will attach great moral value to an agent's being in a certain condition or end-state (where this value is at least in part independent of the agent's choosing, valuing or consenting to being in that condition) and will then urge that paternalistic interference is justified when it will preserve or perhaps promote this value. Another member of this family, which will be attractive to many, is the diminishment of welfare rationale (DWR), which permits interference in order to prevent a serious diminishment in an agent's welfare. And, insofar as there are other kinds of bad consequences for agents (e.g. loss of moral character, religious faith or aesthetic sensitivity) besides losses of freedom or welfare, one may imagine consequentialist principles which permit paternalistic interference in order to preserve these values as well. One may also envision consequentialist principles that permit interference to enhance as well as to prevent diminishments in the above values, and 'mixed' principles which permit interference in order to protect or enhance combinations of the above values.[3] In what follows I shall argue that all of the rationales in this family share certain fundamental defects which have to do with their consequentialist structure and not with the content of the particular end states which they take to warrant interference.

Consequentialist justifications for paternalistic treatment differ fundamentally from those justifications which make reference in some way to the consent of the person so treated. I turn now to an exploration of such justifications. As a number of writers have noted, one of the cases in which paternalistic interference seems most obviously justified is when the person interfered with actually gives his consent to such interference. Consider, to use Gerald Dworkin's example, the case of Odysseus, who 'commands his men to tie him to the mast and refuse all future orders to be set free, because he knows the power of the Sirens to enchant men with their songs.' Here Odysseus explicitly consents to the

---

3 A rationale for paternalistic interference resembling DWR is endorsed, for example, by C.L. Ten in his 'Paternalism and Morality.' Ten would permit paternalistic interference when (but not only when) 'the harm inflicted on the agent is of a severe and permanent type' (C.L. Ten, 'Paternalism and Morality,' *Ratio*, **13** [1971] 56-66). Bernard Gert and Charles Culver base their justification of paternalistic treatment on a mixed consequentialist principle in part: they hold that paternalistic treatment is only justified 'if we are preventing significantly more evil to (the person interfered with) ... than we are causing' (Bernard Gert and Charles M. Culver, 'The Justification of Paternalism,' *Ethics*, **89** [1979] 199-210). Because Gert and Culver hold that paternalistic treatment will always involve violating a moral rule with regard to the person so treated, they also require for the justification of such treatment that one be able to publicly advocate such violations.

subsequent interference with his freedom of action by his men.[4] Their interference does not frustrate Odysseus' attempt to attain those aims he judges most important but rather represents the way which Odysseus chooses to attain his ends. According to a consent-based theory, it is Odysseus' consent and not the fact that in interfering the sailors will preserve something thought to be good for Odysseus (e.g. his freedom or welfare) which justifies interference.

In other cases in which paternalistic interference seems obviously justified, the person interfered with (call her Alice) fails to consent to interference prior to the time at which it occurs but (a) it seems reasonable to attribute this failure to the fact that Alice lacks certain capacities or opportunities to gather information which are necessary for informed consent and (b) it seems reasonable to suppose that Alice will possess such opportunities or capacities in the future and that when she does so, she will restrospectively consent to the interference with no serious prospect of a change of mind. A variety of cases fit this pattern. Imagine, to use an example of Mill's, that Alice is unknowingly about to try to cross a washed-out bridge. If there is not time to warn her it seems justifiable to restrain her at least until the condition of the bridge can be described to her. A consent-based theory will see the considerations which justify interference in such a case as natural extensions of the considerations which justify interference in the Odysseus case. In the Odysseus case, the sailors choose, in interfering, as Odysseus himself has explicitly chosen. In the present case we have no explicit expression of choice to act on before interference, but we can rely on (can, in choosing, be guided by) the next best thing: the requirement that we choose as we may reasonably expect the person interfered with would choose, had she the capacities and opportunities necessary for informed choice. Thus, according to a consent-based theory, interference is

---

4   Some may wish to say that because Odysseus consents to the sailors' treatment, they do not really 'interfere' with him at all (e.g., see Donald VandDeVeer in 'The Contractual Argument for Withholding Medical Information,' in *Philosophy and Public Affairs* **9** [1979-80] 198-205). If I am correct in contending below that justifications of paternalism which appeal to retrospective and hypothetical, consent are a natural extension of those that appeal to actual consent, such persons also *ought* to say, as VanDeVeer does not, that paternalism which is justified by such appeals also does not involve 'interference.' And if they use 'paternalistic' in such a way that paternalism treatment must involve interference, they will find it more perspicuous to express the conclusions of this essay by saying that paternalistic treatment is never justified, that what can be justified is treatment that appears paternalistic, but is revealed by analysis not to be paternalistic at all, since it does not involve interference. I have no quarrel with this way of putting matters; it seems to me that nothing turns on whether my conclusions are expressed this way or in the way I have chosen.

justifiable in the above case because there is every reason to suppose that Alice will retrospectively consent to being restrained once she is informed of our assessment of the condition of the bridge.[5]

In another kind of case in which it is reasonable to expect retrospective consent the person interfered with fails to consent to interference at the time it occurs not because he lacks certain relevant information, but because he temporarily lacks the volitional and deliberative capacities which are necessary for informed consent. If, for example, a highly inebriated friend announces at a party that he can jump without injury from a fifth story window and makes preparations to do so, one is surely justified in restraining him against his will. According to a consent-based theory of paternalistic interference, it is justifiable to restrain him because at the time of interference there is good reason to suppose that, because of his drunkeness, he lacks the capacity for informed choice and consent, and because we may reasonably suppose that he will consent to having been restrained the following morning. (Indeed if he jumps and survives he might justifiably reproach us for having failed to restrain him, on the grounds that we ought to have expected that he would wish to be restrained.)

There are other cases in which a person bent on self-harming behavior may lack the capacity for informed consent and may be unlikely to acquire that capacity in the future. In such cases we may sometimes give a justification for interference which resembles that appealed to in the Odysseus case by invoking the notion of hypothetical consent. We may argue that interference is justified on the grounds that if the person interfered with were to re-acquire the capacity for informed consent, he would consent to the interference. We are, I think, justified in preventing a person who has become permanently deranged from harming himself in certain ways even if it is unlikely he will regain full use of his faculties and consent to our interference as long as it is likely that if he were to regain his capacity for informed consent, he would consent to our having interfered with him.

In the cases considered so far, the person interfered with has either consented to our present interference or fails to consent to the in-

---

5   It is important to understand that on my view, what justifies interference in this case is not the actual occurrence of Alice's subsequent consent, but the fact that it is reasonable to expect that Alice will subsequently consent. Making the justifiability of interference depend on Alice's actual subsequent consent would, as Donald VanDeVeer notes, have the bizarre consequence that whether or not interference is justified would depend upon, e.g., whether Alice is killed by a bolt of lightning before she is able to consent (Cf. Donald VanDeVeer, 'Paternalism and Subsequent Consent,' *Canadian Journal of Philosophy*, **9** [1979] 631-42).

James Woodward

terference at the time at which it occurs because he lacks the capacity to
consent or because he lacks certain relevant knowledge. Is paternalistic
treatment ever justified when a person has not consented to being so
treated, and does not lack either the capacity to consent or relevant information regarding the consequences of his actions? It seems to me
that it is consistent with the spirit of a consent-based rationale to hold
that in cases of this kind paternalistic treatment may be justified if there
is good reason to believe that the agent's refusal to consent is temporary
and that he will come to consent to having been interfered with in the
future. Cases in which a person acts while in the grip of a mood or emo-
tion which is incongruent with his most long term and deeply held
values and projects may fall into this category. Imagine a man who is
plunged into deep grief and depression by the death of his wife and
resolves to kill himself. Such a man may not lack the capacity for informed choice and consent in the way that a seriously mentally ill person or
a small child does, but there may nonetheless be good reason to think
that his inclincation toward suicide is temporary and that when he
recovers from his grief and depression he will consent to having been
restrained (and indeed be grateful for this).

A consent-based theory seems to me to give a plausible rationale for
interference in such cases. There is no reason, within the frame work of
a consent-based theory, to give a pre-eminent status to a person's present choices and desires no matter how transitory or unreflective of his
underlying personality and values these may be. A person, at any moment, is more than the time-slice of his desires and emotions at that moment.

A plausible consent-based criterion for paternalistic treatment thus
might claim that such treatment is justified when and only when it has
either (a) actually been consented to in a free and informed way, or (b)
there is failure to consent to such treatment only because the person affected acts out of ignorance or temporary incapacity in his deliberative
or decision-making abilities and it seems reasonable to suppose he will
consent to the interference once this ignorance or incapacity has been
removed, or (c) the person affected fails to consent to the treatment only because of an incapacity which is not temporary, but nonetheless it
seems reasonable to suppose that he would consent to the interference
if he were to regain this capacity, or (d) while the person interfered with
does not consent to the treatment at present and does not lack the
capacity for rational deliberation and decision-making, it is nonetheless
reasonable to suppose that because of his most deeply held projects and
values he will come to consent to the treatment in the future.

My interest, however, is not so much in arguing for this specific version of a consent-based theory as in exploring the contrast between
those rationales which make reference to the consent of the person in-

terfered with and those rationales which attempt to justify interference by reference to the preservation or enhancement of some good for the agent. It is important to see that when we restrain a would-be suicide on the grounds that he may change his mind about the desirability of suicide, we appeal to a rationale for interference which is quite different from a rationale which makes reference to the preservation of his welfare or freedom of action. The former consent-based rationale would permit restraint of a normally optimistic man who resolves on suicide during a period of deep depression following the loss of his job; it would not permit restraint of a man who gradually develops, over a period of time, a desire to end his life, a desire which is the natural outcome of his most persistent beliefs and values. On the other hand, a diminishment of freedom or diminishment of welfare criterion would presumably permit interference in both of these cases.

Before we turn to a more detailed exploration of the differences between consent-based and consequentialist rationales for paternalistic treatment, it may be useful to remove some possible misunderstandings. Note to begin with that on a consent-based theory there must be (actual, expected, or hypothetical) *consent* to the specific kind of interference contemplated and not just a general recognition on the part of the subject of the desirability of the good which the interference is designed to protect. This point is often not appreciated. Gerald Dworkin, for example, seems to assume that even on a consent-based theory, interference becomes unproblematic once a person comes to see the relevant portions of his conduct as undesirable. Thus, in the case of a smoker, who recognizes the desirability of not smoking but who suffers from 'weakness of will' and continues to smoke, Dworkin writes '[in this case] thee is no theoretical problem. We are not imposing a good on a person who rejects it. We are simply using coercion to enable people to carry out their own goals.'[6]

From the perspective of a consent-based theory this conclusion is too quick, for there are several different cases here which must be distinguished. A person may view certain portions of his conduct as irrational or undesirable and yet consistently refuse to consent to being prevented by another from engaging in that conduct. He may regard smoking as a dangerous habit, fervently wish that he had the will-power to stop smoking and yet consistently and indignantly resist any attempt to coerce him into not smoking. He may attach sufficient importance to other people not having control over this portion of his life that he would prefer not to stop smoking at all if this could be accomplished on-

---

6   Dworkin, 124

ly through such coercion. When this is the case, and there are no grounds for thinking that he will change his mind and no grounds for attributing his failure to consent to interference to incapacity or ignorance, paternalistic interference will not be justifiable according to a consent-based rationale, even if the subject sees the good for the sake of which interference is taken as desirable. On the other hand, a person may not only suffer from weakness of will in the sense that he wishes to stop smoking and does not, but he may be quite willing that others step in to make him stop smoking. In this sort of case paternalistic interference will be justified according to a consent based theory.

Secondly, it is important to recognize that the kind of hypothetical consent which may appropriately be appealed to by a consent-based theory is hypothetical consent of a rather special kind. If we are to take seriously the idea of justifying interference by considerations continuous with those at work in the Odysseus case and the correlative idea of choosing as the subject herself would choose had she the capacity to do so, we must, in employing the notion of hypothetical consent in clause (c) above, hold the agent's actual plans, values and desires as nearly intact as is consistent with imagining her to possess the capacity for rational consent and choice and then ask how she would choose if she possessed such capacities. When the notion of hypothetical consent is employed in his way, I shall speak of hypothetical$_1$ consent.

If, in applying the test of hypothetical consent, we are allowed to imagine a person's projects, values and desires as however different we wish (consistent with some minimal condition of rationality) from her actual projects, values, and desires and if we can justify interference by what a person would 'consent' to if she possessed this novel set of projects, values and desires, then we have moved away from the idea of choosing as the person interfered with would choose and from the kinds of considerations we used to justify interference in the cases described above. If Beatrice is in a coma from which unaided recovery seems unlikely and we are wondering whether it would be justifiable to perform an operation which would allow her to recover, the appropriate notion of hypthetical consent to employ if we wish to construct a consent-based justification for interference is one according to which it makes a difference, in determining what Beatrice would consent to, whether or not Beatrice is a Christian Scientist who has often said that she would not undergo surgery under any circumstances. If Beatrice is such a Christian Scientist, we cannot claim to be appealing to her hypothetical$_1$ consent, in the sense of that expression which is appropriate to a consent-based theory, if we argue that the operation is justified on the grounds that if Beatrice was an Episcopalian or someone who valued her health above all else, she would consent to the interference. If we think that it would be justifiable to perform the operation in this case, we must appeal to considerations which cannot be seen as continous with the considerations which justified interference in the Odysseus case.

For similar reasons we must be careful to distinguish hypothetical$_1$ consent from the kind of hypothetical consent which is appealed to in a 'rational will' argument for paternalistic interference.[7] By a 'rational will' argument, I mean an argument that proceeds in the following way: It is contended that a fully rational agent will always wish to maximize (or at least preserve a minimal level of) certain goods such as welfare or future ability to choose and that if a person fails to do this, interference to preserve those goods is justified on the grounds that he is not rational (since he does not act to preserve the goods in question) and that if he were rational he would consent to the interference (since he would wish to preserve the goods in question).

Obviously if arguments of this kind are thought of as yet another legitimate way of appealing to the consent of the person interfered with, the contrast I have attempted to draw between consent-related and consequentialist justifications of paternalistic treatment will collapse. Given any consequentialist theory according to which it is justifiable to interfere in order to preserve or enhance an agent's possession of G, it can always be argued that any agent who fails to preserve or enhance G is not fully rational, and hence that, by virtue of a rational will arguement, interference is justified. While a full discussion of this argument must be beyond the scope of this essay, it should be clear that the sort of hypothetical consent to which a rational will argument appeals is not hypothetical$_1$ consent. Rational will arguments abstract from the specific plans, values and beliefs of agents in the way in which the appeal contemplated above to what Beatrice would consent to if she were an Episcopalian abstracts from her specific plans, values, and beliefs. The notions of choice and consent appealed to in consent-based theories only have application in those contexts in which individual plans and values are held to matter, in contexts in which it is allowed that two persons can be 'rational' in the sense that they both meet the preconditions for morally effective choice and yet, because of individual

---

7 The characterization of arguments of this sort as 'rational will' arguments is taken from John Hodson's 'The Principle of Paternalism,' *American Philosophical Quarterly,* **14** (1975) 61-71. An apparent willingness to regard such a 'rational will' argument as a natural extension of a consent-based justification of paternalistic interference can be found in Dworkin's 'Paternalism.' A distinction similar to the distinction I have drawn here between hypothetical$_1$ consent and the sort of hypothetical consent appealed to in a 'rational will' argument is also made by Donald VanDeVeer in his 'Autonomy-Respecting Paternalism,' *Social Theory and Practice,* **6** (1980) 187-207.

differences, choose differently. If we think, as the rational will argument does, entirely in terms of agents who are abstract and interchangeable and who, insofar as they are rational, will always 'choose' the same thing, then we have really abandoned the notions of choice and consent, in the sense in which they are employed in a consent-based theory. At least in the case of persons with the general capacities for informed consent, rational will arguments should not be regarded as legitimate appeals to their consent.[8]

One final point: It is sometimes suggested that it is only appropriate to use the word 'consent' where there has been actual consent, and that it is always confused or misleading to speak of hypothetical$_1$ consent. If this suggestion is to amount to anything more than a verbal quibble, it must invole the claim that hypothetical$_1$ consent either plays no natural justificatory role in moral argument or at least no role that very closely resembles the role played by actual consent. But in fact there are many very ordinary cases, having nothing to do with paternalistic treatment, in which it seems natural and appropriate to appeal to hypothetical$_1$ consent in the sense indicated above. Suppose that you wish to use something that Charles owns. Putting aside special cases (in which, e.g., using Charles' property is necessary to prevent serious harm to someone), it seems that the justification for using the property must make

---

8  See my 'The Rational-Will Argument for Paternalism,' in preparation. I might also remark in this connection that a consent-based theory will draw a sharp distinction between those who have had a general capacity for informed consent in the past and have thus had an opportunity to form a distinctive set of values and projects and those (such as small children, persons who have been severely retarded since birth) who have never had this capacity and thus have not formed a distinctive set of values and projects. In the latter sort of case we cannot appropriately invoke the notions of retrospective and hypothetical$_1$ consent and must fall back on something like a 'rational will' argument in determining whether paternalistic interference would be appropriate. It is only in this latter sort of case that a concern with consent collapses in a concern with the sort of consequentialist considerations represented by DFR and DWR. (Even here, of course, one should not ask 'What would be best for any rational agent?', but rather 'What would be best for this kind of child or retarded person?' Thus in the case of normal children, paternalistic treatment should be undertaken with an eye toward, among other things, developing their capacities for informed choice, while this sort of purpose may be inappropriate, because incapable of fulfillment, in the case of the severely retarded.) I might also note in this connection that once this last point is recognized, the worries of writers like Rosemary Carter ('Justifying Paternalism,' *Canadian Journal of Philosophy*, **7** [1977] 133-45) that a consent-based theory like that described above will permit parents to 'distort' their children's values or stunt their capacities in such a way that their upbringing itself manufactures subsequent consent to having been brought up in that way can be seen to be misguided.

reference in some way to Charles' consent. The simplest, most paradigmatic case is one in which you may use Charles' property because he has actually consented to your doing so. But if Charles is not available to consent or is unable to do so, there are many circumstances in which you might naturally and appropriately justify your use of Charles' property by showing that he will or would consent to your use when he has the opportunity or ability to do so. ('I borrowed your rake, Charles. You weren't at home but I was sure you wouldn't mind,' may be a perfectly cogent justification, even if it is sometimes abused. And such a justification remains cogent even if the situation is one in which it is likely that Charles will never have the opportunity or ability to actually consent to my use of the rake.) These justifications for using Charles' property, which make reference to his expected or hypothetical$_1$ consent, stand in sharp contrast to those justifications which appeal to the good consequences of such use for me, or society at large (or, for that matter, Charles); in their focus instead on Charles' values, desires and projects they seem to have a moral force like the moral force of actual consent.


## II

I want now to explore in more detail some of the differences between consent-based rationales for paternalistic treatment and consequentialist rationales like DFR and DWR and to introduce some of the considerations which seem to me to favor the former set of rationales. Let us note to begin with that if (as I believe) we can give sense to the idea that a person with the full capacity for informed consent may refuse to consent (and may be such that there is no prospect of his coming to consent) to interference with some freedom-diminishing course or welfare-diminishing course of action which he is about to adopt, it will follow that DFR and DWR will justify a much wider range of paternalistic interference than a consent-based rationale. For example, it seems reasonable to suppose (and Dworkin seems to agree) that DFR would support legislation requiring automobile passengers to wear seat belts and restricting cigarette smoking (driving without seat belts and heavy smoking are, after all, activities that significantly increase the chances of one's freedom of action being severely limited in the future). DFR also (although Dworkin does not explicitly suggest this) seems to provide prima facie support for legislation limiting the consumption of fried foods and legislation requiring people to have regular medical checkups. DWR and the various enhancement rationales mentioned above would presumably support even more extensive paternalistic interference. By contrast, if it is possible for a person to possess the capacity for informed consent and yet refuse to consent, with no prospects of his coming to consent, to being required to wear seat belts, stop smok-ing, limit his consumption of fried foods, or have regular medical checkups, a consent-based rationale will not justify legislation requiring people to do these things.

In addition to the quite different judgements they seem to yield regarding particular cases, a consent-based theory and the consequen-tialist theories like DFR and DWR are associated with two quite different ways of understanding paternalistic interference. On a consent-based criterion we think of the person interfered with as an independent sub-ject with whose actual, expected or hypothetical₁ permission we assist in achieving his aims. We 'interfere' with this person's activities not to frustrate or alter his aims, or to promote some other value (his freedom or welfare) which he may not wish to see promoted at the expense of his other aims, but rather to better help him achieve his aims. Even as we interfere with the agent's acitivities we interfere in a way that acknowledges or evinces our respect for his status as an agent whose choices are deserving of respect because they are his choices. By con-trast, on a diminishment of freedom or diminishment of welfare criterion, we do not evince respect for the agent's choices because they are his choices, but rather evince respect for some other value – the agent's future welfare or ability to choose – which the agent may not share.

One reason why reliance on a consent-based criterion for pater-nalistic interference rather than DFR may seem paradoxical is this: Underlying the consent criterion is, of course, the idea that an agent's autonomous and informed choices agent are of great moral value and significance. But how can the respect to be accorded to such choices ever require that we allow someone to choose in such a way that his choice diminishes his ability to choose in an informed and autonomous way? If the ability of an agent to choose freely is of great moral significance or value, shouldn't we, other things being equal, always take steps to maximize that value, or at least to prevent its serious diminishment, wherever we can? It is this line of thought which leads Dworkin to DFR and Mill to the conclusion that paternalistic in-terference is justified in order to prevent someone from selling himself into slavery. To retain some form of the consent criterion we must hold that the rationale for paternalistic interference is not to be understood solely in consequentialist terms. One can quite consistently hold, to use Bernard Williams' example,[9] that a world in which two people keep

---

9 Bernard Williams, 'A Critique of Utilitarianism, in J.J.C. Smart and Bernard Williams, *Utilitarianism: For and Against* (Cambridge: Cambridge University Press 1973).

their promises is, other things being equal, morally preferable to a world in which only one person keeps his promise, and yet deny that one ought to break his promise if that is the only way one can get two other people to keep theirs. In a similar way, one can agree that a world in which Alice retains her ability to choose autonomously is morally preferable to a world in which that ability is significantly diminished, and yet deny that it is right to interfere with Alice's autonomous choices in order to promote or preserve the achievement of this more desirable world. On this sort of view, which is embodied in a consent-based criterion, Alice's consent (actual, expected, or hypothetical$_1$) to our interference constitutes a 'side-constraint' on the goal of preventing diminishment in Alice's ability to choose freely. Just as certain 'routes' (namely, those that involve my breaking my promise) to the desirable state of affairs in which Beatrice and Charles keep their promises are not permissible, so certain routes (namely, those that involve interference with her conduct without her actual or hypothetical$_1$ consent) to the desirable state of affairs in which Alice's ability to choose is preserved are also not permissible. The idea is that sometimes respect for a person's free choices requires that she be allowed to choose in a way that may diminish her ability to choose freely in the future. We can thus think of both DFR and a consent-based rationale for paternalistic interference as theories which attempt to assign a fundamental importance to a person's free and autonomous choices, but nonetheless have quite different structures, structures which reflect the general difference between consequentialist and nonconsequentialist moral theories.

We may develop this theme further by noting that a consent-based theory of paternalistic interference, like non-consequentialist theories generally, attaches a great deal of signficance to *who* makes a certain choice or brings about a certain result. (Thus on a non-consequentialist, but not on a consequentialist theory, it will make a great deal of difference, in many cases, whether I commit a murder or simply fail to do something which has the consequence that someone else commits a murder.) DFR, like other consequentialist theories, focuses instead on the end result of an action, being indifferent to who (whether the person whose freedom or welfare is in danger or someone else) chooses or brings about that result, except insofar as this affects the value of the end result. On a theory like DFR or DWR, the person interfered with is thought of as a repository of certain values which are to be protected and anyone who can may (and perhaps ought) to take appropriate steps to protect this value. By contrast, the whole point of a consent-based theory is that who chooses some end which is good for an agent — whether it is the agent or someone else — is morally crucial.

We can further remove the appearance of paradox from a consent-based rationale for paternalistic interference by noting its close connection with the notion of privacy. It is commonly recognized that certain kinds of surveillance may constitute a wrongful infringement of a person's privacy even if this surveillance does not actually result in the diminishment of his welfare or freedom of action. This reflects the fact that a person has a concern with controlling certain aspects of his life that goes beyond his interest in preserving his own welfare or freedom of action. When a hidden camera is used to monitor a person's sex life, he is wronged even if this information is never used to his detriment, and he remains unaware of the surveillance. He is wronged because it is no longer up to him who shall observe (and in one sense, participate in) certain activities which are of fundamental importance to him, and because in consequence he no longer has full control over the character and significance of those activities. In violating a person's privacy, we thus wrong him by showing a kind of disrespect for his status as a person which is at least in part distinct from any wrong we may do him by unjustifiably diminishing his welfare or restricting his freedom. To respect another's status as a person we must, among other things, respect his status as a chooser, and this involves respecting the integrity of certain of his aims and projects, and his control over certain portions of his life.

We can use a natural extension of this line of thought to provide support for a consent-based criterion for paternalistic interference. Once we recognize that a person's interest in controlling certain portions of his life is, at least in part, independent of his interest in preserving his freedom and welfare and that we can wrong a person by showing a disrespect for his status as a chooser, even if we do not diminish his freedom or welfare, it becomes easy to see how it can be wrong to frustrate an agent's purposes, to remove certain portions of his life from his control, even if in doing so we preserve or enhance his freedom or welfare. Just as the right to privacy seems to derive, at least in part, from a more general right which persons possess to control certain portions of their life, to carry out certain projects as they see fit, so we may plausibly maintain that a person's right to be free of the sort of paternalistic interference which would be justified by DFR or DWR derives from a similar basis.

## III

There are a number of additional respects in which consent-based theories seem to me to be superior to consequentialist theories like DFR. To begin with, these two kinds of theories assign a very different significance to individual differences among persons. Consequentialist theories are concerned with the protection and enhancement of some end-state (freedom, welfare, etc.) which is thought of as valuable for all persons. Whether paternalistic interference is permissible is thought of as a question which can be settled without any direct reliance on information having to do with the particular desires, plans, goals or values of the person interfered with. By contrast such information will be of crucial importance in a consent-based theory, for it will in large measure determine what an agent can be expected to consent to.

Consider a concert pianist, Dora, whose hand has become seriously infected in such a way that there is a high probability that she will die of blood poisoning unless the hand is amputated. Suppose, that because of her commitment to her career, she strenuously insists that the operation not be performed — she prefers instead to the the relatively small chance that she will survive with her hand intact.

It seems to me that if potential losses and gains in Dora's welfare or ability to choose can be objectively assessed at all, DFR and DWR yield a very good case for proceeding with the operation against Dora's wishes. It seems reasonable to suppose that the loss in welfare or future ability to choose represented by the loss of Dora's life, discounted by the rather high probability of its occurrence without the operation, will outweigh whatever gain in these values would be produced by Dora's survival with her hand intact, discounted by the small probability of its occurrence. Certainly there is nothing in DFR or DWR which suggests that, in deciding whether interference would be justifiable, one should take into account Dora's distinctive wishes and projects, except insofar as these are (one piece of) evidence for the course of action which is most likely to preserve Dora's freedom or welfare. Except for this last qualification (about which I shall say more below), both DFR and DWR presumably instruct us to treat Dora exactly like Frank, who faces the same situation as Dora but does not attach any greater than average significance to the use of his hands and who enthusiastically consents to the operation.

By contrast, for a consent-based rationale for paternalistic interference these differences between Dora and Frank will matter in a direct and crucial way in determining what should be done. Given that Dora is competent, and that her refusal to consent to the operation derives from her most deeply held plans and values, so that there is no reasonable prospect of a change of heart, there will be no justification for performing the operation on Dora, while performing the operation on Frank will of course be unproblematic.

Cases of this sort can be multiplied endlessly. Consider persons who wish to strenuously pursue religious, intellectual, aesthetic, or political projects when doing so will gravely undermine their physical or mental health or even hasten their deaths. DFR and DWR would presumably provide a rationale for interference in many such cases, while a consent-based rationale would not. Or consider the fact that persons facing unavoidable risks may have different preferences regarding how those risks are distributed over their lives. Suppose that Gus must choose between a high risk operation which if successful will guarantee his survival over the next ten years and a series of treatments which spread the risks he faces out evenly over the ten-year period. Here again it looks as though for DWR and DFR the issue of which alternative Gus should be required to undergo can be settled simply by calculating the pro-babilistically discounted value (whether this is a matter of welfare or freedom) associated with each alternative — presumably if one of these alternatives is seriously inferior to the other Gus must be required to take the other, regardless of his preferences.

From the perspective of a consent-based theory, consequentialist theories like DFR and DWR treat persons as abstract and inter-changeable, as mere repositories or loci of certain goods or values which it is desirable to protect or enhance, regardless of whether these goods figure in the plans or projects of the persons interfered with. By contrast, according to the moral vision which underlies a consent-based theory, persons are not to be thought of in this way. On this view it is central to the very idea of a person that a person will have a distinctive set of goals, values, plans and projects which he has formed and which are constitutive of his individuality. Respect for another's status as a person requires that when we attempt to aid him we do not treat him in a way which abstracts entirely from such considerations. It is, so to speak, not the bare, abstract idea of a rational chooser (and still less the abstract idea of an experiencer of pleasure or a possessor of welfare) which is to be respected, but rather this particular choosing person. When we seek to protect certain values (even those that are 'good' for an agent) in a way that fails to take into account his particular plans and projects, we treat him as a thing or means which can legitimtely be used for purposes other than his own, just as surely as when we ignore his own purposes in order to use him as a means to further some other agent's interest.

At least in the case of DWR it might be responded, however, that this line of criticism is unfair.[10] It may be argued that since whether or not a

---

10  While it is true that whether or not a certain course of action will preserve a per-sons's welfare depends in part on his particular desires, values, and projects, a parallel claim in the case of DFR seems to have little plausibility. Although it is sometimes suggested that if someone who does not plan or desire to do X, is deprived of the freedom to do X, his freedom is not diminished, this surely is a mistake. In the relevant sense the extent of an agent's freedom has to do with

course of action will preserve a person's welfare depends in part on his particular desires, values and projects, DWR is sensitive in an appropriate way to the differences among persons. Thus it may be contended that if it is indeed wrong to force the pianist to undergo the amputation of her hand in the example above, this is because it is likely, in view of the depth of her commitment to playing the piano, that she will be so miserable without her hand, that her welfare will fall to a level which will be significantly below the level associated with her survival with her hand intact, even discounted by the small probability of its occurrence. Similarly it might be argued that if it is wrong to require a Christian Scientist to undergo an operation necessary to save her life, that is because, given the unhappiness she would feel at the violation of her religious convictions, this course of action is not likely to yield significantly more welfare for her than the alternative of allowing her to die.

There are several points worth noticing about his line of argument. Note first that if DWR is not to collapse into a consent-based justification for interference, what a person consents to cannot always be taken as decisive in determining whether a course of action will best preserve her welfare. If the mere fact that Dora refuses to consent to a course of action shows that there are no significant welfare values which can be protected by requiring that course of action, then in fact we have abandoned DWR in favor of a consent-based justification of paternalistic interference. If DWR and similar principles are to retain their distinctively consequentialist features, it must be possible for a person to object strenuously to interference and to be convinced that interference will significantly decrease her welfare — and yet for interference to have just the opposite consequence.

Quite apart from this, it seems to me that to the extent a principle like DWR (or any other consequentialist principle) focuses on individual differences, it will focus on them in the wrong way. On the interpretation of DWR we are considering, what is presumably crucial is how unhappy, miserable, and devastated a person will feel in the long run when his choices are overridden. Suppose, in the example above, that there is good reason to think that if her hand is amputated Dora will not be thoroughly miserable for the rest of her life — she is a cheerful and resourceful sort of person who will probably 'adjust' to the loss of her hand and adopt a new set of concerns and make the best of a bad situa-

---

whether he will have the ability and opportunity to make certain choices or take up certain options if he wishes to do so. Whether he will in fact wish to do so is (at least largely) irrelevant to the question of how free he is.

tion although she may be counted on to object strenuously to having been forced to undergo the operation for the rest of her life. DWR seems to suggest that to the extent this outcome may be expected, imposition of the operation becomes more justifiable, while to the extent that Dora will be plunged into permanent misery or despair by the amputation, imposition of the operation will not be justified. It seems to me that it is simply a mistake to think that these considerations — these features of Dora's individuality — are morally crucial in determining whether paternalistic treatment is justified. To the extent that the character of Dora's subsequent life matters in determining whether it is justifiable to impose the operation on her, it seems to me that it matters in the way a consent-based theory would suggest — that is, that the crucial consideration is whether Dora can subsequently be expected to consent to the operation.

From the perspective of a consent-based rationale for paternalistic treatment, a rationale like DFR or DWR misconstrues the sort of role that Dora's concern about her music plays in her life. On DFR or DWR this concern is taken to be of significance only insofar as it bears on some other value — Dora's happiness or freedom to choose. But this need not (and presumably is not) the way Dora thinks about her piano playing ability — she does not value it only insofar as it contributes to (or is part of) her happiness or freedom to choose. It is presumably because she attaches a value to her music which is independent of the contribution it makes to other values in her life — because she does not think of her music primarily as a way of making herself happy or well or free — that she is prepared to sacrifice (or run the risk of sacrificing) her welfare or freedom in order to have a chance to continue her music. Similarly in the case of a scientist who pursues her research even though in doing so she knows she will very seriously undermine her health, it is typically not the case that she thinks of the research simply as the most effective way of preserving her happiness or welfare (or anything else). Presumably the scientist values both her welfare and research in their own right, as ends, and thinks of these ends as in genuine conflict — she elects to pursue her research *at the cost* of her welfare.

In DWR and DFR, individual differences matter only insofar as they bear on a value (welfare, freedom to choose) which is taken to be of uniformly paramount importance for everyone. The superior sensitivity of a consent-based theory to individual differences consists in the fact that on such a theory a person's values and choices are valued in their own right, and not just in virtue of the contribution they make to other values. A consent-based theory recognizes, in a way that DWR and DFR do not, that individuals differ not only with regard to what is likely to make them well or free, but with regard to the importance they attach to their welfare or freedom or welfare vis-à-vis other values.

I turn now to another respect in which a consent-based theory seems to be superior to consequentialist theories like DFR and DWR. Consider the fact that we are, as a general rule, far more likely to think that paternalistic interference is justifiable when factual rather than (fundamental) evaluative differences are at issue.[11] If a person refuses to undergo an operation which is necessary to preserve his health or life, it seems to many people to matter a great deal, in determining whether it would be justifiable to require him to undergo the operation, whether he refuses because he has not had the opportunity to acquire or reflect on certain information and is in consequence seriously misinformed about crucial factual matters (e.g. about the seriousness of his condition, or the after-effects of the operation), or whether he refuses because, although he appreciates the facts of his situation perfectly well, he objects to the operation on religious grounds. It seems to me that, at least in a situation in which the operation cannot be delayed without great danger, our pre-theoretic judgment is that the case for paternalistic interference is much stronger in the former case than in the latter. Similarly, the case for paternalistic interference seems, pre-analytically, to be much stronger in the case of Henry, who attempts to cross a bridge in a dangerously deteriorated condition because he is ignorant of its condition, than in the case of Jack, who fully appreciates the facts concerning the bridge's condition but wishes to take the risk of crossing it because of the value he attaches to the completion of some other important project.

This difference is, I think, difficult to satisfactorily account for on consequentialist theories. Such theories permit interference whenever a person is about to do something which is seriously damaging to some favored value — the *reason* why this person is about to embark on this damaging course of action is not seen as affecting the justifiability of the interference in any fundamental way. Refusing to undergo the operation or attempting to cross the bridge carry with them the same objective probability of loss whether they are prompted by a 'non-standard' value or by a 'non-standard' factual assessment of one's situation.

By contrast, a consent-based theory is able to account in a natural way for our (usual) greater willingness to interfere when a person's factual assessment differs from ours. According to a consent-based theory, this differential treatment of factual and evaluative differences is justified by two considerations. First, it is, as a general rule, much more likely that those whose factual assessment of their situations differ from our own 'standard' factual assessment can be brought into agreement with

---

11   This fact is noted by Dworkin, 122, but no explanation is offered.

this standard assessment (and hence can be brought to retrospectively consent to our interference) than it is that those whose evaluative assessments differ from our 'standard' evaluative assessments can be brought into agreement with our evaluative assessments (and hence to retrospectively consent to our interference). Secondly, the amount of change a person with an unusual factual assessment of his situation must undergo before he comes to agree with our 'standard' factual assessment is usually smaller than the amount of change required to bring a person with unusual values into evaluative agreement with us.

In the case of Henry, who is simply ignorant of the condition of the bridge, we (justifiably) feel confident that when we have communicated our assessment of the condition of the bridge, he will adopt that assessment and (probably) consent to our having interfered with him. But in the case of Jack, who attempts to cross the bridge because his values differ from our own (because unlike us, he is willing to risk his life to complete a certain project) there are no grounds for the corresponding expectation — no reason to think that when we acquaint him with our evaluative assessment of his situation, he will come to share it, and consent to our interference. Related to this is the fact that the change which Henry must undergo before he will come to consent to an interference seems less deep and fundamental than the change which Jack must undergo. No doubt some factual beliefs a person holds play a fundamental role in his sense of who he is and what matters to him. But the factual beliefs held in the examples above do not seem to be of this sort, while the evaluative beliefs do. The non-standard evaluative beliefs held in the examples above seem to be constitutive of the individual personalities who hold them in a much deeper way than the non-standard factual beliefs held in the above examples. So interfering with the choices of those holding the non-standard evaluative beliefs, especially given the small likelihood of their ever coming to consent to the interference, seems a much more fundamental intrusion into their personalities than interference with the choices of those holding the non-standard factual beliefs.

There is yet another kind of case in which consent-based theory seems to yield results which are intuitively more satisfactory than the results yielded by consequentialist theories like DFR or DWR. Consider cases in which a person is about to do something, either because he is ignorant or temporarily incompetent, which will have results he will find quite undesirable, but which are not such that they will significantly undermine his welfare or ability to choose. Imagine, to use an example which John Hodson uses to make a similar point,[12] that Jane is about to

---

12   John Hodson, 'The Principle of Paternalism'

drink some very foul-tasting but harmless liquid, having mistaken it for water. If there is no opportunity to warn her, and if she can be restrained without significant interference, many people would think it justifiable to temporarily restrain her, at least until we have had an opportunity to explain the situation. Yet since there is no question here of a serious diminishment in Jane's welfare or ability to choose, DFR and DWR seem to provide no justification for interference. Nor does it seem an acceptable strategy to deal with such cases by modifying DFR or DWR to permit interference in order to prevent small or harmless unpleasantries — this would permit a degree of interference with persons' lives that even the most ardent paternalist would surely wish to avoid. By contrast, a consent-based theory provides a natural explanation of why interference is justified in the above case, for it is clear that Jane acts out of ignorance and, in the absence of any evidence to the contrary, it is reasonable to assume that Jane wishes to avoid the foul-tasting liquid and will retrospectively consent to our (minimal) interference once the situation is explained. This sort of case also seems to suggest that it is not, as the consequentialist supposes, the kind or degree of the harm threatened which justifies paternalistic interference, but rather the attitude of the person interfered with toward the harm and the contemplated interference.

## IV

There is one final point I wish to make. In my discussion above I have urged that individual differences among persons must be taken into account in determining the justifiability of paternalistic interference. In a number of cases — perhaps most commonly when a private citizen is contemplating paternalistic interference with a friend, relative or obviously endangered stranger or when a professional is contemplating paternalistic treatment of a client — it may not be unduly difficult to take whatever information of this kind is available into account, in a way that satisfies the requirement that the interferer be guided by the prospects of actual, expected or hypothetical$_1$ consent. But, in many cases in which governments or other large organizations contemplate paternalistic measures, it may be very difficult or very undesirable for them to make (and to act on the basis of) the fine discrimination among individuals that a consent-based theory demands. It may be that the legal system or conceivable administrative agencies lack the (conceptual and material) resources to make such discriminations or to make them accurately. To empower the legal system or other agencies to make such discriminations may have the consequence of entrusting too much to the individual discretion of judges or administrators. It may have the consequence that people find it impossible to anticipate whether their behavior will invite interference. It may simply be that it is thought by most people to be undesirable that the state, or certain other organizations, become implicated in certain kinds of decision-making. It is thus quite likely that situations will arise in which some of those affected by paternalistic legislation can be thought of as giving their (actual, expected or hypothetical$_1$) consent to such legislation and others cannot and in which it is also difficult or undesirable for the state to attempt to distinguish between these two groups. For these and other reasons, paternalistic measures adopted by the state or other large organizations seem to raise distinctive issues which may not be raised by paternalism in other contexts.

While a thorough examination of these issues would require another paper, I might remark that the argument made in this paper does not seem to me to yield the conclusion that legislation restricting self-harming behavior described above is necessarily unjustified if it does not gain the actual, expected, or hypothetical$_1$ consent of all of those affected. What my argument does suggest is that there is no acceptable *paternalistic* justification for imposing such legislation on those who do not consent to it. If the legislation in question is justifiable, the justification will not be that the legislation is for the good of the non-consenting group, but rather must be that the consenting group has a right to make use of the legal system to realize their purpose of self-protection, even if in doing so they restrict the choices of the non-consenting group in certain ways. Since I do not think it at all plausible to hold that only the consent of those affected justifies imposing non-paternalistic restrictions on conduct, the possibility remains open that legislation to prevent people from harming themselves will sometimes be justifiable (although not on paternalistic grounds) even if only a portion of those affected consent to it. As in other cases of non-consensual restrictions on conduct, the justifiability of such restrictions will depend on such matters as the nature, extent and distribution of the harms prevented or the benefits conferred by the restrictions, on whether the restrictions burden fundamental rights, and on the character of the procedures used to arrive at the restriction.

## Select Bibliography

Carter, Rosemary, 'Justifying Paternalism,' *Canadian Journal of Philosophy*, **7** (1977) 133-45.

Dworkin, Gerald, 'Paternalism,' in *Morality and the Law*, ed. Richard Wasserstrom Belmont, CA: Wadsworth 1971) 107-26

Feinberg, Joel, 'Legal Paternalism,' *Canadian Journal of Philosophy*, **1** (1971-72) 105-24.

Gert, Bernard and Culver, Charles, 'The Justification of Paternalism,' *Ethics*, **89** (1979) 199-210.

Hodson, John, 'The Principle of Paternalism,' *American Philosophical Quarterly*, **14** (1975) 61-71.

Husak, Douglas, 'Paternalism and Autonomy,' *Philosophy and Public Affairs*, **10** (1980-81) 27-46.

Ten, C.L., 'Paternalism and Morality,' *Ratio*, **13** (1971) 55-66.

VanDeVeer, Donald, 'Paternalism and Subsequent Consent,' *Canadian Journal of Philosophy*, **9** (1979) 631-42.

VanDeVeer, Donald, 'Autonomy-Respecting Paternalism,' *Social Theory and Practice*, **6** (1980) 187-207.

VanDeVeer, Donald, 'The Contractual Argument for Withholding Medical Information,' *Philosophy and Public Affairs*, **9** (1979-80) 198-205.

Williams, Bernard, 'A Critique of Utilitarianism,' in Smart, J.J.C. and Williams, Bernard, *Utilitarianism: For and Against* (Cambridge: Cambridge University Press 1973).

CANADIAN JOURNAL OF PHILOSOPHY
Supplementary Volume VIII, 1982

# The Ethics of Consent

JOHN KLEINIG, Macquarie University

We would not be far wide of the mark if we suggested that the prevailing social ideology is structured round the presumption that interpersonal and political relationships ought to be, and for the most part are, based on the mutual consent of the parties involved. Liberal democratic theory has secured for consent a crucial role in the justification of political obligation and authority. In law, the maxim *volenti non fit injuria,* to the one who consents no wrong is done, constitutes a defence in cases where one person invades the interests of another. In the bioethical field, there is a preoccupation with the formulation of a standard of 'informed consent' in patient-doctor and subject-researcher relationships. And in the broader domain of ethical theory there is an influential view that consensual acts do not differ in moral quality from self-regarding behaviour.

But closer to the interface of theory and practice, the ideological picture becomes considerably more complicated. Liberal democratic consent theory expresses itself in the practice of voting, but the terminology of 'tacit consent' and 'duty of obedience' is not far under the surface. In criminal law, the *volenti* maxim joins up with another old timer, *jus publicum privatorum pactis mutari non potest,* the arrangements of private individuals cannot change public right, and together they ex-

John Kleinig

clude from criminal immunity some consensual acts deemed to involve (the risk of) serious bodily harm. The doctrine of informed consent struggles to free itself from the doctrine of therapeutic privilege, but finds that living alone creates its own problems. And claims about the moral status of consensual acts look less convincing when the result is exploitation.

Although these problems have attracted some attention, the discussion has generally taken for granted the nature and importance of consent.[1] This, I believe, has had unfortunate consequences. To illustrate: the obvious practical problems surrounding the express consent theory of political obligation have led, not to a reappraisal of consent theory, but instead to an attenuation of the act of consenting into the act of voting or some other act of 'tacit' consent. The preoccupation of theorists has thus come to be with the mechanisms whereby such tacit consent might be registered rather than with its possibility and a general reconsideration of the place of consent in human relationships.

My purpose in this paper is to take some steps towards answering the fundamental questions of the nature and importance of consent. Within its scope I shall not attempt to offer any detailed solutions to the problems I have mentioned, but I am hopeful that we may be better placed to tackle them as a result.

---

1  Detailed treatments of consent are not plentiful. Locke's classic discussion is brief, and commentators almost invariably focus on his doctrine of 'tacit consent.' The most extensive contemporary discussion is found in J.P. Plamenatz, *Consent, Freedom and Political Obligation*[2] (London: Oxford University Press 1968), though see also J. Tussman, *Obligation and the Body Politic* (New York: Oxford University Press 1960) Ch. 2. Plamenatz's views have inspired a small literature on the topic, including F.A. Siegler, 'Plamenatz on Consent and Obligation,' *Philosophical Quarterly,* **18** (1968) 256-61; J.J. Jenkins, 'Political Consent,' *Philosophical Quarterly,* **20** (1970) 60-6; M. Walzer, *Obligations: Essays on Disobedience, War & Citizenship* (New York: Simon & Shuster 1971); P.H. Partridge, *Consent and Consensus* (London: Macmilan 1971); P.J. Euben, 'Walzer's Obligations,' *Philosophy & Public Affairs,* **1** (1971-72) 438-59; F. Snare, 'Consent and Conventional Acts in John Locke,' *Journal of the History of Philosophy,* **13** (1975) 27-35; A.J. Simmons, 'Tacit Consent and Political Obligation,' *Philosophy & Public Affairs,* **5** (1975-76) 274-91 (reworked in *Moral Principles and Political Obligations* [Princeton, N.J: Princeton University Press 1980] Chs. III, IV); A. Weale, 'Consent,' *Political Studies,* **26** (1978) 65-77; C. Pateman, *The Problem of Political Obligation: A Critical Analysis of Liberal Theory* (Chichester: Wiley 1979) Consideration of the nature and importance of consent has also been prompted by discussions of rape; e.g. C.M. Shafer & M. Frye, 'Rape and Respect,' in M. Vetterling-Braggin, F.A. Elliston & J. English (eds.), *Feminism and Philosophy* (Totowa, NJ: Littlefield, Adams & Co. 1977) 333-46; J.A. Scutt, 'Fraudulent Impersonation and Consent in Rape,' *University of Queensland Law Review,* **9** (1975) 59-65; idem, 'Consent versus Submission: Threats and the Element of Fear in Rape,' *University of Western Australia Law Review,* **13** (1977) 52-76; C. Pateman, 'Women and Consent,' *Political Theory,* **8** (1980) 149-68. [See also M.T. Thornton, 'Rape and Mens Rea,' this volume, pp. 119-46 (Eds.).]

The semantic field of 'consent' is quite extensive, and includes terms such as 'agreement,' 'acquiescence,' 'compliance,' 'concurrence,' 'willingness,' 'connivance,' 'condonation,' 'accession,' 'assent,' 'submission,' 'approval,' 'permission,' 'promise,' 'authorization,' 'consensus,' 'concord,' 'endorsement,' and so on. Within this semantic field, 'consent' often functions as a kind of carry-all, and, since the range of concepts implied is rather broad, different accounts appear to be indicated. However, it seems to me that apart from this somewhat generalized use, 'consent' has a quite specific and distinctive function, and it is this that I shall attempt to detail.

In Section I, I argue that consent is not a state of mind, but an act. I detail some of the associations of this act in Section II, suggesting that it is an act in which a person explicitly tends to facilitate the initiative of an other. This is extended in Section III, where it is claimed that the consenting person must act voluntarily, knowingly and intentionally. In this section I look also at the effects of coercion, fraud, deceit and exploitation on consent, and comment on the determinateness of consent and the problems of tacit consent and voting. Consent is argued to be a form of co-operation with the initiative of an other whereby one shares responsibility for it. This co-operation finds expression in the tendency to facilitate the other's initiative. In Section IV, I endeavour to locate consent within a more general theory of social interaction, and argue against three alternative accounts of consent: (1) consent as an institutional notion; (2) consent as a self-assumed obligation; and (3) consent as a kind of promise. In the final section, I try to gauge the importance of consent in relation to utility and respect for persons, and consider what limitations might be placed on consent as an acceptable standard of social interaction.

I

In this first section I want to develop a point that I would have thought obvious except for the number of writers who have been tempted to take a different view.[2] The point I want to make is that consent is to be seen, not as a state of mind, but as a human act.

---

2  The view is expressed most uncompromisingly by Siegler (258), though a number of other writers appear to have drifted into it. For details, see J. Dunn, 'Consent in the Political Theory of John Locke' in G.J. Schochet (ed.), *Life, Liberty & Property* (Belmont, CA: Wadsworth 1971) 136; Partridge, Ch. 2; Simmons (1976), 289-90; Snare, 27-31.

The etymology of 'consent' (L. *consentire:* to feel/think together with), and the range of ideas within its semantic field, have led some writers to believe that its primary, or at least an essential function is to pick out a state of mind, attitude or belief. Consent is seen as 'being of the same mind' as another, as expressing a 'psychological pro-attitude,' or as involving a concurrence of feeling and judgment. More specifically, it is taken to express accord with the acts or projects of another or the desire for their successful completion.

In assessing this view, we need not deny that consent frequently does reflect some sort of concurrence or accord. And we might expect this to be the case especially though not exclusively where what is consented to requires substantial effort on the part of the person consenting. But to focus on this as primary or essential involves a significant misdirection of attention. A concurrence of minds or attitude of accord is neither necessary nor sufficient for consent, and where consent is accompanied by such, it is often convenient and advisable to qualify it as 'wholehearted' or 'unreserved.' For on other occasions it could be reluctant, grudging, thoughtless, guilty or half-hearted.

We can show that a psychological pro-attitude is not necessary to consent by means of the overworked and somewhat dated example of parental consent to a child's marriage. In general, parental consent is accompanied by parental accord. But this need not be the case. The parents may believe that certain of their aspirations will not be realized by the proposed union, or that their child has not yet developed a mature and settled outlook on relationships. Nevertheless, they may indicate that, despite their dislike of the arrangement, they will not stand between the couple. They will, albeit reluctantly, consent. This consent presupposes, not their accord, but their being in a position unilaterally to affect the couple's plans in some tangible way, either by withholding needed support or by intervening to impede or prevent their union.

It is this latter point, to which I'll later return (in Section II), which indicates why accord is not merely unnecessary but insufficient to constitute consent. Accord may remain unexpressed, but even when expressed may be causally impotent with respect to its object. Should I strongly accord with the activities of a South American liberation group or of the sixteenth century Swiss Anabaptists, my accord would not ipso facto amount to consent, in part, because it does nothing, and in the latter case could do nothing, to advance or impede their causes.

This hiatus between consent and accord or some other psychological pro-attitude does not reflect a recent development in the concept.[3]

---

3  In the account of Stephen's martyrdom, where the translators of the King James version of the Bible (1611) state that 'Saul was consenting unto his death' (*Acts*

The seventeenth-century social contractarians did not attempt to argue that either the establishment or perpetuation of political society was dependent on the presence or endurance of a psychological state or attitude called 'consent.' As Locke makes quite clear, consent is that 'act ... whereby [among other things] any one unites his person, which was before free, to any commonwealth.'[4] The question of accord is at best a secondary one. This is true equally, if not especially, of his doctrine of 'tacit consent,' which is constituted by what a person does (or omits to do), and not by what he/she feels or merely believes. The notoriety of this doctrine resides not in any reduction of consent to a state of mind or attitude, but in the kinds of acts which Locke interprets as manifesting such consent.

Without prolonging the point unduly, we may suspect that one of the reasons why consent is sometimes taken to be a psychological pro-attitude lies in its assimilation to the ideas of approval and agreement, where the latter are viewed simply as attitudes. There are two problems with this. One is implicit in our earlier discussion, viz. that parents who neither approve of nor agree with the projects of their children may nevertheless consent to them. But there is a deeper reason, relating to the character of approval and agreement. There is a surface ambiguity to 'approval' and 'agreement' which lends support to the view that they can be merely psychological pro-attitudes. This ambiguity can be expressed by means of the distinctions between 'X approved a' and 'X approved of a' and between 'X agreed to Y's proposal' and 'X agreed with Y's proposal'. Whereas the first sense is taken to presuppose an institutional structure in which the approver/agreer has a position of authority, the second is believed to indicate no more than that X is for a, and, moreover, has grounds for being so. Now, even if this way of making the distinction is accepted, we would have reason to ally consent with approving/agreeing to rather than approving of/agreeing with, for, just as one may approve/agree to something without approving of/agreeing

---

8:1), the point was not so much to indicate Saul's accord with the stoning — though accord there undoubtedly was — as to mark him out as *particeps criminis*.

4 J. Locke, *Two Treatises of Civil Government* (London: J.M. Dent 1924) Bk. II, Ch. viii, Sect. 120. Discussions of Locke can be found in most of the writers mentioned in footnotes 1 and 2. See also T. Waldman, 'A Note on John Locke's Concept of Consent,' *Ethics*, **68** (1957-58) 45-50; H. Pitkin, 'Obligation and Consent I, II' *American Political Science Review*, **59** (1965) 990-9, **60** (1966) 39-52, reprinted in P. Laslett, *et al.*, *Philosophy, Politics & Society*, Fourth Series, (Oxford: Blackwell 1972) 45-85; A. Tassi, 'Two Notions of Consent in Locke's "Second Treatise" ', *Locke News*, **3** (1972) 26-30

with it, so also may one consent to something without approving of/agreeing with it. But the reduction of approving of to a psychological pro-attitude is itself defective, since, as Philippa Foot has strongly argued, approving of, no less than approving 'can, logically speaking, exist only against a background of agreement about the part that other people's views shall be given in decision making.'[5] I should emphasize, however, that in pointing to a similarity between consent and institutional approval, I do not wish to imply that consent is a form of institutional approval. Later (in Section IV) I shall argue that although, in consenting, X may be approving a, consent is not a kind of institutional approval.


## II

I turn now to a more detailed account of the kind of act that consent is. Here I shall argue that in consenting a person tends to facilitate the initiative of an other.

Consent is always consent *to*, where the object of this consent is some act or project, typically the act or project of some other. In the central case, therefore, X consents to Y's request to do a.[6] There is, however, an ambiguity here which may obscure the point. 'Y's request to do a' may be understood either as 'Y's request that Y do a' or as 'Y's request that X do a.' The first interpretation is exemplified by parental consent to a child's marriage, the second by my consenting to write a Conference paper or to arbitrate in a dispute. Although some writers have suggested that two different senses of 'consent' are indicated by this ambiguity,[7] I believe that it is more economical and to the point if we simply make it clear that when we speak of consenting to the act or project of an other, we understand by this the other's *initiative*, which comes to us in a relatively determinate form and to which we are asked to respond.

---

5  P. Foot, 'Approval and Disapproval,' in *Virtues and Vices and Other Essays in Moral Philosophy* (Oxford: Blackwell 1978) 189-203; cf. G. Pitcher, 'On Approval,' *Philosophical Review*, **67** (1958) 195-211

6  More complicated cases, e.g., where X consents to Y's request that Z does a, do not affect the analysis in any significant way. My analysis is also intended to cover cases where a is already going on, and X consents to its *continuation*.

7  E.g. Simmons (1976), 275

A potential difficulty for this account is posed by the fact that in a number of contexts people have wished to speak of consent even though the initiative did not or did not clearly lie with the party to whom the consent was given. For example, in the celebrated *Wright's Case,*[8] X asked Y ('a lustie rogue') to cut off X's hand to enable X to beg more effectively. When charged, Y claimed that X consented to his hand being cut off. Similarly, if X goes to Dr. Y to seek some cosmetic surgery, and signs the appropriate consent form, Y can later claim that X consented to the surgical procedure performed on X. When Locke discusses political obligation, he speaks of its basis in consent even when considering the original compact, although there is never any suggestion that the individuals entering into the agreement are simply responding to the initiative of some other or others.[9]

However, I do not believe that these cases constitute an insuperable problem. For what they involve is something more than, though not exclusive of, what is central to consent. If X invites Y to do a, and Y does so, we need not deny that X consented to a in order to make the point that X did not merely consent but actually invited Y to do a. Our continuing to speak of consent in such cases may simply reflect the rebuttable presumption that a is not the sort of action that X could be expected to initiate. But even if this is not the case, I shall later argue that in continuing to speak of consent in these cases no serious distortion is involved, since the point at issue, namely the location and allocation of responsibility, is generally as well served by one form of locution as by the other.

Given then, that consent typically involves one person acting in response to the initiative of an other, what is the relation between the consenting party and that which is consented to? I think we can most generally and conveniently express this relation as one of facilitation, or better, of the *tendency to facilitate.*[10] Thus, when X consents to Y's doing a, X tends to make a easier for Y to accomplish. Expressing the relation as one of the tendency to facilitate is to put it not only in its most general, but also in its least demanding form. Sometimes it is only if X's

---

8  *R. v. Wright,* 1 Coke on Littleton 194 (127a, 127b); 1 Hale PC 412

9  Locke, Bk. II, Ch. viii

10  For it is possible to envisage circumstances in which consent does not actually facilitate: e.g., if Z proposes to impede a should X consent to Y's request that X participate in a. Circumstances may also arise in which the sought consent will make little or no difference to the act or project in question: e.g., if Y is so superior in power to X that X's unwillingness to submit to Y constitutes no impediment.

consent is forthcoming that a is possible. An obvious corollary of this is that one can consent only to that which is amenable to human alteration.

The idea of facilitation deserves further specification. It is useful, I think, to distinguish between positive and negative facilitation, and then to distinguish these further from what I shall call explicit and implicit facilitation. I do not want to suggest that these are hard and fast distinctions or that it is always easy to know how a particular case is to be categorized. But I hope that the point of the distinction will become clear as the discussion proceeds.

When X's consent involves the positive facilitation of a, X makes some contribution to a's accomplishment, be it by giving Y permission to do a, or by agreeing to do a for Y, or by lending support to Y's request to do a. Where X's consent facilitates a only negatively, X does not stand in the way of Y's doing a. X may refuse or agree not to bring any impediment in the way of Y's accomplishment of a. In itself, the distinction between positive and negative facilitation does not make any significant contribution to the analysis of consent. To see its usefulness we must turn to the second distinction. If the relation marked out by consent is to be understood in terms of facilitation, it must, I believe, be confined to explicit rather than implicit facilitation. Facilitation is explicit where there has been some interchange between X and Y in which X has signified his/her participation in Y's initiative. Where it is implicit, no such signification has taken place, even though X is in a position to have some effect on Y's initiative. Here the language of consent (whether 'express' or 'tacit') becomes inappropriate, and we must resort instead to a range of other possible locutions, depending on certain additional features of the situation. For example, we may wish to say that X acquiesces in or condones Y's doing a.

There has been a common tendency for writers to confuse implicit facilitation with negative facilitation, thus blurring the distinction between acquiescence and consent. The distinction, I believe, can be quite important, since it bears on the degree to which X can be held responsible for a. X's signification of consent prima facie brings into being a high degree of involvement in a, even though that involvement may otherwise show itself in behaviour no more active than would be the case were X merely to acquiesce in Y's doing a.

## III

Consent, I have argued, is an act in which one person tends to facilitate the initiative of another. But not all facilitation, even of an explicit kind, constitutes an act as one of consent. Facilitation is not to be understood as an independent specifying characteristic of consent. It is by virtue of X's responsibility-sharing participation in Y's initiative that X tends to facilitate *a*. It is for this reason that when X consents to Y's initiative, X must act voluntarily, knowingly and intentionally. Sometimes these are run together as part of a general voluntariness requirement, but I think it is of some advantage to clarity if we see them as distinct.

*Voluntariness.* Facilitation, I have observed, is made explicit when one person signifies his/her participation in the initiative of an other. Signification may be accomplished in a variety of ways, depending on the context. It may be 'yes' or some other conventional sign such as a gesture or a signature. Except in formal contexts, we do not usually signify consent by the phrase 'I (hereby) consent,' an interesting difference between consenting and promising to which I shall later return (in Section IV). However, as with other conventional signs which can be distinguished from what they signify, it is possible for a person to signify without expressing consent.

This situation occurs when a person does not act voluntarily. The voluntariness requirement is violated in cases where the person signifying consent acts under coercion, compulsion or duress. This will be so where there is (or is believed to be) some threat of substantial physical, material or psychological harm, including the threat of harm to some other with whom one feels closely identified.[11] Generally in such cases, without the threat consent would not have been signified. A person acting under threat submits but does not consent to the purposes of the other. In law, the distinction between expressing and merely signifying consent is sometimes marked by a distinction between consent and assent.[12] Mere assent is given when a person's conduct conventionally

---

11  Coercion does not have to be intended, and there is sometimes a fine line to be drawn between the case where Y negligently acts coercively and the case where X is predisposed to interpret Y's act as intimidatory, even though its being so reflects neither wilfulness, recklessness nor negligence on Y's part. Cf. the case in which X permitted Y to take 'indecent liberties with her person' because he was a police officer in uniform, and she was worried about what he might do if she refused' (*Commonwealth v. Carpenter*, 172 Pa. Super. 271; 94 A.2d 74 [1953]). On the other side, there are cases where threats are made but are not taken as such, either because what Y believes to be injurious is not taken to be so by X, or because X misunderstands that aspect of Y's initiative. It may be better to view threats as vehicles of coercion rather than as necessarily coercive. Cf. temptations and being tempted.

12  See, for example the U.S. *Restatment of the Law of Torts* (2d) (St. Paul, MN: A.L.I. Publishers 1966) Ch. 3.

John Kleinig

signifies but does not express an agreement to participate or co-operate in the project or act of an other.[13]

It is not always easy to decide whether an agreement to participate in some other's initiative expresses or merely signifies consent. This difficulty sometimes has a conceptual dimension, and arises acutely in the context of total institutions, where inmates or prisoners may be presented with the possibility of benefits or remissions in return for their participation in some therapeutic/rehabilitative or research programme. Do the circumstances of these initiatives render them coercive? For some writers, the issue resolves itself into the question whether such initiatives constitute offers or threats. But this may not be sufficient, since it is at least arguable that offers, no less than threats, may be coercive.[14]

The general situation envisaged here is one in which $Y$ puts it to $X$ that if $X$ agrees/does not agree to $a$, there will be a reasonable probability that $b$. This can be filled out to constitute either an offer or a threat. If $Y$ puts it to $X$ that if $X$ agrees to invest \$5 in some project initiated by $Y$, he/she will be repaid two-fold, then, ceteris paribus, $Y$ is making $X$ an offer. But if $Y$ puts it to $X$ that if $X$ should refuse to invest \$5 in $Y$'s project, $X$ will be beaten up, then ceteris paribus, $Y$ is threatening $X$. Here the determination of offer or threat is dependent on the benefit or detriment which $b$ is believed[15] to constitute. This may also be thought to deter-

---

13 Failure to satisfy the voluntariness requirement comes about not only when behaviour is nonvoluntary, but also when it is involuntary. But since we are more likely to speak of movements than acts in such cases, I shall leave any further discussion aside.

14 Discussions of this issue include R. Nozick, 'Coercion,' in S. Morgenbesser, et al. (eds.), *Philosophy, Science and Method* (New York: St. Martins Press 1969) 440-72, esp. pp. 447-53; reprinted in P. Laslett, et al. (eds.), *Philosophy, Politics & Society*, Fourth Series, (Oxford: Blackwell 1972) 101-35, esp. 112-20; J.R. Pennock & J.W. Chapman (eds.), *Nomos XIV: Coercion* (New York: Atherton Press 1972) esp. essays by Bayles, Gert & Held; H. Frankfurt, Coercion and Moral Responsibility,' in T. Honderich (ed.), *Essays on Freedom of Action* (London: Routledge & Kegan Paul 1973) 65-86; M.D. Bayles, 'Coercive Offers and Public Benefits,' *Personalist*, **55** (1974) 139-44; H. Steiner, 'Individual Liberty,' *Proceedings of the Aristotelian Society*, **75** (1974-75) 33-50; J. Murphy, 'Total Institutions and the Possibility of Consent to Organic Therapies,' *Human Rights*, **5** (1975) 25-45; H.J.N. Horsburgh, 'Moral Black- and Whitemail,' *Inquiry*, **18** (1975) 23-8; D. Lyons, 'Welcome Threats and Coercive Offers,' *Philosophy*, **50** (1975) 425-36; V. Haksar, 'Coercive Proposals (Rawls and Gandhi),' *Political Theory*, **4** (1976) 65-79; D. VanDeVeer, 'Coercion, Seduction and Rights,' *Personalist*, **58** (1977) 374-81; T. Benditt, 'Threats and Offers,' *Personalist*, **58** (1977) 382-4.

15 I think we have to distinguish between what $X$ believes to be beneficial or detrimental and what will turn out to be so. Lottery winners sometimes find their sudden wealth brings more misery than happiness.

mine the coerciveness or otherwise of Y's approach. But there are contextual factors which can complicate this simple picture. Consider the
following cases, where X is an inmate of a total institution (prison,
psychiatric hospital) and Y is a researcher/psychiatrist:

1.  Y puts it to X that since X's release depends on some marked
    improvement being shown in his/her condition, and a pro-
    gramme of drug therapy would be more likely to achieve this
    than alternative therapies, agreement to participate in the pro-
    gramme would significantly improve X's chances of release.

2.  Y puts it to X that since X's release depends on Y's recommen-
    dation, X might agree to participate in a programme of drug
    therapy, it being possible that this would also improve X's con-
    dition.

3.  Y puts it to X that if X agrees to take part in Y's cancer research
    project, X's sentence will be reduced and X will be moved to a
    cell with colour TV and an innerspring mattress.

4.  Y puts it to X that if X agrees to take part in Y's cancer research
    project, X will be moved out of solitary confinement and off a
    bread-and-water regime.

It is reasonable to see Cases 1, 3 and 4 as offers. In each case some
perceived benefit is held out to X in return for his/her compliance. Case
2 is trickier, since Y's approach has both beneficial and detrimental
features. Participation provides some hope for improvement and
release, yet no participation clearly implies the likelihood of discrimination against X. This case has the characteristics of what Hillel Steiner
calls a 'throffer.'[16]

But for present purposes, the key question is: Is coercion involved in
any or all of these cases? It is sometimes claimed that the fact of insti-
tutionalization makes all such approaches coercive, since the unequal
position of inmates makes it inevitable that any agreements they make
will be under duress.[17] I do not think this follows, though in practice I

---

16  Steiner, 39

17  See the opinion in *Kaimowitz v. Department of Mental Health,* Michigan Circuit
    Court for Wayne County, Civil No. 73-19434-AW (10 July, 1973), reprinted in
    W.M. Gaylin, J.S. Meister & R.C. Neville (eds.), *Operating on the Mind* (New
    York: Basic Books 1975) 185-209 and discussed by Murphy.

suspect that coercion is very common. In case 1 for example, provided we grant that X is legitimately institutionalized, then he/she is presented with a very reasonable choice. The only justification for releasing X is X's fitness to resume non-institutionalized life, and Y's offer is the best that could be expected. Ceteris paribus, there is no reason to see Y's offer as coercive. What we say about Case 2 depends significantly, I think, on what it is that counts in any decision X makes. If Y's implied threat is a significant factor, then his/her throffer is coercive. But if it is the hope of improvement and, with it, release, we may be reluctant to see X's agreement as having been coerced.[18] Case 3 has the appearance of a non-coercive offer, since the TV and innerspring mattress might be seen as luxuries or bonuses rather than basic necessities. However, we need to know more before we can decide the matter. If prison conditions are harsh and inhumane, then such an offer will be coercive. This comes out more clearly in Case 4, where the offer is clearly coercive, since X has a right to humane treatment which is not dependent on his/her willingness to participate in Y's project. If we can risk a generalization from these cases, it might be that where X has reason to expect b (or even something less than b) from Y on less costly terms than those offered by Y, Y's offer is coercive.

*Knowledge.* An apparent consent may be vitiated by certain kinds of ignorance. (1) If X is incapable of understanding the nature of a, then he/she cannot be said to have consented to a's being done. Very young children and those with severe learning difficulties or brain damage may not be able to comprehend the nature of their acts sufficiently to consent to anything. For the rest, the capacity to consent may vary with the particular nature of a and our access to the means of comprehending it. This has been acknowledged in medical contexts, where an explicit standard of informed consent to surgical procedures has been developed. Advances in medical technology, bringing with them risks which may not be appreciated by patients, either because the information is not publicly available or because the terminology is too esoteric, have made it necessary to spell out the knowledge requirement in detail.

(2) If X is suffering from no defect of understanding, but is kept ignorant of the character of a by Y's deception, then X cannot be said to have consented to a's being done.[19] The so-called manufacture or manipula-

---

18   If I do not punch you when I am tempted to do so because I believe it would be wrong, is my restraint coerced because there is also a law forbidding assault?

19   To determine whether X has, albeit ignorantly, *consented* to a, we must find out whether X's ignorance of the character of a was culpable. If it is, we are inclined

tion of 'consent' in political contexts in fact serves to nullify it. However, the issue has received most discussion in legal contexts, where a somewhat anomalous situation exists. The position is adequately summarized by Perkins:

> The general rule is that if deception causes a misunderstanding as to the fact itself (fraud in the *factum*), there is no legally recognized consent, because what happened is not that for which consent was given; whereas consent induced by fraud is as effective as any other consent, so far as direct and immediate legal consequences are concerned, if the deception relates not to the thing done, but merely to some collateral matter (fraud in the inducement).[20]

The difference can be illustrated by the following two cases. In Case 1, patient $X$ is being treated by her gynaecologist $Y$, who introduces what she believes to be an inert instrument. She later discovers that he has been having intercourse with her. This, according to Perkins, is fraud in the *factum*. In Case 2, patient $X$ is being treated by her gynaecologist $Y$, who induces her to have intercourse with him on the false pretext that it will be therapeutically beneficial. This, according to Perkins, is fraud in the inducement. Case 1 falls within the classic definition of rape, whereas Case 2 does not.

Before I comment on this distinction, I want to soften it up by referring to another case, which appears to fall mid-way between the other two. In Case 3, $X$ gets into bed in the dark, and submits to intercourse with $Y$, falsely believing that it is her husband. Legal opinion on the matter differs. Some consider it to be a case of fraud in the inducement, since the woman consents exactly to what is done (sexual intercourse); others consider it to be a case of fraud in the *factum*, since the woman's consent is to an innocent act of marital intercourse, while what is actually perpetrated upon her is an act of adultery ... she did not consent to adulterous intercourse.'[21]

At the heart of the issue lies Perkin's phrase: 'merely to some collateral matter.' What is merely collateral cannot be decided by a simple process of inspection. Acts do not come to us in neatly labelled packages. Descriptions are given to acts, and the description we give of any particular act reflects a judgment about the nature and importance

---

to say that $X$ was foolish (etc.) to consent to $a$; otherwise we are reluctant to describe $X$ as consenting to $a$. In certain circumstances, not only $Y$'s deception but also incompetence or negligence can help to negate $X$'s apparent consent.

20  R.M. Perkins, *Criminal Law*[2] (Mineola, NY: Foundation Press 1969) 964-5

21  Perkins, 966

of its contextual features, relative to certain ends. The movement of my finger may be described as no more than that, but depending on whether other contextual features are taken into account and how they are described, my act could be characterized as pulling a trigger, firing a shot, assassinating the President, removing a dictator, liberating the proletariat, saving the country, or effecting a turning point in history.[22] The descriptions are not necessarily exclusive, though any one description may be challenged by another which selects other contextual features or rates them differently. Returning to the earlier examples, we note that Case 2 is excluded from the purview of rape legislation because it is judged that even though X was deceived, she nevertheless consented to extra-marital intercourse. But to believe that this is a satisfactory description of her conduct is to make a contestable judgment about the relative importance of the various features of the situation. It is not the only possible description of her behaviour, and some other description is arguably preferable. For example, it might be claimed that what she consented to was not extra-marital but therapeutic intercourse, though what she got was not therapeutic but merely extra-marital intercourse. My point here is that it may be grossly misleading to describe X has having 'consented to extra-marital intercourse,' even though it is in some sense 'true.' It is misleading in the same way that it is misleading to describe someone who has killed the President as having pulled the trigger. In making this point it is not my intention to deny that deception *may* concern merely collateral matters and thus not serve to vitiate consent. Case 2 *may* be an example of this, but it is not something which we can decide without a close look at the surrounding circumstances and the values we and those involved bring to bear on them. Had Y induced X to have intercourse in exchange for a $20 note, which later turned out to be counterfeit, we might be less inclined to deny that X consented to extra-marital intercourse, though this is not because our description of X's act has become somehow less evaluatively laden.

We can, perhaps, put the foregoing point even more strongly by insisting on the intentionality of consent. Even though what X consents to is extensionally equivalent to extra-marital intercourse, the intensional character of consent makes it inappropriate to describe what she *consented* to as extra-marital intercourse. She consented only to what she intended, viz. therapeutic intercourse.

Closely associated with the knowledge requirement is the relatively *determinate* character of consent. When X consents, X does not general-

---

22  See, e.g. Joel Feinberg's discussion of the 'accordion effect' in *Doing and Deserving* (Princeton, NJ: Princeton University Press 1970) 133ff.

ly consent to anything at all, but to some determinate act *a*, and to what is known to be normally associated with *a*. This should not surprise us, since consent implies responsibility, and it is irresponsible to accept unlimited responsibility.[23] To say that a completely indeterminate or carte blanche consent is irresponsible is not of course to say that it is impossible. However, as I shall later argue, it subverts one of the chief presumptions of consent, namely, that it is the act of a responsible agent.

In claiming that consent is determinate, I do not wish to imply that what is consented to must always be spelled out before it can be properly included. Often, consent is given in a context in which reasonably specific parameters are implicit. Thus, to cite some familiar legal examples, the proprietor of a store who places a large box of matches on his counter for the convenience of customers does not consent to the whole box being taken away;[24] the girl who willingly eats a fig does not thereby consent to eat the deleterious drug concealed within it;[25] and the wife who consents to intercourse does not consent to communication of the disease with which, unknown to her, her husband is infected.[26] Even in those familiar situations in which one person says to another 'Do whatever you like,' certain parameters are generally implicit. Such situations are bounded by a set of mutual understandings which limit the range of possibilities to those acts for which the consenting party would be willing to share responsibility. Notwithstanding these contextual parameters, consent always carries with it a certain element of risk, since in consenting to the act or project of an other we do so in the knowledge of the other's freedom. Should *X* fail to establish *Y*'s credentials, *X* may not be able to relieve him/herself of all responsibility for what *Y* subsequently does.

Determining the limits of consent is not without its problems, particularly in those cases where there is an apparent embodiment of consent in public institutions. For example, in most legal jurisdictions it is considered that when a woman undertakes her marriage vows she consents to intercourse with her husband at his rather than their mutual

---

23  Harry Beran has brought to my attention J.G. Fichte's discussion of irrevocable contracts in *Sämmtliche Werke* (Berlin 1845) Vol. VI, pp. 158-61.

24  *Mitchum v. State*, 45 Ala. 29 (1871)

25  *Comm. v. Stratton*, 144 Mass. 303 (1873)

26  *State v. Lankford*, 29 Del. 594; 102 A. 63 (1917)

convenience.[27] And elected governments are frequently quick to claim a mandate for whatever they may have included in their election platform. Despite the conventions, it cannot really be argued that consent is given to what it is said to be given. Since in consenting to Y's doing a, X comes to share responsibility for a, we cannot determine the limits of X's consent without taking into account what X believed he/she was doing, whatever the conventions involved. I am not suggesting that the conventions can be ignored, but neither can they be completely determinative.

*Intention.* In the *Second Treatise of Civil Government,* Locke argues that 'every man that hath any possession or enjoyment of any part of the dominions of any government doth hereby give his tacit consent, and is as far forth obliged to obedience to the laws of that government, during such enjoyment, as any one under it, whether this his possession be of land to him and his heirs for ever, or a lodging only for a week; or whether it be barely travelling freely on the highway.'[28] This, I would argue, involves an unjustifiable extension of the notion of consent, since it removes it altogether from what a person perceives him/herself to be doing. We have already noted a difficulty in inferring the expression of consent from its signification. It is no less problematic to infer its signification from acts of the kind mentioned by Locke. We may wish to argue that someone enjoying these benefits ought to consent to uphold the arrangments that make them possible, but this would not be the same as saying that such a person tacitly does so. If X consents to Y's doing a, then X must realize that this is what he/she is doing. The theory of tacit consent is simply a post facto attempt to legitimize an existing political arrangement. Whether voting theory represents an improvement on this is a matter to which I shall soon return.

But what do we say about the case where X signifies his/her consent to Y's doing a with the intention of deceiving Y? Does X consent to Y's doing a? It is, I think, generally argued that just as a promise is a promise whether or not there is an intention to deceive, so consent is consent even if it is given deceptively. This I wish to dispute. It depends on what I believe to be the mistaken view that consent is a kind of promise. However, we do not need to pursue that here in order to see that the

---

27  At present, only Sweden and the states of Oregon, Michigan and South Australia recognize an offence of rape within marriage. See further, J. Scutt, 'Consent in Rape: the Problem of the Marriage Contract,' *Monash University Law Review,* **3** (1977) 155-88.

28  Locke, Bk. II, Ch. viii, Sect. 119

deceptively intended signifying of consent does not amount to consent. For the point of consenting is different from that of promising. When *X* consents to *Y*'s doing *a*, *X* so acts as to become a full participant in the implementation of *a*. By a 'full participant' I do not mean an 'enthusiastic participant,' but one who will be clearly implicated when responsibility for *a* is allocated. Now where consent is deceptively signified, *X* does not assume responsibility for *a*. That may not of course leave *X* morally unscathed, but if that is the case it is not because *X* participated in *a* but because *X* deceived *Y*.[29] Suppose *X* is a narcotics detective who infiltrates a drug ring. The occasion arises when *X* is asked to take part in a particular operation. *X* agrees to do so, but reports the matter, and when the operation gets under way the members of the ring are rounded up. *X* has acted deceptively (and in this case perhaps justifiably), but does not bear any responsibility for the attempt at *a*, for *X*'s efforts are not directed at *a*'s facilitation.[30] In other words, *X*'s deceptively signified consent does not amount to an expression of consent on *X*'s part.

So far in this section I have endeavoured to locate consent squarely within the domain of responsible (v. non-responsible) behaviour. It expresses a form of co-operation with or participation in the act or project of an other, such that the consenting party becomes, with the other, a bearer of responsibility for the act or project to which consent is given. In contemporary liberal democracies, this standard of co-operation is frequently said to be satisfied in the political domain by the practice of voting: 'the vote ensures that government is by consent.' We may distinguish weaker and stronger versions of this claim. On the weaker versions, those elected to public office govern by consent, even if only a minority of eligible voters participate, since all are at liberty to express a preference. The dubious presumption here is that those who do not vote have no firm preference, and/or will be more or less satisfied whatever the outcome. On the stronger and more plausible versions, a person's uncompelled and witting participation in the voting process constitutes his/her consent to its outcome, even if the elected candidate is not the one voted for. The stronger versions are well-represented by John Plamenatz:

> Where there is an established process of election to an office, then, *provided the election is free,* anyone who takes part in the process consents to the

---

29  In some cases, particularly where *Y* would not have done *a* had he/she not believed that *X* had consented, *Y* may be able to defend his/her involvement by reference to *X*'s deception.

30  In this case, I think we must assume that *X* has not expressed his/her agreement by lying to officials, killing policemen, etc.

> authority of whoever is elected to office ... The citizen who votes at an election is presumed to understand the significance of what he is doing, and if the election is free, he has voluntarily taken part in a process which confers authority on someone who would otherwise not have it. He may bitterly regret the election of the successful candidate and may not even have expected it, but if the election was free and he freely took part in it, he consented to the authority of the man elected.[31]

Plamenatz's phrase about understanding the significance of what one is doing has occasioned some difficulty, but what he presumably means is that if voting is to register consent, the voter must know that he/she is participating in a process whose recognized function is to produce a decision which is binding in circumstances where unanimity is impossible. It is Plamenatz's view that this and the voluntariness requirement are satisfied in most liberal democracies.[32]

However, the matter is not as clear-cut as defenders of the stronger versions would have us believe. Even if we agree with Singer that 'there is a conceptual connection between consenting and voting'[33] it does not follow of any particular voting situation that it satisfies the requirements for registering majority consent. For the social practice of voting can frustrate the point of voting in a number of ways. Use of the gerrymander, discrimination against particular/potential candidates, manipulation of opinion via the media, the multiplicity and almost expected fraudulence of election promises, and so on, cast serious doubts upon the claim that election results constitute some mandate based on popular consent.

The now almost endemic distortion of the voting situation in liberal

---

31  Plamenatz, 171. Similar views are expressed by Plamenatz in his earlier *Man and Society:* 'When you vote for a person or party that wins an election you directly consent to his or their authority, and you also consent indirectly to the system of government. Even when your vote is cast for persons who intend to change the system, you consent until it is changed ... For the purpose of an election is to give authority to the people who win it, and if you vote knowing what you are doing and without being compelled to do it, you voluntarily take part in a process which gives authority to those people. It does not matter what your motive for voting is, any more than it matters what your motive is in making a promise' ([London: Longmans 1963) Vol. I, 239-41).

32  Australian legislation, which makes voting compulsory, runs into some sort of difficulty on Plamenatz's account. Whether the possibility of registering an informal vote meets this difficulty is questionable.

33  P. Singer, *Democracy and Disobedience* (Oxford: Clarendon Press 1973) 50. Singer, however, allows that participating in the voting procedure may not imply actual consent.

democratic communities has done much to diminish the credibility of inferences to consent from participation in the vote. The widespread cynicism expressed in the graffiti reminder that 'whoever you vote for a politician gets in' is more compatible with government under sufferance or by acquiescence than government by consent. This also calls into question attempts to rescue voting, which argue that whether or not voting expresses actual consent to its outcome, the participant voter nevertheless places him/herself under obligation to accept it, since the act of participation induces in others a belief that one will.[34] Whether such a belief is induced is to be decided, not a priori, but by seeing what serious expectations are in fact engendered. I doubt whether, in the contemporary climate, participation creates any strong general expectation of conformity.

There is a further problem for the supposed nexus of voting and consent, which arises primarily from the lack of control which the individual voter has over the voting initiative. The voter may be presented with what he/she believes to be an unacceptable choice, but in which it is better to participate than not to participate. Consider an election involving two candidates, one moderate and the other fascist. Voter X may be determined to reject the fascist candidate, come what may, but believe that for the present the most acceptable way is to vote for the moderate. X knows what elections are for, but this does not mean that should the fascist candidate win, X has thereby consented to the outcome. X, after all, did not set up the initial choice situation, and even though he/she may recognize the point of the voting process, this does not mean that it cannot operate in unacceptable ways.

Voting, therefore, even if it meets Plamenatz's stated conditions, cannot be taken for granted as a mechanism of consent. Between its point and its practice there is a good deal of room for deflection.

Before moving to the next stage of the argument, I want to make three brief annotations:

(1) Consent *extends,* but does not thereby *transfer* responsibility.[35] There is a view, commonly aired in libertarian circles, that if X consents to Y's doing a to X, where a is known to constitute some injury to X, Y does no wrong. The assumption underlying this is that if X consents to Y's doing a

---

34  Singer, 50. Singer speaks of this as quasi-consent.

35  An affirmative answer to the question 'Will you take responsibility for this?' will not serve to transfer responsibility if the initiative is an irresponsible one. In this paragraph I have used material from my 'Consent as a Defence in Criminal Law,' *Archiv für Rechts- und Sozialphilosophie,* **65** (1979) 329-46.

to X, X assumes or takes over responsibility for a. X may be foolish to do so, but Y has not violated X's rights or otherwise acted wrongly. This, however, seems to me to be mistaken. For in consenting to Y's act, X does not reduce Y to an instrument of his/her will. Y does not have to do what X consents to his/her doing. Y, too, is a responsible agent, and may and ought to refrain from doing a because of its harmfulness to X. Y's lack of respect for X's person is not substantially diminished by making the injury done dependent on X's consent. Given the harmful nature of a, Y should not even have seriously considered it (assuming, of course, that there were no strong moral reasons for doing so). And the appeal to X's consent illegitimately detaches X's freedom from its embodiment in X. For it is the character of harm to limit the options available to a person.

(2) Closely related to the preceding point is the question whether *exploitation* negates consent. Some difficulty is posed by an ambiguity in the notion of exploitation. Marx used the term to characterize the relationship between classes in a class-based society. In respect of capitalist society he believed that workers were exploited since they were forced to produce a surplus which was not compensated for but appropriated by the capitalist class, partly as profit.[36] Because Marx saw this relationship as forced — since workers were not owners of the means of production and thus had to sell their labour power to alien interests in order to survive — he would not have considered exploitation to be compatible with genuine consent. However this somewhat technical use of 'exploitation' departs from a more commonplace normative understanding precisely on the point of coercion. On this commonplace view, exploitation (normatively considered) involves taking advantage of others' vulnerability or (less normatively) dispositions. No violation of the other's autonomy is implied. A sponger may exploit another's generosity, children may exploit the love of their parents, a man may exploit the insecurity of a woman, advertizing firms may exploit the gullibility of the public and politicians may exploit the fears of the citizenry. It would be difficult to argue that these cases of exploitation involve coercion. Rather, they involve one party's playing on some character trait of the other for the purpose of securing some advantage. As a consequence of the non-

---

36 See, e.g. L. Crocker, 'Marx's Concept of Exploitation,' *Social Theory & Practice,* **2** (1972) 201-13; N. Holmstrom, 'Exploitation,' *Canadian Journal of Philosophy,* **7** (1977) 353-69; A. Buchanan, 'Exploitation, Alienation and Injustice,' *Canadian Journal of Philosophy,* **9** (1979) 121-39; G.A. Cohen, 'The Labor Theory of Value and the Concept of Exploitation,' *Philosophy & Public Affairs,* **8** (1978-79) 338-60; also J. Tormey, 'Exploitation, Oppression & Self Sacrifice,' *Philosophical Forum* (Boston), **5** (1973) 206-21.

coerciveness of exploitative relations, we may want to condemn not only the exploiting party for his/her demeaning use of the other, but also
the exploited party for a weakness of character. There is a further point,
however, which links the commonplace notion of exploitation with
something like the Marxian. This is, that exploitation which is uncheck-
ed may well bring into being unequal relations which will then find expression in power relations. Exploitation then, may be the precursor of
coercion.

(3) In discussing the relation of consent, I have been careful to speak of
the consenting party's bearing of responsibility for that which is consented to. I have not expressed the point in terms of praise- and
blameworthiness. For, although the ascription of praise and blame
presupposes that the matter of responsibility has been settled, responsibility alone is not sufficient to determine praise- or blameworthiness.

## IV

We are now in a better position to understand the context of consent
relationships. So far I have argued that when $X$ consents to $Y$'s initiative,
$X$ explicitly tends to facilitate that initiative, and in doing so comes to
share in responsibility for it. In this section, I want to extend this account
and then to defend it against three alternative accounts: (1) consent as
an institutional notion; (2) consent as a self-assumed obligation; and (3)
consent as a kind of promising.

A world which places high importance on the securement and determination of consent is one which also places high importance on the
autonomy and responsibility of individuals. It is not uncommon to see
this in individualistic terms. Consent is seen as a free interaction between atomic individuals, who confront one another with their self-
created projects, seeking to elicit support for their implementation or
advancement. But this involves a serious distortion of the background to
relationships of consent. For the individuals who seek and give consent
are not independent atoms, but beings whose existence presupposes
and depends on a structure of social relationships. The human individual does not develop into an autonomous being naturally, inward-
ly structured like a seed, needing only a catalyst to bring those inbuilt
resources to full bloom. It is true that on a gross biological level there is
some sort of analogy between human beings and plants. But beyond
these biological contours they are constituted by a range of capacities
for development (learning) which depend in large measure for their
structuring as well as their nurture on social existence. It is only through

social existence that there can be an 'I' of recognizably human proportions, and it is largely through that social existence that this human 'I' can persist. Consequently, the projects of such individuals are not the creations of isolated organisms, but reflect in their conception and prosecution the stamp of social existence.

Autonomy, likewise, has to be understood not against but in terms of social existence. The core of personal autonomy, what Harry Frankfurt[37] calls 'reflective self-evaluation,' or the capacity to form not only desires to do this or that, but also desires that these desires be other than what they are, is developed in a social setting, and its content is also socially conditioned. To be autonomous, a person must possess a high degree of internal integration and coherence. This will involve emotional maturity and stability, self-awareness, and the ability to persevere at a task. There needs also to be a willingness to take the initiative in interpersonal transactions and an ability to respond constructively to the initiatives of others. In addition, a person must have access to information relating to his/her situation, and developed skills enabling its processing and evaluation. It is not possible to divorce our conception or possession of these qualities from social existence.

As social beings our lives may and do intersect often and in a great number of ways. Not only do we initiate projects which depend on the restraint and co-operation of others, but we are also possible participants in projects of others which require our restraint and initiative. Some combination of initiative and response seems to be essential in any social arrangement in which responsibility and autonomy are generally valued and encouraged, rather than restricted to some élite or class. Within the context of an ongoing social existence, consent constitutes, from the point of view of the initiator of some project, a limitation on the conditions under which it is acceptable to involve an other. From the point of view of the respondent, it constitutes a basis for involvement compatible with his/her continuance as an autonomous being, that is, as both initiator and respondent.

This account of the character and setting of consent can now be usefully distinguished from certain alternative accounts:

(1) *Consent as an institutional notion.* A number of writers have explicated consent as though it belonged to the domain of institutional structures. I have in mind those accounts in which 'X consents to Y's doing a' is analysed as 'X approves/authorizes Y's doing a.' Plamenatz and

---

37  H. Frankfurt, 'Freedom of the Will and the Concept of a Person,' *Journal of Philosophy*, **68** (1971) 5-21

38  Plamenatz, 169, etc.

Simmons[39] sometimes express themselves in this manner. Approval and authorization are institutional acts. They presuppose a framework in which there are offices and duties, roles and responsibilities, rights and powers, and approval and authorization belong with notions such as license, ratify, confirm, permit, commission, empower, legalize, and so on. The mistake in such analyses, I believe, is that they improperly generalize from the effect which consent has in certain restricted contexts to the function of consent in general. Signing a consent form does authorize a doctor to perform a particular operation, but these days parents who consent to their child's marriage do not authorize anything but indicate (at the minimum) that they will not make it difficult, given that they have some ability to do so. The pre-requisite for seeking consent is the advantageous position of the person from whom consent is sought, and although that advantage is sometimes exhibited in institutional status, it need not be.

(2) *Consent as a self-assumed obligation.* It is commonly argued[40] that if $X$ consents to $Y$'s doing $a$, $X$ assumes an obligation which involves, at the very minimum, non-interference with $Y$'s initiative. It is inferred from this that the act of consenting is most fruitfully understood as the assumption of an obligation. Simmons criticizes this by arguing that the obligation generated by consent is only secondary; its primary purpose is to authorize another's actions and, in so doing, create for or accord to another a special right.[41] Weale[42] shows the inadequacy of Simmons' position with respect to third party consent; that is, where $X$ consents to $Y$'s doing $a$ to $Z$. If neither $X$ nor $Y$ have a right to do $a$ to $Z$, then, in consenting to it, $X$ cannot authorize it. But Weale nevertheless agrees that the obligation involved in consenting is only secondary. Consent, he suggests, is best understood not as the illocutionary act of assuming an obligation, but as the perlocutionary act of intentionally inducing another's reliance upon one.[43] An obligation follows secondarily from 'the general utilitarian principle that where others have planned their own future conduct relying on an undertaking one has voluntarily given, then one is obligated not to act in violation of the undertaking in question.'[44] Now, I agree with Weale to this extent, that any obligation aris-

---

39   Simmons (1976), 276

40   E.g., by Pateman, Weale

41   Simmons (1976), 276

42   Weale, 67. Weale does not explicitly discuss Simmons.

43   Weale, 68f

44   Weale, 69

ing from consent is consequent upon the perlocutionary force of consenting. But this, I believe, does not show consent to be a perlocutionary act. I suggested earlier that X may *signify* his/her consent to Y, intending that Y rely on him/her, but without *expressing* consent, since the signification is intended to deceive. Consent is not given, though reliance is induced. Contrary to Weale's claim, it is as an illocutionary act that consent has to be understood. What X does in consenting to Y's doing *a* is to act so as to share responsibility for *a* with Y. We can see this better if we do not limit ourselves to the particular vantage points of X and Y, but look at the transaction from the point of view of someone outside it. From this point of view, I think it becomes much clearer that the question about whether X consented to Y's doing *a* is basically a question about X's complicity.[45]

(3) *Consent as a kind of promise.* Weale, and, indeed, many others, see consent as a form of promising — a kind of passive promising, in which one undertakes to do or refrain from doing something where the initiative lies with an other. No doubt this is one reason why consent is seen as placing oneself under an obligation, for it is common to view promising as the paradigmatic instance of placing oneself under an obligation. Although I do not go along with Pateman's suspicion of passive promising — as though, in consenting, a person does not show him/herself to be 'capable of independent judgement and rational deliberation,'[46] I do accept the point that a promise is the 'free creation of a relationship of obligation.' The point of the words 'I promise,' when freely uttered, is to bind the utterer. And this is not the point of consenting. Compare 'Will you promise to do *a*?' and 'Will you consent to do *a*?' The intention of the two questions is quite different. In the former question, the recipient is being asked to take part in a social practice whereby he/she binds him/herself to do *a*. In the latter question, the hearer's free participation in *a* is being sought. Perhaps as a reflection of this, we rarely promise without using the words 'I promise,' whereas consent, though it must be signified, is not usually, except in legal or quasi-legal contexts, given by means of the words 'I (hereby) consent.'

---

45 It may be worth repeating here that X's responsibility in regard to Y's acts is not determinable *only* by considering whether X consented to what Y was doing. If X feigns sleep and does not resist when Y approaches to fondle, X may be in no moral position to disclaim all responsibility for what is done. Consent is simply one form of co-operation with an other — a form whereby one comes to share an equal burden of responsibility with the other for some determinate act or project initiated by the other.

46 Pateman, 21

## V

When Y initiates some project whose facilitation X can effect by contribution or restraint, and Y seeks that contribution or restraint, why should he/she attempt to bring this about via X's consent? Several rationales have been proposed, but ultimately they come down to considerations of utility or respect for persons.[47] Here I shall consider what is at stake in each of these approaches, and indicate why I think the latter holds out more promise.

(1) By utility, I here understand any determination of the value or propriety of a particular form of interaction by reference to its consequences for either individual or the general happiness. This leaves a number of questions about utility unresolved, but gives us sufficient for present purposes.

I think it is significant that arguments for the utility of consent are usually introduced in limited contexts, for it gives us reason to suspect that they are at best supplementary to some more general argument.[48] In a therapeutic situation, for example, it is sometimes argued that X is likely to be more concerned about and better able to judge of the utility of a particular procedure than Y, its initiator. Requiring X's consent will serve to minimize gross risks, and will reassure people generally that they will be at least informed about what the risks are. The suspicion that utilitarian arguments are at best supplementary is borne out by the fact that they are only weakly presumptive. In therapeutic situations, at least, there is frequently good reason for thinking that particular patients are not good judges of what will be best for them. And in non-therapeutic situations, where it is desired to use body wastes such as urine or placental tissue for experimental purposes, risks are minimal and public benefit potentially considerable. What strong utilitarian reason could there be for requiring consent in such cases? Yet even in such cases there is a strong demand that consent be first obtained.[49] That, of course, does not show it to be justifiable, but it suggests that there is another source of the demand for consent.

(2) It is most commonly argued that respect for persons requires that where Y's project needs or would benefit from X's participation, Y

---

47   In posing these as alternatives I must beg certain questions.

48   See, e.g. R.M. Veatch, 'Why Get Consent?', *Hospital Physician,* **11** (1975) 30-1.

49   It is generally argued that use of body wastes without consent breaches a person's privacy, since the analysis of such wastes may provide information considered to be of a private nature (e.g. concerning drug use, diseases).

should first obtain *X*'s consent. At the heart of this there lies a conception of the individual as an autonomous being, whose autonomy constitutes the basis of claims against interference by others. This autonomy, sometimes expressed as the right to self-determination, lends itself to two apparently different interpretations. On the first, *absolutist* interpretation, autonomy/the right to self-determination picks out

> categories of decisions which an individual must be permitted to make, even if others believe the individual decides irrationally or incorrectly. It indicates that an implicit weighing of the interests of competing decisionmakers has already taken place and that the balance has been resolved in favour of individual choice.[50]

Requiring the consent of the individual, then, is seen as recognition of the absolute determination which ought to be allowed to the individual with respect to matters which do not limit the like autonomy of others. On the second, *relativist* interpretation, autonomy/the right to self-determination picks out a pre-eminent interest of individuals, but one which may be balanced against other interests which the individual or others may have, and which may, on occasion, be overridden in favour of these other interests. The absolutist position absolutely rejects strong paternalism.[51] The relativist position provides only a strong presumption against it. The absolutist position absolutely opposes any encroachment on the individual's private domain for the sake of social interests. The relativist position offers only a strong presumption against it.

Autonomy, whether viewed in absolutist or relativist terms, is central to respect for persons, since it represents that level of personal development in which moral agency is fully exemplified. It is as the subject and object of morally significant determinations that the idea of a person, as someone to whom respect is due, gets its grip. The requirement that personal interactions be based on the consent of those involved, acknowledges and safeguards autonomy. Utilitarian justifications of consent, unless they undergo substantial modification, cannot constitute such acknowledgement or safeguard.

In assessing the relative merits of absolutist and relativist positions, it is not obvious to me that the former is to be preferred, unless it be for

---

50 C.H. Montange, 'Informed Consent and the Dying Patient,' *Yale Law Journal,* **83** (1974) 1643

51 By 'strong paternalism' I mean interferences for a person's (supposed) good without regard to that person's decision-making capacities (consent). It is to be distinguished from 'weak paternalism' in which there is (or is believed to be) a defect in the person's decision-making capacities (inability to consent).

pragmatic reasons. The intellectual and moral myopia of those with social power may make us wary of any 'thin edge of the wedge' which might lead to oppressive inroads on individual autonomy. But apart from this, there are a few considerations which favour the relativist account.

(a) Not all encroachments on a person's right to self-determination are of equal significance. If the right to self-determination is construed on the model of a piece of territory over which one has jurisdiction[52], there is a clear difference between a temporary trespass which does not interfere with any significant projects of the occupier and the permanent alienation of a substantial part of that territory. Equally there is a clear difference between an interference intended to prevent an occupier from planting a crop and one intended to prevent the occupier from rendering the land permanently useless. Therefore it is not obvious why the boundaries of the territory must represent absolute rather than presumptive barriers to the intrusions of others. To this it may be replied that territorial incursions of whatever kind qualify a person's agent-status. But, except in a restricted sense, this need not be so. Agent-status is not an ahistorical possession. Agents are continuants with futures as well as presents and pasts, and in considering the propriety of some invasion, future as well as present status must be taken into account. In cases where they conflict, the balancing of future against present status may sometimes tip the scales in favour of the former.

(b) When emphasizing the value of autonomy, it is important not to forget that the capacities in virtue of which an individual is a self-determining being are not 'natural' endowments but the products of a social environment. It is not an atomistic individual who stands as the raison d'être of moral accounting, but a socially developed and socially dependent being who has duties which arise not only from the rights of others, but also from the dependence of those rights on a certain form of social existence. There is a ground for limitation here analogous to a taxation burden, in which individuals, by being required to contribute, make possible public facilities which increase the range of available social options.

(c) These considerations are reinforced when our concern is not with simple self-regarding behaviour but with consent situations, in which an additional party is involved. Where $X$ consents to $Y$'s initiative, and this is reasonably believed to be injurious to $X$, $X$'s person is not respected by $Y$ even though the initiative has been made dependent on $X$'s consent. For by focusing solely on $X$'s consent and not the connection between con-

---

52  This model is commonly employed by absolutists.

sent and *X*'s continuing status as an agent, *Y* has removed consent from its raison d'être in personhood. It is a key failure of libertarian doctrines that they have a present but no future.[53]

## Select Bibliography

Freedman, B., 'A Moral Theory of Informed Consent,' *The Hastings Center Report*, **5**:4 (1975) 32-9.

Kleinig, J.I., 'Consent as a Defence in Criminal Law,' *Archiv für Rechts- und Sozialphilosophie*, **65** (1979) 329-46.

Pitkin, H., 'Obligation and Consent, I, II,' *American Political Science Review*, **59** (1965), 990-9, **60** (1966) 39-52.

Plamenatz, J.P., *Consent, Freedom and Political Obligation*², (London: Oxford University Press 1968).

Scutt, J.A., 'Consent versus Submission: Threats and the Element of Fear in Rape,' *University of Western Australia Law Review*, **13** (1977) 52-76.

Simmons, A.J., *Moral Principles and Political Obligations* (Princeton, NJ: Princeton University Press 1980).

Snare, F., 'Consent and Conventional Acts in John Locke,' *Journal of the History of Philosophie*, **13** (1975) 27-35.

Weale, A., 'Consent,' *Political Studies*, **26** (1978) 65-77.

---

53 Numerous people have commented on the successive drafts through which this paper has passed, and they can be held at least partly responsible for its patchwork-quilt-like appearance. I am particular indebted to David Armstrong, Harry Beran, Tony Coady, Bruce Langtry, Don Mannison, Carole Pateman, Chris Provis, Michael Stocker and Robert Young.

CANADIAN JOURNAL OF PHILOSOPHY
Supplementary Volume VIII, 1982

# Rape and Mens Rea

M.T. THORNTON, Victoria College, Toronto

'Actus non facit reum nisi mens sit rea.'[1] But when is a mens rea? In the last twenty years discussions of this question have been stimulated by controversial decisions in the English House of Lords in the cases of *Smith, Morgan* and *Majewski.*[2]

The case of *Smith* decided that a man might be guilty of murder if a reasonable person, knowing the circumstances, would have foreseen that death would result even if the agent himself did not so foresee. This appeal to the 'reasonable person' imports what is known as the 'objective test' as opposed to the 'subjective test' of the agent's actual foresight or knowledge. The case of *Morgan* inclined per contra to the subjective test. Here the agent who believes that the woman consents is held to be

---

1 Sir Edward Coke *Institutes of the Laws of England,* Third Part, p. 6

2 Cases referred to are listed at the end. Many of the English cases, including both the House of Lords and Court of Appeal judgements in *Morgan*, can be found in J.C. Smith and B. Hogan, *Criminal Law: Cases and Materials* (London and Toronto: Butterworths 1975).

not guilty of rape even though a reasonable person would have believed otherwise. The case of *Majewski*, however, veers away from the subjective test. Here, if a man voluntarily intoxicates himself so as to be unaware that he is assaulting someone, then he may still be guilty of assault.

The decision in *Smith* was not supported in Canada because the Canadian Criminal Code (Sections 212, 213) explicitly defines the mental element in murder. However the decisions in *Morgan* and *Majewski* have been affirmed by the Supreme Court of Canada in *Pappajohn* and *Leary* respectively. In this paper I shall be concerned with the *Morgan-Pappajohn* ruling on rape.[3]

The controversy over whether the test of criminal responsibility should be always subjective or sometimes or always objective is a moral issue with ancient roots, for it has strong connections with the traditional retributive v. utilitarian debate over punishment. The subjectivists claim that someone is not guilty, and therefore not liable to punishment, unless s/he is 'culpable' or 'responsible' where these concepts are interpreted 'retributively' as referring to the actual state of mind (intention or knowledge) of the person who did the act. The objectivists claim that it is justifiable to hold someone responsible who has fallen below a prescribed standard of conduct which it is reasonable to expect from members of the community with a view to ensuring the general public welfare. In this respect they accept the utilitarian thesis that responsibility depends on the good effects of holding people responsible rather than on their 'guilty mind' at the time they committed their crimes. Some utilitarians, however, go further than the objectivists. They urge the abolition of mens rea altogether or endorse the creation of 'strict liability' offences not requiring mens rea.[4]

### Mens rea

The five 'mental elements' relevant to mens rea are (i) intention, (ii) knowledge, (iii) recklessness, (iv) negligence, and (v) blameless in-

---

3 I discuss the *Majewski-Leary* ruling on drunken crimes in 'Making Sense of Majewski,' in *Criminal Law Quarterly,* **23** (1981) 464-91.

4 E.g. Barbara Wootton, *Crime and the Criminal Law* (London: Stevens 1963). For arguments in favour of strict liability see also R.A. Wasserstrom, 'Strict Liability in the Criminal Law,' in J.J. Thomson and G. Dworkin (eds.) *Ethics* (New York: Harper and Row 1968) (reprinted from the *Stanford Law Review* **12** [1960]), discussed below. References to Wasserstrom's article in the text are to the reprinted version.

advertence. Although all of these may be said to involve psychological states, only the first two *are*, properly speaking, psychological states.

## (i) Intention and (ii) knowledge:

The dividing-line between 'intention' and 'knowledge' has often been blurred in the law because in the great majority of cases either is sufficient mens rea. In *Hyam* Lord Diplock said:

> I agree with those of your lordships who take the uncomplicated view that in crimes of this class [murder] no distinction is to be drawn in English law between the state of mind of one who does an act because he desires it to produce a particular evil consequence, and the state of mind of one who does the act knowing full well that it is likely to produce that consequence although it may not be the object he was seeking to achieve by doing the act. (63)

The lack of a legal distinction leads to a lack of a conceptual distinction between intention (in the proper sense implying purpose) and knowledge. For our purposes, however, 'intention' and 'knowledge' may be understood in their ordinary senses.[5]

## (iii) Recklessness:

In recklessness the agent realizes that a certain circumstance may obtain or a certain consequence may follow, but nevertheless acts when it is unreasonable to do so given that circumstance or consequence. The agent acts in disregard of the risk that the circumstance may obtain or the consequence may follow. Recklessness thus contains a subjective element (knowledge or awareness of risk) and an objective element (unreasonableness of taking that risk).

## (iv) Negligence:

Negligence is usually defined by reference to 'a reasonable person.' A person acts negligently when s/he acts in a way in which a reasonable person would not have acted:

> A man acts negligently when he brings about a consequence which a reasonable and prudent man would have foreseen and avoided. A man acts negligently with respect to a circumstance when a reasonable man would

---

5 The English Law Commission's *Report on the Mental Element in Crime* (Law Com. No. 89, H.M.S.O. 21st June 1978) uses 'intention' and 'knowledge' in their ordinary senses (paras. 41-9) but also says that 'a person should be regarded as intending a particular result of his conduct if ... he has no substantial doubt that the conduct will have that result.'

> have been aware of the existence of the circumstance and, because of its existence, would have avoided acting in that manner.[6]

Negligence is 'inadvertent' because the agent does not consciously realize the risk that the circumstance may obtain or the consequence may ensue. A high degree of negligence is called 'gross negligence' or, misleadingly, 'recklessness.' Following the usual practice nowadays I use 'reckless' to imply 'advertent.'

Because negligence is inadvertent, J.W.C. Turner has suggested that there can be no degrees of negligence on the ground that there can be no degrees of inadvertence: inadvertence is a 'nullity' and 'of nullity there can be no degrees.'[7] This argument has been refuted by H.L.A. Hart.[8] 'Degree of negligence' does not mean 'degree of inadvertence.' Rather, it refers to the degree of unreasonableness in not taking due precaution. Gross negligence occurs when it is highly unreasonable not to take the relevant precautions.

*(v) Blameless inadvertence:*
An agent is blamelessly inadvertent if s/he performs an act which has a harmful consequence but any reasonable person would have failed to foresee that consequence, or if s/he fails to consider a circumstance which any reasonable person would have failed to consider.

The great issue between subjectivists and objectivists is whether (i), (ii) and (iii) or also (iv) should be sufficient for criminal responsibility. Those who endorse 'strict liability' offences regard (v), blameless inadvertence in regard to some circumstance or consequence, as compatible with criminal responsibility.[9]

A subjectivist, as I am using the term, is one who requires intention, knowledge or recklessness with regard to all elements in the actus reus. But H.L.A. Hart has proposed that negligence, properly understood, should also be included under the subjective standard.[10]

---

6  J.C. Smith and B. Hogan, *Criminal Law* (Fourth edition, London and Toronto: Butterworths 1978) 53-4

7  J.W.C. Turner (ed.), *Kenny's Outlines of Criminal Law* (18th edition, Cambridge: Cambridge University Press 1964) 34-5

8  H.L.A. Hart, *Punishment and Responsibility* (Oxford: Oxford University Press 1970) 148-9. Page references in the text are to this work.

9  Thus in *Prince* it was held that a man was guilty of unlawfully taking an unmarried girl under sixteen out of her father's possession although he believed on reasonable grounds that she was over sixteen.

10  Hart, ch. VI

He has two reasons for saying this. First, he thinks that intention and knowledge are important for criminal responsibility only because they show that the agent could have chosen to act in conformity with the law. He argues that a negligent person also could have acted in conformity with the law and that those who exclude responsibility for negligence are subscribing to 'a form of the ancient belief that possession of knowledge of consequences is a sufficient and necessary condition of the capacity for self-control' (150). But his argument rests on a false premise. The reason why subjectivists oppose responsibility for negligence is not that the negligent person lacks the capacity for self-control but that s/he does not *choose* to bring about the harmful consequence s/he brings about. It is, they think, what one *chooses* to do, not what one *could have done,* which is important for responsibility.[11]

Hart's second argument is that negligence is not to be judged simply by appeal to 'a reasonable person.' Instead of asking 'Would a reasonable person have foreseen what would happen?', we should ask 'Is it reasonable to expect that *this* person would have foreseen what would happen?' (153-6). The latter, he says, is a 'subjective,' while the former is an 'objective,' question. However this introduces a different sense of 'subjective' in which it means that the standard of reasonableness is geared to the particular person involved rather than to the invariant standard of the 'reasonable person.'[12] It would simply be a

---

11   Thus Dickson J in *Leary:* 'A person is accountable for what he wills. When, in the exercise of the power of free choice, a member of society chooses to engage in harmful or otherwise undesirable conduct proscribed by the criminal law, he must accept the sanctions which that law has provided for the purpose of discouraging such conduct' (486). Philosophers generally assume that the ability to act otherwise is a necessary condition of responsibility; but (a) it does not follow that it is a sufficient condition, and (b) in any case the assumption needs to be examined; see Harry G. Frankfurt, 'Alternate Possibilities and Moral Responsibility,' *Journal of Philosophy,* **66** (1969) 829-39.

12   Cf. *Hudson* (a case of sexual intercourse with a defective) where the appeal judges adopted 'the subjective approach, that is to say, that, if an accused man succeeds in establishing to the extent known as the balance of probabilities test that he himself did not know and that he himself had no reason to suspect the woman to be a defective, then he succeeds in his defence.' The defence of provocation, which requires that a reasonable person would have lost self-control in the defendant's situation, is also moving towards a variable standard. In *Bedder* (1954) the House of Lords decided that the defendant's impotence had no bearing on the reasonableness of his loss of self-control. Presumably the ordinary resaonable man is not impotent! But since 1961 the reasonableness of the defendant's reaction has been gauged, in New Zealand, by whether the provocation 'was sufficient to deprive a person having the power of self-control of an ordinary person, but otherwise having the characteristics of the offender, of

play on words to assert that a subjectivist about negligence (one who favours a variable standard) is a subjectivist about mens rea (one who favours a requirement of intention, knowledge or recklessness).

To avoid confusion 'subjectivist' will be used in the latter sense only; and the question at issue is whether criminal responsibility should require intention, knowledge or recklessness as to all elements in the actus reus (subjective mens rea, for short). In the case of rape the actus reus is having sexual intercourse with a woman without her consent.[13] Hence if subjective mens rea is required, it follows that unless the agent either intended the intercourse to be without the woman's consent or knew that she did not consent or was reckless as to whether or not she consented, he cannot be guilty of rape. The objectivist, on the other hand, says that if the agent commits the actus reus of rape and unreasonably believes that the woman was consenting, then he is still guilty of rape. Thus the objectivist views rape as a crime of negligence, for if the agent unreasonably believes that the woman consents when she does not consent, he is negligent as to whether or not she consents.

So the crucial question is 'Does an honest but unreasonable belief in the woman's consent negative the mens rea of rape?' This is the question which was discussed and answered affirmatively in Morgan.

## D.P.P. v. Morgan

An R.A.F. sergeant, Morgan, invited other R.A.F. men to his home for the purpose of having intercourse with his wife. The trial judge directed that they could not be guilty of rape if they honestly believed that the woman consented, provided that their belief was a reasonable one. The Court of Appeal upheld their conviction but allowed appeal to the House of Lords, having certified the following to be a point of law of general public importance: 'Whether in rape the defendant can properly be convicted notwithstanding that he in fact believed that the woman consented if such belief was not based on reasonable grounds.' Three out of the five law lords replied No; but all of them held that Morgan and the others had been rightly convicted.

---

the power of self-control' (Crimes Act, 1961, s. 169 [2]). This obviously and, I believe, rightly affirms a variable standard. (I am indebted to Peter Singer for drawing my attention to the unfortunate Bedder. The development of the English law on provocation is discussed in Smith and Hogan, Criminal Law, 294-308.)

13 I omit the objectionable qualification 'not his wife.'

The majority held that rape is a crime requiring subjective mens rea and that an honest belief in the woman's consent is incompatible with the mens rea of rape. Therefore a *Morgan* defendant (as I shall call him) is not guilty of rape.

The opinion of the minority was intended to accord with the majority opinion in *Tolson*. Here, in Stephen J's words, it was held that 'an alleged offender is deemed to have acted under that state of facts which he in good faith *and on reasonable grounds* believed to exist when he did the act alleged to be an offence' (37; my emphasis).

*Tolson* was a case of bigamy. The majority in *Morgan* decided that the statutory offence of rape is not altogether comparable to the statutory offence of bigamy (*per* Cross p. 352, Hailsham p. 362, Fraser p. 382). On the face of it, however, the relevant statutes appear more similar than the lords allowed. The Sexual Offences Act (U.K. 1956) says 'It is an offence for a man to rape a woman' and 'Rape consists in having unlawful sexual intercourse with a woman without her consent by force, fear or fraud' (*Archbold,* quoted in *Morgan* p. 358). The Offences against the Person Act (U.K. 1861) says 'Whosoever, being married, shall marry any other person during the life of the former husband or wife .. shall be guilty of an offence ...'. In both cases there is a clause, 'without her consent,' 'being married,' which specifies the circumstances in which the act, sexual intercourse or marriage, becomes an offence. If *Tolson* says that an honest and reasonable belief that one is not married is required in order to negate the mens rea of bigamy, why did the majority in *Morgan* not say that an honest and reasonable belief that the woman is consenting is required in order to negate the mens rea of rape? There is no indication in the bigamy statute that the element 'being married' is not governed by subjective mens rea. So on what ground is it contended that subjective mens rea does not extend to 'being married' in bigamy but does extend to 'without her consent' in rape? If one really believes in subjective mens rea, then surely one cannot accept the *Tolson* rule. And this is exactly the conclusion which Smith and Hogan reach in their textbook on criminal law:

> It is submitted that the mens rea of bigamy ought to be, not an intention to go through a ceremony of marriage, which is a perfectly innocent intention, but an intention to go through a ceremony of marriage knowing that, or being reckless whether, one is married already.[14]

Here they explicitly reject Lord Fraser's opinion in *Morgan* (p. 382). And so they should if they wish to be consistent subjectivists. The fact re-

---

14   Smith and Hogan, *Criminal Law* 687

mains that *Tolson* provides a very good precedent for the claim that only an honest and reasonable belief in consent should be permitted to negate the mens rea of rape.

Nevertheless it is evidently true that if intention and recklessness are required, negligence as to the woman's consent is not enough. Assuming that rape does require subjective mens rea we must next ask whether a belief in the woman's consent is necessarily incompatible with the mens rea of rape. It may seem that they are obviously incompatible. This indeed was what *Morgan* said. Nevertheless two philosophers, E.M. Curley and Anthony Kenny, have argued that in fact they are not incompatible: one can believe in the woman's consent and still possess the mens rea of rape.[15]

Curley's argument is that a *Morgan* defendant is reckless, not merely negligent, because he does advert to the risk that the woman may not consent: '... we must assume that he considered the possibility that she was not consenting and rejected it' (348). However, to dismiss a possibility is not to disregard it. If someone is reckless then s/he must at the time of the act appreciate that there is a risk but perform the act regardless. If someone thought at an earlier time that there was a risk but then decided later that there was no risk and accordingly performed the act, it would be unjust to describe that person as reckless. Hence Curley's argument, however appealing, is inconclusive.

Another consideration which Curley adduces is that '... the law already recognizes, under the heading of wilful blindness, the possibility that mistake about a material element may coincide with recklessness regarding that element' (ibid.). But this will only prove Curley's point if every *Morgan* defendant is wilfully blind with respect to the woman's consent. No doubt some are; and since in such a case they will be held not to have had an honest belief in the woman's consent they will not be acquitted. It is important to bear in mind that a *Morgan* defendant *may be* closing his eyes to the facts; but this does not show that every *Morgan* defendant is reckless.

Kenny's argument also relates to recklessness and is based on an interpretation of Lord Hailsham's remarks in *Morgan*. Lord Hailsham had said that 'the prohibited act is and always has been intercourse without consent of the victim and the mental element is and always has been the intention to commit that act, or the equivalent intention of having intercourse willy-nilly not caring whether the victim consents or no' (362).

---

15 E.M. Curley, 'Excusing Rape,' *Philosophy and Public Affairs*, **5** (1975-76) 325-60; A. Kenny, *Freewill and Responsibility* (London: Routledge and Kegan Paul 1978) ch. 3. Page references in the text are to these works.

Kenny construes this as saying that indifference to the woman's consent is sufficient mens rea and points out that it is possible both to believe that the woman consents and to be indifferent as to her consent: 'even if the belief was honestly held, its unreasonableness may be evidence of that indifference to the woman's consent which is sufficient for mens rea' (p. 62).

The flaw in Kenny's argument is that indifference is not the same as recklessness, and it was recklessness, not indifference, which Lord Hailsham was asserting to be sufficient for mens rea: 'if the intention of the accused is to have intercourse nolens volens, that is recklessly and not caring whether the victim be a consenting part or not, that is equivalent on ordinary principles to an intent to do the prohibited act without the consent of the victim' (357). Recklessness in rape involves adverting to the risk that the woman does not consent. An element of indifference to (or disregard of) the risk is involved because the person continues in the act despite the perceived risk.[16] Thus indifference is related to recklessness but not identical to it.[17]

Kenny quotes (p. 60) Lord Simon's statement in *Morgan:* 'The mens rea is knowledge that the woman is not consenting or recklessness as to whether she is consenting or not' (363). So it is surprising that he takes indifference, rather than recklessness, to be sufficient mens rea. However, he recognizes (p. 62) that it is recklessness, not indifference, which is now, by the Sexual Offences (Amendment) Act (U.K.) 1976, said to be sufficient mens rea for rape. He comments:

> The effect of the Act does not, in fact, seem to be quite the same as the result of the ruling in *Morgan.* For it seems that an honest belief in consent is in no way incompatible with recklessness about consent; and if that is so an honest and unreasonable belief in consent will not always negate mens rea in rape. ... It is surely perfectly possible that a man might believe that a woman consented while knowing from the circumstances of the case, that there was a risk that she did not. (63)

---

16 Indifference in this sense does not imply 'having no attitude pro or con.' The reckless rapist may well hope that the woman does consent.

17 The formula 'intentionally doing X not caring whether or not *p*' was held to be an inadequate definition of recklessness in *Briggs;* and the English Law Commission has opposed defining recklessness in terms of indifference, *Report*, para. 64. In *Australian Criminal Law* (2nd edition, Melbourne: Law Book Co. Ltd. 1970) 160, Colin Howard points out (anticipating Kenny) that 'it is perfectly possible for D both to believe that he has V's consent and to intend to carry out his purpose whether or not he has that consent,' but infers (unlike Kenny) that the latter formulation fails to define the mens rea of rape.

Since the Act was intended to codify the *Morgan* ruling that an honest even if unreasonable belief always negates mens rea in rape, it would be very odd if there were such a disparity. In fact Kenny is flying in the face of unanimous legal opinion which maintains that a mistaken belief is incompatible with recklessness. Glanville Williams holds that 'an act is not reckless as to a circumstance in respect of which the agent is *mistaken*.'[18] Colin Howard says: 'If D is reckless as to the true state of affairs he has no significant belief one way or the other and therefore cannot have made a relevant mistake.'[19] The Advisory Group on the Law of Rape agreed.[20]

So far as I can determine this apparently unanimous opinion goes back to a famous nineteenth-century civil case, *Derry v. Peek,* a case concerning fraud. There Lord Herschell held that 'fraud is proved when it is shown that a false representation has been made (1) knowingly, or (2) without belief in its truth, or (3) recklessly, careless whether it be true or false' (374). He continued:

> Although I have treated the second and third as distinct cases, I think the third is but an instance of the second, for one who makes a statement under such circumstances can have no real belief in the truth of what he states. (ibid.)

In the same vein J.C. Smith says that for a deception to be 'deliberate or reckless,' 'it is sufficient that D makes a statement which he knows to be false or does not believe to be true.'[21] It follows that an honest belief in the statement's truth excludes mens rea. Nevertheless it does seem possible, as Kenny suggests, that one might at the same time advert to the risk that it is false.

In *Morgan* the majority were apparently so concerned with the (true) assertion that a reasonable belief is not necessary to rebut recklessness that they simply assumed, what does not follow, that an honest belief is

---

18  Glanville Williams, *Criminal Law: The General Part* (2nd edition, London: Stevens 1961) 149

19  Howard, 160

20  *Report of the Advisory Group on the Law of Rape* (Cmnd. 6352, H.M.S.O. 1975) para. 56. (This is discussed further below; references in the text are to paragraphs of the report.) See also *Pappajohn* per Dickson J at pp. 494, 497, McIntyre J at p. 515. However, Smith and Hogan are slightly more circumspect: 'Where the law requires intention or recklessness with respect to some element in the actus reus, a mistake, whether reasonable or not, *which precludes both states of mind* will excuse' (*Criminal Law,* 182; my emphasis).

21  J.C. Smith, *The Law of Theft* 2nd edition, London: Butterworths 1972) para. 201

sufficient to do so. But it does seem that it is only an honest belief *plus* some further ingredient (not, admittedly, the reasonableness of the belief) which provides a defence. Some support for this view can be derived from Lord Cross's judgment in *Morgan* when he says that a man has not committed rape 'if he believed that the woman was consenting to the intercourse and *would not have attempted to have it but for his belief'* (352; my emphasis). Obviously such a man would not be reckless, since the reckless rapist acts whether or not the woman consents. However, it does not follow (did Lord Cross think it did?) from the fact that the man believed in the woman's consent that he would not have acted as he did but for that belief.

Although Lord Cross provides a sufficient condition for denying recklessness, it may not be the case that he provides a necessary condition. For instance, it does not seem that someone who believed in the woman's consent and had not adverted to the possibility that she did not consent would be 'reckless' even if it were not the case that he would not have attempted to have intercourse but for his belief. The only safe course here is to return to the definition of recklessness, which requires that the agent adverts to a risk and unreasonably disregards it. It follows that an honest belief in the woman's consent negates recklessness only if either he does not advert to the risk that she is not consenting or he does not unreasonably disregard that risk.

These considerations show that a *Morgan* defendant should be cross-examined as to whether and why he did not believe that there was a risk that the woman was not consenting, as well as on his belief that she was consenting. Otherwise it will be impossible to prove that the man's belief in the woman's consent does not negate the mens rea of rape.

This concludes the first part of our inquiry: if the mens rea of rape is interpreted in the subjectivist manner, an honest even if unreasonable belief in consent can exclude recklessness and thus can excuse. Reasonableness is not necessary for an acquittal. In the remainder of this paper I shall argue that it would be preferable to require that only an honest and reasonable belief can excuse. This change would, as was said earlier, convert rape into a crime of negligence; so we must first consider negligence in general.

## Crimes of negligence

Although subjectivists like to assert that subjective mens rea is required for major criminal offences, they agree that manslaughter is an exception.[22] Causing death by means of an unlawful act is manslaughter by the Canadian Criminal Code (Section 205). There is also an offence of causing death by criminal negligence (Section 203). 'Criminal negligence' is defined in terms of a 'wanton or reckless disregard for the lives or safety of other persons' (Section 202). Trying to frighten someone and accidentally killing him would be an example (see *Leblanc*).

The rationale for negligent manslaughter is obvious. Causing a person's death is the worst thing one can do to him (her). Accordingly, one should take all reasonable steps to avoid that risk. Negligence reveals a moral fault when the cost of such negligence is very high.

Jerome Hall has said that 'the thesis that inadvertent damage reflects a moral fault is difficult to accept.'[23] He rejects the idea that negligent persons are lacking in a moral regard or ethical sensitivity towards other people. In cases of causing death through negligent driving, for instance,

> It seems much more probable that a dull mind, slow reactions, awkwardness and other ethically irrelevant facts were the underlying case. (138)

Hence, the argument goes, punishment for negligence is punishment for stupidity not for wrongdoing; hence it is unfair and unjust. Now one can agree that punishment for stupidity is unjust without agreeing that stupidity never engenders wrongdoing. I may be an incompetent sailor; there is nothing wrong in that. But it is nevertheless wrong for me, being such a sailor, to take a boatful of people through dangerous waters, in the absence of any emergency which might justify doing so. If the people drown then I am to blame precisely because no reasonable person would have embarked on that course of action.

More generally, we have to recognize that, living together in a society where one person's actions can so easily harm another, each of us has some sort of moral duty to take a modicum of care in regard to the welfare of others. Obviously this duty does not extend to circumstances or consequences which no reasonable person would foresee; but it does imply that gross negligence towards others is culpable.

---

22   E.g. Smith and Hogan, *Criminal Law,* 308-20. Although some subjectivists dispute that there is a distinct type of 'negligent manslaughter' (cf. the discussion in Glanville Williams, *Textbook of Criminal Law* [London: Stevens 1978] 224-33), all agree that 'constructive' manslaughter, i.e. killing by an unlawful act, does not require subjective mens rea.

23   Jerome Hall, *General Principles of Criminal Law* (2nd edition, Indianapolis: Bobbs-Merrill 1960) 136. Page references in the text are to this work.

In his article on 'Strict Liability in the Criminal Law' R.A. Wasserstrom has argued that responsibility for negligence is equivalent to strict liability, i.e. to liability for acts where the agent is blamelessly inadvertent with respect to some circumstance or consequence. He writes:

> If the objection to strict liability is that the defendant's state of mind is irrelevant then a comparable objection seems to lie against offences founded upon criminal negligence. For the jury in a criminal negligence prosecution asks only whether the activity of the defendant violated some standard of care which a reasonable member of the community would not have violated. To the extent that strict liability statutes can be interpreted as legislative judgments that conduct which produces or permits certain consequences is unreasonable, strict criminal liability is similar to a jury determination that conduct in a particular case was unreasonable. (465-6)

There are two points here, one concerning states of mind, the other concerning reasonableness.

As to the first it is undoubtedly true that the subjectivist is opposed to crimes of negligence just as he is opposed to strict liability offences, simply because neither requires subjective mens rea with respect to every element in the actus reus. (But most subjectivists prefer the former to the latter since negligence does at least imply *some* 'fault.') However, it is also true that negligence, unlike strict liability, can be understood in terms of a 'variable standard,' as we noted earlier. As well as asking whether the defendant violated some standard of care which a reasonable person would not have violated, the jury can ask whether the defendant was in a position to behave as the reasonable person would.[24]

Whether or not negligence is interpreted according to a variable standard, I would still wish to argue that negligence is different from strict liability. This brings us to the second point. Pace Wasserstrom, strict liability statutes do not say that certain conduct is unreasonable but only that it is punishable. Of course this means that, in the opinion of the legislators, it is reasonable to make, e.g., selling adulterated milk an offence of strict liability. But it does *not* mean that anyone who sells adulterated milk, being blamelessly inadvertent as to its adulteration, is acting unreasonably. The reasonableness of the law does not imply the

---

24 In fairness to Wasserstrom it should be said that he was probably thinking of the views of Oliver W. Holmes who held that the standards to which everyone is required to conform 'require him at his own peril to come up to a certain height. They take no account of incapacities, unless the weakness is so marked as to fall into well-known exceptions, such as infancy or madness' (*The Common Law,* Lecture II: The Criminal Law, Boston, 1881, 50). Holmes' view is criticised by Hart, 242-4.

unreasonableness of breaking it, since a person who is blamelessly inadvertent is not acting in an unreasonable way. But Wasserstrom has failed to see this distinction.

I conclude that the establishment of crimes of negligence does have a moral foundation. Responsibility for negligence is not the same as strict liability. Whether or not strict liability is justified will be considered later.

### Negligent rape

Crimes where a defendant's mistaken belief should be required to be reasonable as well as honest are those where the agent's negligence implies a disregard or lack of respect for others. If A harms B and could with a moderate use of reason have foreseen and avoided the harm, then in so acting A has shown a disregard of B. This disregard need not be a conscious disregard, i.e. recklessness, but a *lack* of regard or care. People who don't care about other people simply assume that their actions will not adversely affect others. There is a sort of belief (and it is an honest belief because those who hold it really are like that) which, so far from being incompatible with, actually manifests a disregard of others. (Again, this need not be recklessness in the legal sense.) The underlying moral precept is the principle of respect for persons; and where this is absent, the agent who performs the actus reus of rape or homicide may reasonably be brought within the criminal law. It is not negligence per se but negligence as manifesting a lack of regard for others which constitutes the moral fault. In *Smith (David)* it was held that an honest even if unreasonable mistake as to ownership of property is a sufficient defence to a charge under the Criminal Damage Act. This is quite acceptable because (i) no person is harmed, and (ii) such damage can be made good through a civil suit requiring only (civil) negligence. This case has nothing to say about homicide or rape where a person is harmed and the harm cannot be made good through a civil suit.

In the case of rape I would argue that a man who believes without reasonable grounds that the woman consents is not behaving with a respect for her as an autonomous being with her own point of view, but is, rather, regarding her simply as a medium of his pleasure. Thus it is the antithesis of an interpersonal relationship. One noticeable aspect of the *Morgan* defence cases (*Plummer and Brown* in Canada, *Cogan and Leak* in England, as well as *Morgan* itself) is that three parties are involved: the woman, the agent and a 'go-between.' The go-between tells the agent that the woman desires sex or intimidates her so that she offers no resistance. The agent believes the go-between (the woman's husband in *Morgan* and *Cogan and Leak)* or interprets the absence of resistance as consent. The fact that the agent takes his cue from the go-between not from the woman suggests that he is not too concerned about what the woman thinks and feels in the situation. Where the go-between is the husband, the agent perhaps considers the husband as proprietor of his wife and spokesman for her. The availability of the *Morgan* defence means that it is those whose attitude to women is the most reactionary who will have the best defence. The boor who honestly believes that however much a woman may struggle and protest she nevertheless desires sexual intercourse would be a perfect candidate for a *Morgan* defence (though it is of course doubtful whether a jury would acquit him. It is cheering but hardly satisfactory that judges and juries often compensate for inadequacies in the law.)

Even an avowed defender of the *Morgan* decision, Glanville Williams, seems to support these arguments when, in discussing a defendant who claims 'he had no idea whether the woman was consenting or not,' he writes:

> It would be consistent with principle to say that this is no defence, since a man who has intercourse with a woman should positively believe that she is consenting, not just have no opinion on the subject. If he does not know, he must find out.[25]

But if it did not occur to the man that the woman was not consenting how can he be reckless in the legal sense implying advertence to risk? To say that he *should* have a positive belief is to say that a reasonable person would have a positive belief, i.e. the agent is being negligent. I agree that this is culpable! And to say that 'he must *find out*' (my emphasis) implies that his belief must rest on reasons; (it can't imply that the belief must be true since ex hypothesi it is false.) Thus Williams also believes that a man has a duty to a woman to make sure that she is consenting.

The principal objection to *Morgan* is that it attends too much to the subjective state of mind of the accused and too little to what is due to the victim. This view was expressed in *Morgan* by Lords Cross and Simon. Although Lord Cross agreed with the majority as to the existing law, he thought that it would be perfectly justifiable to require that belief in the woman's consent must be reasonable:

> it can be argued with force that it is only fair to the woman and not in the least unfair to the man that he should be under a duty to take reasonable care to

---

25  Williams, *Textbook* 434

ascertain that she is consenting to the intercourse and be at the risk of a prosecution if he fails to take such care. (352)

Lord Simon, believing with the minority that the existing law required
an honest and reasonable belief in consent for acquittal, said:

The policy of the law in this regard could well derive from its concern to hold a
fair balance between victim and accused. ... A respectable woman who has
been ravished would hardly feel that she was being vindicated by being told
that her assailant must go unpunished because he believed, quite
unreasonably, that she was consenting to sexual intercourse with him. (367)

He points out that the Sexual Offences Act (U.K., Section 6) requires for
acquittal an honest and reasonable belief that the woman is over sixteen, presumably to protect her. Why should not the law also protect a
woman by demanding an honest and reasonable belief in her consent?

The decision in *Morgan* caused an outcry which led to the creation
of an Advisory Group on the Law of Rape. They were concerned with
what the law of rape should be, not what it is; but in the end they simply
affirmed *Morgan*. Their report is of some interest as a defence of the
status quo as defined by *Morgan*.

Their first argument is that criminal offences, 'grave' ones at least, require subjective mens rea:

there are cases where negligence is a basic concept as, for example, traffic offences, or is a subsidiary element in certain other offences, but we are here
concerned with a grave crime carrying with it liability to imprisonment for life
and, in the case of such a crime, this principle is generally maintained. (para.
51)

However manslaughter is also a 'grave crime' carrying a possible life
sentence, but it does not require subjective mens rea. The Committee's
argument is broken-backed because the judge can always give a lighter
sentence to a man who honestly believed that the woman consented
than to a man who knew she did not. The Court of Appeal lowered
Morgan's sentence to seven years and his co-defendants' to three years.
And Cogan was sentenced to two years after conviction by a jury which
believed that he honestly but unreasonably believed that Mrs. Leak was
consenting. (He was acquitted on appeal under the *Morgan* defence.)
Clearly, then, there is no practical possibility that a negligent rape will
be punished with life imprisonment.

Another argument in the report is that if negligent rape were introduced then juries 'who have a strong sense of fairness' might be reluctant to convict (para.60). However Cogan's jury convicted him knowing
that his rape was negligent.

A third argument is that differences in different people's sexual relationships 'might present the jury with a somewhat unrealistic problem in having to decide whether the defendant's conduct fell below the standard of some hypothetical reasonable man' (para. 61). However, it is not the accused's conduct but his belief in the woman's consent which is to be judged reasonable or unreasonable. A failure to bring forward positive evidence or to explain away contrary evidence clearly makes the belief unreasonable.

Another argument is that juries do not have to accept the defendant's assertion that he honestly believed the woman consented: 'in deciding to do so or not they are entitled to take the view that the less reasonable they find it to be, the less likely is it to be true' (para. 67). In putting forward this consideration the Committee no doubt wished to undercut Bridge J's view in the Court of Appeal hearing on *Morgan*:

> The rationale of requiring reasonable grounds for the mistaken belief must be in the law's consideration that a bald assertion of belief for which the accused can indicate no reasonable ground is evidence of insufficient substance to raise any issue requiring the jury's consideration. (14-15)

Here I agree with the Committee. As Lord Bramwell said in *Derry v. Peek,* we must avoid 'a confusion of unreasonableness of belief as evidence of dishonesty and unreasonableness of belief as itself a ground of action' (352).

Two further arguments are intended to allay any worries about *Morgan* cases. First, 'In many cases this "defence" would be a desperate defence to advance' (para. 69); 'This is particularly so when the signs of lack of consent are obvious, as when it is established that the man has used violence or threats of violence, or has been armed with a weapon.' This is correct, but the Committee apparently does not see the logical consequence, viz. that the *Morgan* defence will for this very reason tend to minimize rape convictions where the woman does not resist. The Committee thinks that by promulgating the view that 'lack of consent is the crux of the matter and this may exist though no force is used' (para. 20), they will dispel the 'erroneous assumption' that 'the woman must show signs of injury or that she must always physically resist before there can be a conviction for rape' (para. 21). But if a rapist can plead an honest even if unreasonable belief when there are no such signs of resistance, how will convictions for rape be obtained?

Second, 'Once the jury has reached the conclusion that she did not consent, the accused will normally appear a liar, and his claim that he nevertheless believed in consent is likely to be rejected' (para. 69). However, so far from comforting the Committee this likelihood should, properly speaking, upset them! The suggestion that the defendant who claims that he believes the woman consented when the jury thinks she did not will in lieu of further evidence be considered a liar seems to contradict the Committee's view that it is for the prosecution to prove that he is not a liar, i.e. that he intentionally or recklessly raped her (paras. 17, 24, 44-5).

A similar attempt to minimise the effect of *Morgan* is also to be found in *Pappajohn,* where Dickson J said:

> The ongoing debate in the Courts and learned journals as to whether mistake must be reasonable is conceptually important in the orderly development of the criminal law, but in my view, *practically unimportant* because the accused's statement that he was mistaken is not likely to be believed unless the mistake is, to the jury, reasonable. (499; my emphasis)

It is hard to see how a ruling which led to the quashing of a conviction (*Cogan and Leak*) can be 'practically unimportant.' Dickson J thinks that the *Morgan* ruling alters nothing because

> Although 'reasonable grounds' is not a precondition to the availability of a plea of honest belief in consent, those grounds determine the weight to be given the defence. (499-500)

Instead of the judge throwing out the accused's defence because his belief was not reasonable, the jury will throw it out because, not being reasonable, it was not a belief; and fortunately juries have an 'uncanny ability to distinguish between the genuine and the specious' (500). Obviously the learned judge wants to have his cake and eat it. On the one hand he insists on subjective mens rea. On the other he wants the public to be as much protected as if a reasonable belief in consent were required. But if *Morgan* makes no difference then there is something wrong with judicial procedure; and in fact it has made a difference, so there is a moral issue here which is not to be glossed over.

The final and most important argument of the Committee is intended as a rebuttal of the sort of view presented by Lords Cross and Simon in *Morgan* (quoted above). The Committee felt that there is 'a real objection' to this sort of view:

> If carried to its logical conclusion the argument would lead to the abandonment entirely of any requirement of a guilty mind, for the harm suffered by the victim is the same whatever the man's intention may be. We are concerned with criminal not civil law, not only with harm, but with culpability. (74)

But this of course is precisely the point which Lords Cross and Simon were making: the law is concerned *both* with harm *and* with culpability. It must hold a 'fair balance' between victim and accused. In fact the Committee's objection is a perfect example of the 'thin end of the wedge' argument beloved of conservative thinkers.

If they honestly believed that the law is concerned equally with harm and with culpability, they would see that in cases where the harm is great what constitutes culpability is less. This would probably seem irrational to them because they think that the graver the actus reus the more mens rea should be required. The reverse is true. The greater the harm that our acts produce the more we should be careful to prevent that harm. Hence if the harm can reasonably be foreseen we are culpable. I do not deny at all that intentional homicide or rape is worse than negligent homicide or rape, but only that the latter is not culpable.

One could agree with the Committee if it were strict liability rather than negligence which was being proposed. If even an honest and reasonable belief in the woman's consent was insufficient to rebut a charge of rape, the balance would have swung too far towards 'harm' and away from 'culpability.' One does not have to be a retributivist about culpability to feel that a defendant must have had a fair opportunity to conform to the law's requirements and that if he hasn't then it is unfair to hold him criminally or morally responsible.[26]

## Strict liability

The arguments in favour of strict liability are utilitarian in nature, which is not to say that all or even most utilitarians actually favour strict liability.

In his article 'Strict Liability in the Criminal Law,' Richard Wasserstrom has suggested (a) that strict liability can serve a deterrent function, and (b) that the requirement of a voluntary act under the agent's control is all that is necessary for culpability or 'fault.' (He is not prepared wholeheartedly to endorse these suggestions but thinks they have not been adequately refuted.)

On (a) he writes:

> It is at least plausible to suppose that the knowledge that certain criminal sanctions will be imposed if certain consequences ensue might induce a person to engage in that activity with much greater caution than would be the case if some lesser standard prevailed.
> In the second place ..., it seems reasonable to believe that the presence of strict liability offences might have the added effect of keeping a relatively large class of persons from engaging in certain kinds of activity. (457)

---

26 See Hart, especially ch. II, VI, VII.

Here it is appropriate to consider that, although superior deterrence provides a utilitarian justification for a punishment, it does not follow that every punishment which is a superior deterrent is thereby automatically justified on utilitarian grounds; the benefit of superior deterrence may be offset by negative effects. And even if a punishment is prima facie justified on utilitarian grounds (it brings a balance of positive over negative utilities), another punishment which provides the same positive utilities and fewer negative utilities is preferable by the utilitarian principle. Thus, cutting off someone's hand may be a more effective deterrent against stealing, but other moral considerations are relevant before it can be considered a justified punishment. Capital punishment may perhaps be justified on utilitarian grounds, but if life imprisonment brings the same positive utilities and fewer negative ones it is to be preferred.

Suppose that Wasserstrom is right in suggesting that if people know they cannot adduce excuses by way of mitigation or exculpation, they will be more concerned to conform to the law. Nevertheless this system might be unjustified if, as R.B. Brandt suggests, it 'would lead to serious insecurity':

> Imagine the pleasure of driving an automobile if one knew one could be executed for running down a child whom it was absolutely impossible to avoid striking! One certainly does not maximize expectable utility by eliminating the traditional excuses.[27]

So the utilitarian need not be overly impressed by the argument from superior deterrence.

But is strict liability a more effective deterrent? If another system would provide the same benefits without arousing the same antipathy it would be preferable.

Wasserstrom says that under a strict liability system people might be induced to behave with much greater caution and others might be induced to keep out of certain activities altogether. But how much caution do we want people to show? Surely only as much as they can reasonably be expected to show. And whom do we wish to keep out of these activities? Surely only those who do not show as much care as people can reasonably be expected to show. The moral seems clear: the imposition of liability where people have not shown as much care as they can reasonably be expected to show would achieve the same end as strict liability is intended to achieve. But the cases where people have

---

2    Brandt, *Ethical Theory* (Englewood Cliffs, NJ: Prentice-Hall 1959) 493

not shown as much care as they can reasonably be expected to show are, precisely, cases of negligence.

Wasserstrom says that 'if it is conceded that strict liability statutes have an additional deterrent effect, then a fairly plausible utilitarian argument can be made for their perpetuation' (459). But we need not necessarily make this concession or draw this inference.

Existing strict liability offences should be transformed into crimes of negligence. In cases like *Prince's* and negligent rape, if that were made an offence, the burden of proving negligence should be on the prosecution. In so-called 'regulatory' or 'public welfare' offences the burden of proving due diligence (lack of negligence) should be on the defendant. The reason for placing the onus on the defendant is the utilitarian consideration that this would expedite the work of the courts. In *City of Sault Ste. Marie* the Supreme Court of Canada decided that the defence of due diligence is available for some regulatory offences; but they said that the defence would not be available where 'the legislature had made it clear that guilt would follow proof merely of the proscribed act' (302). The Supreme Court has thus gone some way towards ending a situation where people are resentful of the law because they are held accountable whether they have tried to conform to the law or not bothered.

Wasserstrom's second argument seeks to present a weaker conception of 'fault' than the one I have been arguing for. According to this conception there must be 'some sort of causal relationship between the accused and the act in question' (464); those accused must be 'persons who intentionally engage in certain activities and occupy some peculiar or distinctive position of control' (465). This conception is weaker than the requirement of negligence because according to the latter, but not the former, 'The mere fact that there was control over the general activity may be insufficient to justify a finding of fault in every case in which certain results ensue' (ibid.). Wasserstrom's weak conception of fault seems to be the one favoured by utilitarians such as Schlick and Nowell-Smith.[28]

Schlick holds that punishment is concerned with the 'formation of motives' by way of reform and deterrence and that 'the question regarding responsibility is the question: Who, in a given case, is to be punished?' (60-1). He says that 'the "doer" is the one upon whom the motive must have acted in order, with certainty, to have prevented the act (or called it forth, as the case may be)':

---

28 M. Schlick, 'When Is a Man Responsible?', in B. Berofsky (ed.), *Free Will and Determinism* (New York: Harper and Row 1966) (reprinted from his *Problems of Ethics*, tr. D. Rynin). Page references in the text are to the reprinted version. P. Nowell-Smith, 'Freewill and Moral Responsibility,' *Mind*, **57** (1948) 45-61. References in the text are to this article.

> The question of who is responsible is the question concerning the correct
> point of application of the motive. (61)

If we take a strict liability case like *Prince*, where the defendant was
found guilty of taking an unmarried girl under sixteen out of her father's
possession although he honestly and reasonably believed she was over
16, we shall find that Prince is responsible in Schlick's sense because
punishing him deters others and also has a reforming effect on him. It
might be thought that 'reform' is inapplicable since Prince was not at
fault. This is true, but Schlick cannot say so: Prince can be reformed in
Schlick's sense (60), i.e. he can be induced not to repeat the act. Thus to
say that someone is at fault is, for Schlick, to say that there are utilitarian
reasons for applying sanctions to him (her).

We have already canvassed the objections to this view. Instead of
asking 'Who is responsible?' it asks 'Whom is it efficacious to hold
responsible?'. But for someone to *be* responsible it must be fair as well as
efficacious to hold that person responsible.

It cannot be the case that 'X is at fault' *means* 'There are utilitarian
reasons for applying sanctions to X' because it is not self-contradictory to
affirm the one and deny the other. Of course one can redefine the word
'fault' any way one wishes. But this still leaves us with the moral question
of whether strict liability is justified (on utilitarian or on other grounds).

Nowell-Smith's theory of responsibility is designed to resolve two
problems:

> One is the problem of determining what classes of action are voluntary; the
> other the problem of showing a connection between being voluntary and be-
> ing liable to praise or blame. ... If the theory I have suggested is correct, the se-
> cond problem should come first and is simply the empirical problem of
> deciding what characteristics are alterable; and the solution to this problem
> then provides the criterion for deciding what actions are voluntary. (58-9)

The criterion of voluntariness is whether an action can be attributed to a
characteristic which is alterable through reward or punishment:

> To say that a man could have acted otherwise is to say that he might have been
> the sort of person who would have acted otherwise, and to attribute his acting
> as he did to his moral character, as opposed to some amoral [non-moral?]
> defect, is to say that his action was due to one of the characteristics that can be
> altered by means of rewards and punishments. (59)

Again Prince comes out guilty: his punishment can certainly affect his
character so that he will not act that way again (he might become
homosexual), hence he is 'liable to blame.'

The objection to this is, again, that 'liable to blame' does not mean
'alterable through punishment.' So it might be more straightforward to

stop talking about responsibility and simply concentrate on controllability.[29] Indeed there seems to be little difference in practice between persuasively defining 'responsibility' as 'controllability' and saying that responsibility is not the important issue, controllability is. Either way responsibility in the traditional sense has been excluded from the discussion. But this cannot be done without a moral justification. I conclude that Wasserstrom's second argument adds nothing to his first.

While utilitarian arguments do not seem to favour strict liability over negligence, considerations of justice and fairness clearly favour negligence over strict liability. Thus there is no good reason to deny that an honest and reasonable belief in the woman's consent should be a sufficient defence to a charge of rape.

## Conclusion

Subjectivists appear to be more concerned with promulgating the doctrine of subjective mens rea than with considering the interests of actual and potential victims. Since an honest belief in the woman's consent is more easily argued for than an honest and reasonable belief, the *Morgan* ruling favours the defence. Defence counsel would always prefer as many mental elements to be required as possible. Also, judges have become more subjectivist in recent years, perhaps in reaction and in proportion to the growing chorus of those who favour the 'non-punitive' approach of 'abolishing' mens rea.

In the case of homicide and rape, and possibly in other cases not considered here, a requirement of subjective mens rea does not appear to be justified in the light of all the relevant factors, social wellbeing, fairness, liberty, etc.

The thesis that no negligent (inadvertent) wrongdoing is as reprehensible as any reckless (advertent) wrongdoing seems to me impossible to sustain. Surely there are some risks which people *ought* to advert to? Surely taking a risk advertently can be less serious than not adverting to the risk? For instance, someone who consciously takes a risk from a good motive, hoping that the risk will not turn into reality, seems less culpable than someone who is so intent on satisfying his own ends that it does not appear to him that there is a risk. Yet the former is reckless, the latter negligent. It may be objected that the former is not really

---

29  As B.F. Skinner does in *Beyond Freedom and Dignity* (New York: Knopf 1971).

reckless because the good motive makes the risk-taking justifiable. On this point Smith and Hogan write:

> Whether the risk is justifiable depends on the social value of the activity involved, as well as on the probability of the occurrence of the foreseen evil. It is an objective question — that is, it is a question to be answered by the jury and D's opinion is irrelevant.[30]

Since the defendant may have misjudged the social value of his action despite his good motive, it follows that his conduct may be reckless. On the other hand a good motive can lead to a lighter or even no punishment. Similarly, I suggest, a lack of advertence could (and does) lead to a lighter or no punishment. What is objectionable is the idea that lack of advertence automatically excludes responsibility. (No one suggests that a good motive automatically exculpates.) Only the dogma that no one is responsible for a harm unless s/he has willed it, brought it about knowingly, could persuade anyone otherwise. It is not sufficient that people may be made responsible for negligent harm in a civil suit. Society also has an interest in deterring negligence which violates the principle of respect for persons; so it is legitimate that there should be criminal responsibility for serious negligent harm.

Surely a man should take care to find out whether or not a woman is consenting? If her role were simply to gratify the man's desires, the situation would be different. In that case violating a woman's body would be like damaging her property, where an honest albeit unreasonable belief negates mens rea. To require that belief in the woman's consent be both honest and reasonable is to require that the man treat the woman as an equal partner in sexual intercourse.

It is sometimes said that women (some at least) do not want to be equal partners; perhaps they are masochistic, or perhaps they have fantasies about being overpowered by a dominant male against their will. All this may possibly be true, in some cases, but it is irrelevant. If the man *knows* that the woman is like that, then it becomes reasonable for him to believe that she is consenting, despite her protestations (though even in that case it might not *be* reasonable). But if he does not know that she is like that, then it is certainly not reasonable and he should find out whether or not she is consenting. It should not be sufficient, as it is under *Morgan,* that he believes that she is like that, if he has no good reason for so believing. Stereotyped sexist attitudes to female psychology are a poor excuse for rape.

---

30  Smith and Hogan, *Criminal Law,* 53

## Appendix: Proposed Revisions to the Canadian Criminal Code

In Bill C-53 (first reading January 12th, 1981) the ┌ _┘eral Government proposes to replace existing non-consensual sexual offences with new offences of 'sexual assault' and 'aggravated sexual assault.' To accommodate these new offences some sections would be repealed and the existing Sections 244 to 246 (which define assault) would be extensively revised.

Section 244 (5) would incorporate the *Pappajohn* decision into the Code:

> 244. (5) Where a question is raised as to whether the accused believed that the complainant consented to the conduct that is the subject-matter of the charge, the jury shall be instructed, in determining the honesty of that belief, to consider, along with any other relevant matter, the presence or absence of reasonable grounds for that belief.

This statement was evidently derived from the post-*Morgan* Sexual Offences (Amendment) Act (U.K.) 1976:[31] reasonable grounds are to be considered only in relation to the question whether the defendant honestly believed in the complainant's consent; a reasonable belief is not required.

In my view Section 244 (5) should be amended so as to require a reasonable as well as honest belief. Since Section 244 applies to all forms of assault, such an amendment would go beyond my principal thesis, which was concerned only with rape; and it might be thought that such a far-reaching change in the law of assault would be objectionable. I do not think it would.

In the first place, the principle of respect for persons to which I have appealed applies to assault as well as to rape. It is not at all unreasonable to require that the accused's belief that the complainant consented to the application of force should be both honest and reasonable.

In the second place, it is not even clear that the law of assault would be changed. Neither in its existing form nor in the form proposed in Bill C-53 does the Code specify a mental element with regard to consent in assault. Section 244 (1) (a), as proposed in Bill C-53, would make a person guilty of assault when 'without the consent of another person, he applies force intentionally to that other person, directly or indirectly.' (The present Section is in relevant respects similar.) Here 'intentionally' qualifies the application of force, not the consent. Indeed it would be

---

31    See Smith and Hogan, *Criminal Law,* 400-1

plausible, given the word order, to infer that strict liability obtains in respect of absence of consent.

In the third place, even if the law of assault would be changed, that change would not transform assault into 'criminal negligence': subjective mens rea would still be required in regard to the act and its consequences, whereas 'criminal negligence' connotes negligence as to the *harm done* by the act (Sections 202-4 of the code).

In the fourth place, it is practically inconceivable that a defendant could claim an honest albeit unreasonable belief in cases of non-sexual assault, whereas this claim is not only conceivable in cases of rape, it has been successful at least twice, as we have seen. In the case of rape the lack of consent is all that is required in order to turn a normally pleasant activity into a forcible act; but in ordinary cases of assault the act is forcible independent of the complainant's lack of consent. This leads to a distinction between rape and assault, which has been noticed by Glanville Williams.[32] Williams points out that on a charge of assault a 'defendant could set up a defence of his belief in the victim's consent only if he believed that the victim had manifested his consent to that very kind and degree of force before it was applied; and such manifestation would almost necessarily have to be by words.' In the case of rape, on the other hand, 'the defence of belief in consent would amount to a defence that he thought the woman was not resisting and that he inferred from the lack of resistance that she was a willing party.' It would seem to follow that in assault the plea of an honest albeit unreasonable belief would fail (and so far as I know it has never been attempted), whereas in rape or sexual assault it can and does succeed.

I conclude that the extension of the requirement of a reasonable belief to all cases of assault would have no untoward consequences. Bill C-53 emphasizes that submission and lack of resistance to an assault do not constitute consent.[33] But the efficacy of this will be lost if, as

---

32 Glanville Williams, *The Mental Element in Crime* (Jerusalem: Magnes Press, Hebrew University 1965) 49-50

33 Section 244 (3) and (4). In Section 244 (3) it is stated that '*no consent* is obtained where the complainant submits or does not resist by reason of (a) the application of force ...' (my emphasis). In Section 244 (4) (b) it is stated that 'consent shall *not necessarily* be inferred from the fact that the complainant submitted to or did not resist the application of force' (my emphasis). Section 244 (3) (a) evidently refers to the case where the victim is forced to submit to intercourse: this is 'no consent.' But 'application of force' in Section 244 (4) (b) must refer to the act of intercourse itself: where a woman submits to intercourse this is 'not necessarily' consent. To remove any appearance of a discrepancy, the phrase 'the application of force' in sub-section (4) might be altered to 'the conduct that is the subject-matter of the charge.'

Williams suggests, a belief in consent inferred from lack of resistance is a defence to a charge of rape.[34] I would therefore urge that Section 244 (5) be amended.

Bill C-53 does not require subjective mens rea in respect of all offences. For instance Section 249 would preserve the rule laid down in *Prince*.[35] If our legislators are still prepared to enact strict liability statutes, then there can be no objection in principle to requiring that a belief in consent be reasonable in order to negate a charge of sexual assault.

## CASES

Cases are listed under each country in the order in which they are referred to. Page references in the text are to reports of these cases as indicated below. 'R.v.' and 'v. R.' have been omitted.

ENGLAND

*Smith, D.P.P. v.* [1960] 3 All E.R. 161.

*Morgan, D.P.P. v.* [1975] 2 All E.R. 347 (House of Lords); *Morgan* [1975] 1 All E.R. 8 (Court of Appeal).

*Majewski, D.P.P. v.* [1976] 2 All E.R. 142.

*Hyam v. D.P.P.* [1974] 2 All E.R. 41.

*Prince* [1874-80] All E.R. Rep. 881.

*Hudson* [1965] 1 All E.R. 721.

*Bedder v. D.P.P.* [1954] 2 All E.R. 801.

*Tolson* [1886-90] All E.R. Rep. 26.

*Briggs* [1977] 1 All E.R. 475.

*Derry v. Peek* [1886-90] All E.R. Rep. 1.

*Smith (David)* [1974] 1 All E.R. 632.

*Cogan and Leak* [1975] 2 All E.R. 1059.

---

34  See my discussion (under *'Negligent rape'*) of the Report of the U.K. Advisory Group on the Law of Rape.

35  See footnote 9. Section 166 in Bill C-53 likewise excludes a defence of mistaken belief.

CANADA

*Pappajohn* (1980) 52 C.C.C. (2d) 481.

*Leary* (1977) 33 C.C.C. (2d) 473.

*Leblanc* (1975) 29 C.C.C. (2d) 97.

*Plummer and Brown* (1975) 24 C.C.C. (2d) 497.

*City of Sault Ste. Marie* (1978) 20 Crim. L.Q. 300.

## Select Bibliography

Curley, E.M., 'Excusing Rape,' *Philosophy and Public Affairs,* **5** (1975-76) 325-60.

Feinberg, Joel, and Hyman Gross (editors), *Responsibility* (California: Dickenson 1975).

Hacker, P.M.S., and J. Raz (editors), *Law, Morality, and Society* (Oxford: Oxford University Press 1977).

Hart, H.L.A., *Punishment and Responsibility* (Oxford: Oxford University Press 1968).

Kenny, Anthony, *Free Will and Responsibility* (London: Routledge and Kegan Paul 1978).

Mackie, J.L., *Ethics: Inventing Right and Wrong* (Harmondsworth: Penguin Books 1977).

Pickard, Toni, 'Culpable Mistakes and Rape,' *University of Toronto Law Journal,* **30** (1980) 75-98 and 415-20.

Wasserstrom, R.A., 'H.L.A. Hart and the Doctrines of *Mens Rea* and Criminal Responsibility,' *University of Chicago Law Review,* **35** (1967) 92-126.

Wootton, Barbara, *Crime and the Criminal Law* (London: Stevens 1963).

CANADIAN JOURNAL OF PHILOSOPHY
Supplementary Volume VIII, 1982

# Moral Contracts and the Morality
# of Abortion

A.T. NUYEN, University of Queensland

The question concerning the morality of abortion has been debated thoroughly over the past fifteen years, so thoroughly that it is difficult to add anything new to the debate. However, as the number of arguments has become numerous, it is still possible to formulate a new moral stance based on a new combination of old arguments. In what follows I shall develop and defend a moral stance based on the concept of moral contract and the concept of intentional pregnancy. Though these concepts are not new, the way they will be interpreted and combined here is unique.

The analysis that I shall provide presupposes that the traditional arguments either for or against abortion are problematical. (In what follows, 'for' and 'against' are used in the moral sense only.) The first part of this paper is devoted to surveying briefly the principal arguments and to showing why they are problematical. In the second part I shall discuss a couple of arguments which I regard as of the right sort, although they too seem unsatisfactory. Finally, I shall attempt to indicate in my own way whether and when abortion is morally permissible.

# I

Characteristic of all controversial issues, abortion has attracted a diversity of views ranging from one extreme to the other. With some notable exceptions, various writers have fastened on two main points: the status and the rights of the unborn. Concerning the status of the unborn, the question is whether the unborn, whether it be a zygote, or an embryo, or a fetus, is a human being. Related to this question is whether the unborn, if it is a human being, is a person. Concerning the rights of the unborn, the usual question is: does the unborn have the right to life? Many writers regard these two aspects as two sides of the same coin, that is, the solution to one problem supplies the solution to the other. Thus, for instance, it is often argued that, since human beings have the right to life, if the unborn is a human being then it has the right to life, hence abortion is morally wrong. However, some writers insist that there are certain necessary characteristics that an entity should possess for it to have moral rights including the right to life, and that being a human being is not sufficient. They argue, for instance, that only persons, or human beings with certain characteristics, should be regarded as members of the moral community to be accorded with moral rights. This is the general picture. Let me now look at some arguments more closely.

John Noonan's view[1] must surely be regarded as an extreme view. Noonan adopts what might be called a theological definition of being human. The defining criterion is: 'If you are conceived by human parents, you are human' (p. 126). The trouble with Noonan's view is that someone who does not share his theology will find it difficult to accept his condemnation of abortion. Also, when incorporated into an argument against abortion, his criterion proves to be problematical. One such argument is as follows: Human beings have the right to life, a fetus is human (conceived by human beings), hence the fetus has the right to life. But this is a bad argument: it equivocates between 'human' and 'human being' in the premises. The term 'human' in the second premise means something like 'genetically human.' But to be genetically human is not necessarily to be a human being.

At the other extreme, we are likely to find equally bad arguments. According to one, a fetus, or more so an embryo, cannot be a human being because it does not look anything like one: it is only a fuzzy lump of tissues. This is a bad argument because it bases the essentiality of humanity on appearance. Many things that look like human beings

---

1  J.T. Noonan, Jr., 'Abortion and the Catholic Church: A Summary History,' *Natural Law Forum*, **12** (1967) 85-131

(e.g., science-fiction robots) are not human beings. The argument is also dangerous. It can be, and in fact has been, used to justify highly immoral practices such as slavery. It should be noted parenthetically that the argument from appearance has been used by the people in the opposite camp as well. Thus, they will ask us to look at a twelve-week-old fetus to see for ourselves that it has eyes, the outlines of arms and legs, that, in other words, it looks like one of us. The trouble of course is that a monkey also has eyes, arms and legs, but a monkey is not a human being.

The argument from appearance also leads to imprecision. When exactly does the fetus look sufficiently like a human being for abortion to be morally wrong? This is admitted by Becker,[2] who has advanced probably the most sophisticated argument from appearance. However, Becker contends that imprecision is 'a practical problem of a sort endemic to law and morality' (p. 346). But I am not so sure that the morality of abortion has to be subject to this kind of imprecision.

Let me pass over these difficulties and consider what useful purpose a definition of human being may serve. As pointed out earlier, the interest in such a definition arises from the assumption that once the question 'What constitutes a human being?' is settled, the question concerning the rights of the unborn and the morality of abortion will be settled more or less automatically. Unfortunately, this assumption is false. The ascription of moral rights does not follow automatically from the ascription of the status of human being. Furthermore, the fact, if it is a fact, that embryos and fetuses have the right to life does not necessarily mean that abortion is always morally wrong. The moves from 'human being' to 'having rights' including the right to life or the right not to be aborted, and from 'right to life' to 'the immorality of abortion,' have to be argued for, and not assumed. But many writers either ignore this requirement, or adopt a linguistic strategy to side-step it. The side-stepping can be done by *defining* a human being in such a way that anything that is a human being has the right to life. This way, it is analytic that a human being has the right to life. The next move is to define 'having the right to life' in such a way that this entails that abortion is morally wrong. Now these two linguistic manoeuvres amount quite clearly to begging the question. The issue cannot be settled by pure verbal manoeuvres.

Some writers recognize the need to argue for the move from being a human being to having the right to life. Thus, pro-abortionists such as

---

2 L.C. Becker, 'Human Being; The Boundaries of the Concept,' *Philosophy and Public Affairs*, **4** (1974-75) 334-59

Tooley and Warren[3] argue that human beings do not necessarily have rights; only persons, or human beings with certain characteristics, have rights. Fetuses do not have these characteristics and so are not persons and do not have the right to life. By implication, abortion is morally permissible. The trouble is that by Tooley's criterion, namely self-consciousness, very young infants are not regarded as persons. Tooley therefore is forced to argue that not only is abortion is morally permissible, but so also is infanticide. As it happens, my moral intuition does not sanction infanticide. I suggest that most people share this intuition. It should be noted also that Tooley has not provided the link between 'not having the right to life' and 'abortion is permissible.' For these reasons, the argument that I shall put forward later is preferable to Tooley's.

While Tooley relies exclusively on self-consciousness as the criterion of personhood, Warren mentions a number of criteria (p. 55) and contends simply that the fetus does not satisfy any of them. But again, it is not clear to me whether Warren's thesis does away with infanticide. Also, like Tooley, Warren does not say why the fetus's not being a person entails that it can be aborted.

So far I have not said very much about the step from 'having the right to life' to 'the immorality of abortion,' the converse of which has been assumed by Tooley and Warren. All that I have said is that this step cannot be simply assumed; it has to be explicitly argued for. I think that the moment one pays attention to this point, one realizes that the bulk of the verbal exchanges in the abortion debate has been either futile or misdirected. For, even if the fetus or embryo is human, or is a human being or a person, or whatever you will such that it has the right to life, it does not follow that abortion is morally wrong. My thesis is that the morality of abortion does not hinge at all on the notion of the right to life. That is, when there is no right to life, it may still be wrong to abort, and when there is right to life, aborting may still be permissible. Animals do not have the right to life, at least not in the same sense that we have, yet it may still be wrong in some cases to kill animals. And we adults certainly have the right to life, yet it is not immoral on someone's part to kill someone else in justifiable self-defense. Clearly then, to establish the right to life is a long, long way from establishing the immorality of abortion. It follows that all the efforts to determine the humanity or the personhood of the unborn in an attempt to establish the right to life are misdirected and most probably futile.

---

3   M. Tooley, 'Abortion and Infanticide,' *Philosophy and Public Affairs*, **2** (1972-73) 37-65, and M.A. Warren, 'On the Moral and Legal Status of Abortion,' *The Monist*, **57** (1973) 43-62

In this respect, I agree with English[4] who says that 'if a fetus is a person, abortion is still justifiable in many cases; and if the fetus is not a person, killing is still wrong in many cases' (p. 233). I also agree with her when she says that 'the concept of a person cannot and need not bear the weight that the abortion controversy has thrust upon it' (p. 234). However, her reason for saying the latter differs from mine. Her reason is that 'no single criterion can capture the concept of a person and no sharp line can be drawn' (p. 233). But, as I have indicated, the morality of abortion simply does not hinge on any such criterion. It follows, a fortiori, that it does not hinge on the unborn's *potentiality* to become a human being, or a person.

## II

Having dispensed with the bulk of the literature on abortion, let me turn to a couple of papers which present the right sort of arguments. One well-known paper is by Thomson.[5] Thomson very generously grants that a fetus is a person, and that it has the right to life. She then proceeds to build a credible defense of abortion. Thomson's main point is that the right of the fetus, if it has one, has to be weighed against the right of the pregant woman. If her life is in danger then, since she too has the right to life, abortion for her cannot be morally wrong. But even if her life is not in danger, she still has the right to do whatever she wishes with her own body. Under certain circumstances, this right cutweighs the right of the unborn. Backing up this claim is Thomson's famous violinist case: you have been kidnapped and plugged into a sick violinist; to unplug you from him means to kill him; while the violinist has the right to life, does it mean that it is morally incumbent on you to accede to this situation? Thomson's answer is no. It is the violinist's life versus yours. You have the moral right to protect your own life. Even if you are in no danger, merely inconvenienced, being plugged into the violinist, you may still refuse to allow your body to be used in this way. To drive home the point, Thomson asks us to consider another example: 'I am sick unto death, and the only thing that will save my life is the touch of Henry

---

4  J. English, 'Abortion and the Concept of a Person,' *Canadian Journal of Philosophy,* **5** (1975) 233-43

5  J.J. Thomson, 'A Defense of Abortion,' *Philosophy and Public Affairs,* **1** (1971-72) 47-67

Fonda's cool hand on my fevered brow ...' (p. 55). Thomson says that it would be nice of Henry Fonda to provide this touch. In fact, he ought to do it. But all the same, Thomson points out that she does not have the right to Fonda's touch, and it will not be immoral on Fonda's part to refuse to give it. She argues, and I think quite correctly, that while she has the right to life, this right does not entitle her to Henry Fonda's hand or to any part of his body. Similarly, granted that the fetus has the right to life, this right does not entitle it to the use of the body of any person. If Fonda has not done anything immoral when refusing to provide the touch to save Thomson's life, then the pregnant woman has not done anything immoral when refusing to provide her body to save the life of the unborn.

Thomson's argument is restricted, of course, to cases where the woman had taken all reasonable precautions and cannot be said to be responsible for the pregnancy that may accidentally result. There are other cases and what Thomson would say about them is not clear. For instance, she says that it would be 'indecent in the woman to request an abortion ... if she is in her seventh month, and wants the abortion just to avoid the nuisance of postponing a trip abroad' (p. 65). It is interesting to note that Thomson says 'indecent' and not 'immoral.' Whether they mean the same thing is not clear. Furthermore, what would Thomson say about the same woman if she were in her sixth, or fifth, or fourth, month? Does the stage of pregnancy matter and why? Clearly, Thomson remains inconclusive in quite a few cases. Thomson is aware of this but contends that it is an advantage: 'I am inclined to think it a merit of my account precisely that it does *not* give a general yes or a general no' (p. 65). I, too, am inclined to think that our moral principles need not give a blanket yes or no. However, our principles must be strong enough to say yes or no in *specific* cases. If we can't give a blanket yes or no, nor can we do so in specific cases, our principles are worthless. There is another disadvantage in Thomson's account: what if we are not as generous as Thomson and refuse to grant that the unborn is a person, or for that matter, a human being? At best, Thomson's account is inapplicable under this condition, and at worst, it sanctions abortion in every case.

The fact, if it is a fact, that a fetus is not a human being does not mean that we can do whatever we like with it. I have said that it is wrong to kill animals for no good reasons. It is even wrong to uproot trees and shrubs for no good reasons. However, if one is going to argue as though humanity or personhood does not matter then one has to show why killing is sometimes permissible when the unborn is treated in one way, and sometimes not when treated in another way. English is the only writer that I know of who has tried to do this. Granted that fetuses are human beings, or persons, her case is similar to Thomson's. But granted that they are not, her case is based on what she calls 'psychological facts': 'Our psychological constitution makes it the case that for our ethical theory to work, it must prohibit certain treatment of non-persons which are significantly person-like' (p. 241). She goes on to say that in the early stages of pregnancy, abortion can hardly be compared to murder for psychological reasons, but 'in the latest stages it is psychologically akin to murder' (p. 242), and 'abortion is not always permissible because of the resemblance of a fetus to a person' (p. 242).

I think that this argument is unsatisfactory. Firstly, I have already said that 'resemblance' is a very weak criterion, far too weak to perform any task in this abortion debate. Secondly, it is not good enough to say: '[It] is wrong to torture dogs for fun or to kill wild birds for no reason at all. It is wrong, period ...' (p. 240). I think that the 'psychological constitution' that English speaks of must prohibit this form of treatment of dogs and birds despite the fact that they don't look anything like persons. I think that it should also prohibit certain treatment of lower forms of life, including vegetable life. If our 'psychological constitution' singles out person-like entities for attention, and allows anything whatsoever to happen to entities which do not look like persons, then I am sure that the resulting ethical system will be defective.

In the case of abortion, contrary to English, I am disinclined to give psychological facts a role to play. Psychological facts are often pure emotions. To give emotions a role to play in what is already a highly emotional issue is to invite disaster. What we need are level-headed people with clear and logical arguments, not emotions. And what role should psychological facts play anyway? Given a particular pregnancy, are we to take a X-ray picture of the fetus, publicize it, and then conduct an opinion poll to determine the common psychology concerning the case?

# III

For an ethical system to work, we need more than English's 'psychological constitution,' we need some moral imperatives as well. I have already mentioned one such imperative: it is wrong to destroy life, whether it be human life, or animal life, or vegetable life, for no good reasons. The demand of 'good reasons' becomes stricter as you move higher up the ladder to higher forms of life. In the case of abortion, the freedom and dignity of the woman are often good enough reasons to destroy fetal life, if it has to be destroyed at all. (I shall return to this point later.) However, I believe that the morality of abortion must be governed by another, more specific, imperative which makes it morally wrong to breach a moral contract, an imperative similar to, but much stronger than, the Kantian imperative that we should keep our promises.

I regard the conscious decision to get pregnant as the symbolic signing of a moral contract to bring up a child. Once such a contract has been made, it is wrong to breach it; that is, it is wrong to seek an abortion. But with whom has the moral contract been made? It may be thought that a contract requires at least two parties, and that, consequently, there is something wrong with the idea of the moral contract to bring up a child because at the time the decision to get pregnant is made, conception has not taken place, and there isn't an entity with which one makes the contract. It is tempting to answer this objection by saying that the contract must be made between the man and the woman concerned. However, this answer is unsatisfactory, as it implies that without the consent of the man, a pregnancy has no moral basis. There is no reason why the woman should rely on the man to formulate successfully a moral commitment. A woman may wish to become pregnant, and to raise the child on her own, or together with a man who is not the child's natural father. With artificial insemination, the woman is totally free to make the kind of decision we are referring to. The proper answer to the objection is that in a moral contract, it is not necessary to have two parties: one can certainly commit *oneself* morally to a certain thing or to a certain behaviour. Thus, a woman can be said to enter into a moral contract *with herself* to bring into existence a human being. A moral contract differs from a legal contract. In the latter, it is true that there must be at least two parties to an agreement: there is no point in making a legal contract binding just oneself. In the moral sense, on the contrary, not only that it makes sense to bind oneself morally, one may even say that the moral contract that one makes with oneself has a stronger binding force. While it is wrong to cheat, it is more wrong to cheat oneself than to cheat someone else. Moral contracts that one makes with oneself are designed to preserve the self. Contracts that one makes with other people are designed to preserve a society of a certain kind. Self-preservation is more vital than the preservation of a society.

At this point, it is necessary to introduce the distinction between intentional and unintentional pregnancies. Intentional pregnancies are planned, and often wanted pregnancies. They are the results of conscious decisions followed by sexual or other acts leading directly to the pregnancies. (For the 'other,' I have in mind test-tube conceptions.) Unintentional pregnancies are unplanned, and often unwanted. They are not the results of conscious decisions to become pregnant. If the pregnancy is unintentional, it cannot be said that any moral contract has been entered into. For the making of a moral contract is a conscious and intentional act. It follows that if an unintentional pregnancy is terminated, the woman cannot be said to have acted immorally. She has not breached any moral contract, as no such thing exists. Thus, it does not matter how the woman becomes pregnant, whether it be due to rape, or due to the failure of contraception, so long as the pregnancy was unplanned, unintentional, abortion is morally permissible. The advantage of my position as distinct from Thomson's and English's is that we can say without hesitation that a frightened fourteen-year-old schoolgirl who got herself pregnant due simply to her ignorance about the facts of life, may *of course* seek abortion.[6]

It is quite possible that, after unintentionally getting herself pregnant, the woman then decides to carry the pregnancy to term. If so, then she is deemed to have made a moral contract not to abort the fetus, despite the fact that the pregnancy itself has been unintentional. Cases such as this should be treated in the same way as intentional pregnancies, where it would be immoral to breach the contract, that is, to seek abortion. The second advantage of my position as distinct from Thomson's and English's now becomes clear: Both Thomson and English say that it is wrong (or 'indecent') for a woman in her seventh month of pregnancy to seek abortion in order to avoid the inconvenience of postponing an overseas trip; whereas I want to say that it is wrong for her to seek abortion for such a frivolous reason, whether she is in her first month, or ninth month of pregnancy. My position allows us to condemn an abortion at any stage of pregnancy, provided that such an abortion amounts to a breach of the moral contract the woman has made with herself.

The third advantage of my position is that we may in general rule that an abortion performed at a late stage of pregnancy is morally wrong. This is so *not* because the fetus has acquired any particular characteristic. It is so because to have carried the pregnancy this far, the woman must have decided to carry it to full term: she must have made the moral contract not to abort the unborn child. It does not seem credible to say that the woman has not been able to make up her mind in the past seven or so months whether to have the baby or not. Unless there are special circumstances then, to seek abortion at a late stage could only mean a breach of the moral contract.

But it is not difficult to imagine special circumstances that may arise: the woman may discover at a late stage that, for instance, to carry the

---

6   Compare this with Thomson's statement: '... a sick and desparately frightened fourteen-year-old schoolgirl, pregnant due to rape, may *of course* choose abortion ...' (p. 66).

pregnancy to term will endanger her life. It is then up to the woman to decide whether the moral contract that she has entered into is flexible enough for her to escape morally unscathed. If she decides to seek an abortion, she certainly has not done so for a frivolous reason, and moral condemnation from bystanders is unjustified.

For me then, abortion is essentially a matter of private morality, concerning the woman alone. But this does not mean that there is no role for public morality to play. As a matter of public morality, I have no objection to the idea that the state should take an interest in the unborn, and should, where possible, protect the life of the unborn. What I do object to, however, is the idea that in order to carry out this protective function, the state conscripts certain individuals to carry the burden. In a similar vein, I do not object to, and in fact positively endorse, the idea that the state should provide a national defense system to protect its citizens from external agressors. But I object to the practice of conscripting certain young people for this purpose.

It is now time to look at the term 'abortion' more closely. For me, abortion does not necessarily mean the killing of the fetus. By the notion of 'abortion' I mean simply the freeing of the fetus from the mother. In practice, of course, abortion invariably results in the death of the fetus. But this is just a function of the current state of medical technology. It is not, and should not be, brought about intentionally or deliberately. Already in at least a few cases, if newspapers are to be believed, fetuses taken from the womb by abortionists are discovered to have a chance of living. This chance is not great, but the most obvious cause of their death is neglect. If it is at all possible to keep the fetus alive outside the womb, then it should be kept alive unless there are reasons why it should be destroyed (for example, if the baby, allowed to live, will grow up with severe deformities.) I envisage that in the future the state will be able to take a more active interest in the unborn without conscripting the pregnant mothers to bear the burden. I envisage that medical technology will progress to the stage where it is possible to transplant a fetus from one woman to another, or to transplant the fetus to an artificial incubator so that it may continue to develop. When that happens, abortion will no longer mean killing in practice. When that happens, public morality demands that the state take over and protect the life of the fetuses, just as it has the function to protect other forms of life against wanton destruction. Recent medical cases show that we are not all that far from the day when this is possible. Thus, recently, a woman in New Zealand conceived (and later gave birth to a healthy baby) *after* she had had a hysterectomy.[7] In another case involving a woman in North

---

7   *The Brisbane Courier Mail* (Brisbane: May 17, 1979) 3.

Carolina, the fertilized egg slipped out of the uterus and developed to full maturity in her abdomen.[8] Commenting on these cases, a medical scientist speculated that it would be possible for *men* to carry the fertilized egg to full term. Under these conditions, my position is that the state can either call for volunteers to carry the fetuses, or ensure that artificial incubators are used. For now, all I want to say is that the notion of abortion does not necessarily entail the notion of killing the fetus.

Finally, given what I have just said about fetuses, my position necessarily rules out infanticide. I assume that any woman who carries the pregnancy to term must have decided in those nine months preceding birth to have made a moral contract not to kill the child. I am not saying that she is morally bound to raise the child, unless of course this is part of her moral contract. She may have decided only to bring the pregnancy to term, and adopt the baby away at birth. As a matter of private morality, I fail to see any circumstances under which infanticide is justifiable. As a matter of public morality, I want to see the state take an interest in newly born babies and give them the necessary protection and care. Unlike the case of the unborn child, the state even now can certainly perform its protective function towards neonates without conscripting anyone to bear the burden. Whoever will look after these babies are paid-for volunteers. All things considered then, infanticide is morally objectionable, irrespective of whether young infants are or are not persons with certain characteristics.

I shall end this discussion with a postscript. What if the woman who has decided happily to carry the pregnancy to term, discovers at a late stage that the child, if born, will have severe physical and mental deformities? May she then terminate the pregnancy? The termination of the pregnancy in this case is strictly speaking not an abortion in the sense in which I use this term. What the woman wants to do, or is considering doing, in this case is not just to be rid of the fetus: she wants to kill the fetus. This is akin to euthanasia. The morality of euthanasia is something else and deserves a full, separate treatment.

---

8   *The Brisbane Courier Mail* (Brisbane: July 20, 1979) 6

## Select Bibliography

Bayles, Michael D., 'Harm to the Unconceived,' *Philosophy and Public Affairs,* **5** (1975-76) 292-304.

Becker, L.C., 'Human Being: The Boundaries of the Concept,' *Philosophy and Public Affairs,* **4** (1974-75) 334-59.

Brody, Baruch, 'Thomson on Abortion,' *Philosophy and Public Affairs,* **1** (1971-72) 335-40.

English, J., 'Abortion and the Concept of a Person,' *Canadian Journal of Philosophy,* **5** (1975) 233-43.

Feinberg, J. (editor), *The Problem of Abortion* (Belmont, CA: Wadworth 1973).

Finnis, John, 'The Rights and Wrongs of Abortion: A Reply to Judith Thomson,' *Philosophy and Public Affairs,* **2** (1972-73) 117-45.

Narveson, Jan, 'Semantics, Future Generations, and the Abortion Problem: Comments on a Fallacious Case Against the Morality of Abortion,' *Social Theory and Practice,* **3** (1975) 461-85.

Noonan, J.T., Jr., 'Abortion and the Catholic Church: A Summary History,' *Natural Law Forum,* **12** (1967) 85-131.

Nuyen, A.T., 'Moral Contracts and the Moral Self,' *Idealistic Studies,* **11** (1981).

Thomson, J.J., 'A Defense of Abortion,' *Philosophy and Public Affairs,* **1** (1971-72) 47-67.

Thomson, J.J., 'Rights and Deaths,' *Philosophy and Public Affairs,* **2** (1972-73) 146-59.

Tooley, M., 'Abortion and Infanticide,' *Philosophy and Public Affairs,* **2** (1972-73) 37-65.

Trammell, Richard Louis, 'Tooley's Moral Symmetry Principle,' *Philosophy and Public Affairs,* **5** (1975-76) 305-13.

Warren, M.A., 'On the Moral and Legal Status of Abortion,' *The Monist,* **57** (1973) 43-62.

Werner, Richard, 'Abortion: The Moral Status of the Unborn,' *Social Theory and Practice,* **3** (1974) 201-22.

CANADIAN JOURNAL OF PHILOSOPHY
Supplementary Volume VIII, 1982

# Justification or Excuse: Saving Soldiers at the Expense of Civilians

PAUL WOODRUFF, University of Texas at Austin

## 1. Introduction

When soldiers find it morally comfortable to kill civilians and the public accepts such actions easily, philosophers are inclined to ask whether their comfort and acceptance rests on a misunderstanding. If it does, then philosophy could save lives by clearing up the problem. But most recent discussion has been about the wrong issue — *whether* killing non-combatants is wrong, and if so, *why*.[1] That is all beside the point.

---

1 The chief contributions of this kind are: G.E.M. Anscombe, 'War and Murder,' in *Nuclear Weapons: A Catholic Response,* ed. Walter Stein (New York 1961); Thomas Nagel, 'War and Massacre,' *Philosophy and Public Affairs* 1 (1971-72) 123-44; the discussions of Nagel's essay by R. B. Brandt (ibid., 145-65) and R. M. Hare (ibid., 166-81); and George I. Mavrodes, 'Conventions and the Morality of War,' *Philosophy and Public Affairs* 4 (1974-75) 117-31.

Recently there has been a debate over whether the rule against killing civilians can be based on the principle of self-defense: Robert K. Fullinwider, 'War and Innocence,' *Philosophy and Public Affairs* 5 (1975-76), 90-7; and Lawrence A. Alexander, 'Self-Defense and the Killing of Noncombatants: A Reply to Fullinwider,' *Philosophy and Public Affairs* 5 (1975-76) 408-15.

In this essay I use 'civilians' as a synonym for 'non-combatants,' and make no effort to solve the problem of saying exactly what it is to be a civilian, since, in the sort of case I discuss, no one would question the civilian status of the victims.

Soldiers who kill civilians, in my experience, believe already that it is a bad thing to do. That they consider their actions at least prima facie wrong is evident from their readiness with excuses and justifications. Indeed, many of them take care to silence their consciences in advance with arguments of self-exoneration for the wrongs they are about to commit. We may reasonably hope that these soldiers would find it harder to kill civilians without those arguments to relieve their anticipated guilt. The others, the ones who have no qualms about killing civilians, are not likely to be restrained by arguments of any kind. So a practical moral discussion of the problem should study the arguments soldiers of good character use to prepare themselves for killing civilians. The important issue is whether those arguments are sound. If they are not, so much the better. But if some of them *are* sound, we will need to ask what practical consequences follow from the sound ones — whether soldiers are morally free to kill civilians in certain circumstances, or whether the situation is more complicated. It may turn out, for example, that one soldier may clear himself by shifting blame to another. If so, the other may be surprised to find that he carries the burden of exoneration.

This essay addresses the following specific question: can a soldier at war clear himself of blame for killing civilians on the grounds that he does so to save his own life? Soldiers who say they can do that usually invoke the principle of self-defense, the familiar rule that justifies killing an attacker in private life under certain conditions. If they do so correctly, then their actions against civilians would be justified and therefore morally right in the last analysis. But on close examination we find that the common principle of self-defense does not apply, because the civilians in question cannot be counted as attackers under the principle. What makes the soldiers' argument persuasive is not the principle of self-defense but another very different sort of rule, the excuse of self-preservation. This has the effect of shifting moral blame from the killers to their commander, whether or not he ordered or condoned the killings, as we shall see. So the soldiers' argument succeeds as an *excuse* but not as a *justification,* and the killing of civilians in a soldier's self-defense is wrong in the final analysis. Someone, though not necessarily the killer, is to blame for it, and someone is morally obliged to prevent it.

The basis for this conclusion is a strong distinction between *justification* (which makes an action right) and *excuse* (which reduces blame for an action that is wrong). The distinction allows us to make more sophisticated final evaluations than 'right' and 'wrong.' We can say also 'wrong but excusable,' a useful epithet for actions like those atrocities of war that strike us as evil necessities, actions whose particular agents we have no wish to blame, but actions we would nevertheless like to prevent. The practical power of this distinction, which has been neglected by philosophers, is illustrated by the result of this essay — an argument for evaluating operations orders in the light of the excuses they make available to the soldiers they govern.

A number of issues are easily confused with the one at stake here, and should be dismissed at once. (1) The argument does not help decide what should be done with soldiers who have already committed atrocities against civilians. Its interesting results are for choices about how to wage war in future. (2) It does not treat the *laws* of war or the legal definition of a war crime. (3) The argument is independent of wider moral questions about the overall justification of wars. I do not ask whether wars themselves may be justified in defense of nations, nor whether any action necessary to the defense of a nation is *ipso facto* justified. My concern is with the moral evaluation of actions taken in a war *not known to be just*. I impose that limitation because I suspect that few wars are *known* to be just.

## 2. Introducing Miles Atrox

I shall examine the arguments of a specimen of *Miles Atrox* whom I call Miles. Let us assume Miles has certain common and highly plausible moral beliefs: (1) Killing people is ordinarily wrong, but (2) there is nothing wrong with killing (if you must) someone who attacks you. In other words (and he acknowledges this formulation as well), you have the right to kill anyone who attacks you if you must to survive his attack, but killing people in other cases violates their rights. (3) War, he thinks, is often necessary, but a very bad thing, and the less of it the better. (4) Civilians should be spared the horrors of war, in his opinion, and not harmed unless they take active part in combat. Miles adheres to these beliefs absolutely, and will not abandon them whatever the consequences. In particular, Miles' moral beliefs are the same in war as they are in other circumstances. Nevertheless, Miles would not blame a soldier in combat harshly for breaking his moral rules. It is hard, he thinks, to blame anyone for what he does in fear of his life.

Miles has massacred thousands of civilians, and is confident he has done no wrong. How can this be? It is not that Miles holds a false theory of ethics. Indeed, he knows no theory whatever about the basis of right and wrong, but like most of us draws practical consequences from unsystematic moral beliefs that are, as far as they go, unexceptionable. Where Miles goes wrong, if he goes wrong, is in applying his beliefs. It is not that he loses his head in a tight situation. Far from it. Miles is an experienced officer, cool under fire, and always has reasons for what he does. I want to consider a case in which his reason for killing civilians is the defense of himself and his unit. Miles argues that his action is justified by the principle of self-defense.

I shall argue that this is an improper use of the principle as it is commonly understood. In my argument I appeal freely to common language, common sense, and common law. I do this without apology to Miles, since his is clearly meant to be the common principle of defense, the rule that permits killing attackers but not innocent persons. I shall take 'innocent' here to mean 'not an attacker' and devote the core of this paper to an explication of the relevant sense of 'attacker.' It turns out that the civilians Miles killed were not attackers in the sense required by the principle of defense.

### 3. The Situation

Miles is pilot and aircraft commander of an armed reconnaissance helicopter ('hunter-killer'). His mission is to search for and destroy enemy units moving at night, and to defend his aircraft and crew against all attacks. He is instructed to fly low over areas in which the enemy operates, so as to draw fire and thereby to locate the enemy. He is also instructed to return fire immediately when fired upon.

Miles often kills harmless civilians while carrying out his mission. Here is a typical case. Flying low at night over an area densely populated by civilians known to be neutral or friendly (and in either case harmless), he thinks he sees tracer ammunition coming towards him from the ground. Believing that he is under fire, he smothers the ground beneath him with incendiary rockets. It turns out that the ground is a village guarded by friendly militia, and that he has burned the village, killing or maiming a number of civilians. Subsequent investigation fails to determine who fired the offending shot or why he fired it, and does not confirm Miles' contention that he was under fire. If there was an attack, it appears the village was not involved.[2]

Miles argues that he has done no wrong. He acted in self-defense against what appeared to be an attack. If he had not countered immediately, he might have been shot down. It was not safe to take

---

2 Based loosely on a case investigated by the author in Chau Doc Province in 1970.

evasive action, or to wait to ascertain his location or the origin of the fire threatening him. He could not tell in the darkness whether the shots came from the forest or the village, and even if he could have told the difference, he could not be absolutely sure that the village did not harbor an enemy. Miles is not sorry about the civilian casualties. They were unavoidable accidents of war. They may even have a salutory effect, in deterring civilians from letting people shoot at helicopters from their village.

Miles' argument raises these questions about the principle of self-defense:

    a)   Does the principle justify killing non-attacking bystanders to repel an attack?

    b)   Does the principle justify killing persons to deter an attack?

    c)   If one places oneself in danger of an attack, by inviting or provoking it, does the principle justify killing the attacker in order to survive that attack?

To answer these questions, we need to examine the common views — to which Miles subscribes — about the rights and wrongs of repelling attacks. Under examination, Miles reveals two deep-seated convictions:

    1)   It is not wrong to kill someone who attacks you, if you must do so to save your life from that attack.

    2)   It is wrong to blame a person fully for *anything* he must do to save his own life.

I shall distinguish these convictions by calling them the principles of self-defense and self-preservation respectively. They represent different kinds of exculpation, and we shall need to persuade Miles not to confuse them.

## 4. Two Kinds of Exculpation[3]

Miles' acknowledged beliefs presuppose a distinction. Though (as he thinks) killing human beings is generally wrong, there are two sorts of circumstances in which he would withhold blame from a killer:

---

3   The distinction I make here entered philosophical discussion with J.L. Austin's 'A Plea for Excuses,' *Proceedings of the Aristotelian Society,* **57** (1956-57) 1-30. I do not fully agree with Austin's use of the relevant terms, but there is not space here to discuss my disagreement.

*Justification.* Sometimes, Miles thinks the killer had a right to kill (as in self-defense), and so did nothing wrong in killing.

*Excuse.* In other cases Miles thinks that the killing was wrong, but does not blame the killer for it (or reduces the blame due him) for such reasons as these: (1) He may sympathize with him, thinking his action natural in the circumstances (if the killer were in a state of panic, for example). (2) He may hold someone else responsible for the killing (as when someone is forced to kill by an evil master). An excuse must be in proportion to the wrong it is supposed to cover; he thinks of the circumstances cited in the excuse as balancing the wrong. The distinction Miles presupposes is rooted in common usage and reflected in common law. It is, however, often blurred, so we must state it clearly.

The chief difference between justification and excuse is this: You cannot be excused for an action unless there is something wrong with it; but if an action is justified, in the final analysis there is *nothing* wrong with it, though we would not justify an action unless it seemed wrong or belonged to a type that is generally wrong. A successful excuse for wrongdoing shows that an agent should not be blamed for what he did; the justification of an action shows that, appearances to the contrary, it is right. Of course, an action may be justified and still not be the best thing to do in the circumstances. It is faint praise to say of someone that he was within his rights; and there is a sort of blame reserved for those whose actions are justified but not, for example, generous or merciful. But we are not concerned in this essay with that sort of blame. Principles of justification do not discriminate between actions presumed to be right; similarly, it is not a principle of justification that tells us to choose the better of two actions presumed to be wrong. For even a lesser wrong cannot be chosen with justification. A justification does not, strictly speaking, admit that there is anything wrong in the final analysis with what it justifies. Suppose a wicked tyrant orders you to murder a man who has not attacked anyone. If you fail, he threatens, he will kill a family of five. Suppose that you attribute to such persons the right to life. Then you would be mistaken if you argued that the family's danger *justified* your murder of the one; for neither the tyrant's threat, nor the family's need, vitiates that man's right to life. If you kill him, however, you are a candidate for excuse. If the threatened family is your wife and children, then your excuse might exonerate you completely. Of course, you will think differently if you deny the man's right to life in these circumstances. But that has two unfortunate consequences. First, after the killing we will have little with which to reproach the tyrant if the victim's rights were not violated. Second, tyrants will have the power by issuing such threats to negative a person's moral rights. Since Miles has no wish to deny the right to life of such a person, we need not argue the point anyway.

Miles may not agree that I have correctly stated the distinction he presupposes. He might argue that if you are fully excused for an action, your action is not wrong. It means nothing, he might say, to call an action wrong unless you are prepared to blame the person who did it. But there are excellent reasons for speaking as I do about excuses. If you repeat an action covered by an excuse, you may wear out your excuse. But it is not so with justification. For example, it is an excuse that you acted to save your life. But the more people you kill under that excuse, the worse; so it must have been wrong on the first occasion. On the other hand, you are justified in killing your attacker to save your life, and that goes for any number of attackers. So it is important to keep in mind that a fully excusable act remains wrong.

Miles' argument confuses justification with excuse by applying simultaneously the principles of defense and self-preservation to the same case. His amalgam of the two principles lets him think he can justify killing civilians when he is under attack by someone else. But we shall see that the principle of defense does not apply at all to Miles' situation, and that the principle of self-preservation does not *justify* Miles' action. However, the weaker principle yields a surprising result — it shifts the burden of argument from Miles to his superior.

## 5. Defense

We must not let Miles' tendency to excuse acts of self-preservation obscure his other principles: that it is ordinarily wrong to kill human beings, but that it is not wrong to do so when you are under attack and have good reason to think you can survive only by killing your attacker. Miles' belief on this point is common, and is represented in the common law.

We have been calling this the principle of *self*-defense, but it is merely a special case of the more general principle of defense. To defend under the wider rule, you do not need to be under attack yourself. The violent defense of any innocent victim is justified if it is necessary to save the victim's life. This also is generally recognized in law and morality.

The principle of defense is not a special case of the excuse of self-preservation. (1) The principle of defense is stronger, in that it claims to exculpate completely in every case to which it applies. Like all excuses, the excuse of self-preservation carries more weight in some of the situations in which it applies than it does in others. (2) The principle of defense does not discriminate among victims; but the excuse of self-preservation draws some of its force from the idea that saving one*self* from danger is naturally irresistable. (3) The principle of defense depends on a distinction that makes no difference to the principle of self-preservation – the distinction between attacker and innocent person. The principle of defense is good only for acts against *attackers,* whereas the principle of self-preservation applies indifferently to acts reasonably deemed necessary for the survival of the agent, and so may extend to acts against the innocent. (If you must kill innocent persons to survive an attack, your attacker is responsible, as we shall see [below, p. 171, cf. n. 8]. But you are not *justified* in doing so. And it would be better [though supererogatory] for you not to kill the innocent persons in the first place.[4])

To describe the moral difference between innocent and attacker, it helps to translate 'wrong' as 'violation of a moral claim.' Then, since it is usually wrong to kill people, we can say that humans usually have moral claims over one another that their lives be respected. Unless he attacks you, a person generally keeps intact his claim on you. To kill an innocent (non-attacking) person, therefore, would be to transgress a moral claim and could not be justified. For nothing wrong is justifiable. But when an attacker attacks, he cuts the ground from under his claims over the person he attacks in so far as he makes it necessary for that person to kill him to survive.

Whether this is really so, and why it is so if it is, are questions we need not answer here. Our question is whether the principle of defense warrants Miles' conclusion. To answer that, we need to say what it is to be an attacker; for our purposes that is to say what it is to endanger someone's life in such a way as to give him the right to kill you. Is an attacker anyone who endangers another's life? Or must one be guilty of something to be an attacker?

Clearly, an attacker endangers his victim's life by performing an *act.* Can we stop there, or must we go on to ask whether the victim has good reason to believe that the supposed attacker is *responsible* for endangering the victim's life? Suppose I induce my enemy under hypnosis to attack me, in the hope that I may kill him with the justification of self-

---

4 Lawrence Alexander's principle of self-defense is an ingenious combination of the principles of defense and preservation. It permits you to kill anyone (attacker or not) whom you must to save your life, but enjoins you (in effect) to prefer killing attackers over innocents. This is probably good advice but not the principle of defense, for that has always been held to apply only in cases of attack. However much, for example, a fetus endangers the life of the woman who carries it, the woman cannot justify destroying the fetus by the principle of defense. For she is not under attack by the fetus. I owe the point to Baruch A. Brody, 'Abortion and the Sanctity of Human Life,' *American Philosophical quarterly*, **10** (1973) 133-40.

defense. Or suppose I booby-trap my room for the same purpose, so that his turning a light switch would kill me. In neither case would it be justifiable for me to kill my enemy in self-defense, apparently because *I* am responsible, not he, for the danger to my life. So we cannot escape the issue of responsibility for endangerment.[5]

On the other hand, you are not required to find your attacker *guilty* before you kill him. If you were, you would not be justified in saving yourself from attacks by a lunatic, or a child, or by a person who thought you were someone else. Killing in self-defense is not justified as punishment; if it were you would be justified in killing your attacker whether or not it were necessary to save your life. But according to the principle of defense, you may kill your attacker *only* if you have good reason to believe it necessary to do so to save your life from his attack. So the attacker does not need to satisfy the conditions that justify punishment; he need not be guilty of anything. However, he must be causally responsible by some act for endangering your life. To understand the principle of defense, we need a sense of 'causally responsible' not so narrow as 'guilty,' but narrow enough to exclude such innocent attackers as the one hyponotized by his victim.

A person is causally responsible by an act for anything caused by that act, unless another's responsibility supervenes. We need to distinguish between an attack and an innocent act necessary to the success of someone else's attack. Consider the case of the devious attacker. He leads you to a crowded field where an Olympic competition is in progress. At the crucial moment he pushes you into the path of a pole-vaulter. You are hemmed in by the crowd and will surely be impaled and killed unless you stop the jumper, who is so intent on his goal that he does not see you. You can stop him by shooting him with a heavy pistol. But would you be justified? Surely not on the grounds that he had attacked you. In such a case it will do you no good to kill your devious attacker. The jumper seems not to be an attacker at all; between you and him occur conditions that warrant no more than the excuse of self-preservation. In such a situation a pair of people, through no fault of either, face a danger that no more than one of them can survive. Of course, if you *do* shoot the jumper, your devious attacker will be responsible, in as much as your shooting is a natural response to his putting you in danger. His being responsible is a powerful excuse for you, but it does not put you in the right; it does not undercut the jumper's

---

5   Baruch Brody (p. 134) uses the example of the booby-trapped room to make the opposite point. He thinks that the victim may consider the switchturner as an attacker. But if the 'victim' himself booby-trapped the room, the situation seems to change.

claim on you that you respect his life. That claim you would violate, and so you would do wrong in circumstances that incline us to excuse you. It is worse if you put yourself in danger. Then you make the excuse of self-preservation hollow indeed. Suppose you trip and fall in the jumper's path, or suppose you arrive at that point while crossing the field in a straight line as part of your initiation into a secret society. In those cases you alone are causally responsible for your plight; no one has by endangering you given up his claim that you respect his life.

Your attacker by the principle of defense, then, is any person who performs an act necessary to your being in danger *unless:*

(i) The supposed attacker puts you in danger without knowledge or intent *and* there is another person who has acted or is acting with the intent to put you in that danger, the latter act being necessary for that danger to you. (This excludes as innocent anyone whose acts are, without his knowledge, part of a devious plan of attack.)

(ii) The supposed attacker puts you in danger without knowledge or intent, and you put yourself into that danger with or without knowledge or intent. (So no one who unintentionally contributed to your endangering yourself counts as your attacker. Of course, he may still be answerable to you for damages, if he is negligent for example; but that is another matter.)

These two exclusions reflect the general principle that the chain of responsibility linking a person with unintended or unforeseen consequences of his actions is cut if someone else intervenes (with knowledge and intent) to bring about those consequences.[6] The same consideration is part of the grounds for the last exclusion:

(iii) You knowingly and intentionally put yourself in danger, whether or not the supposed attacker acts with knowledge or intent, *unless* you do so as a necessary response to his attack on a person (or perhaps on a person's rights). This excludes from attacker status, for example, anyone who joins you in a dangerous fight you helped to start. Obviously you cannot acquire the *right* to kill your enemy by starting or even joining with him in mortal combat, unless you do so in defense of someone, or perhaps of someone's rights. Much hangs on what it is to put yourself in danger. Acting routinely or exercising one's rights in the face of an unusual threat should not count as putting yourself in danger.

More conditions are necessary for a complete account of what it is to be an attacker. We want to exclude one who endangers another by accident, and not to admit without qualification one who does so by

---

6 Cf. H.L.A. Hart and A.M. Honoré, *Causation in the Law* (Oxford: Clarendon Press 1959) 128ff.

negligence. But precision on those matters is beyond the scope of this paper.

We are now able to make clear the intuitive distinction between *attacker* and *innocent* needed for the principle of defense. In those terms the distinction is misleading, for 'innocent' would seem to mean either 'guiltless' or 'harmless.' But the attacker need not be guilty (he could be a child) and the non-attacker need not be harmless (he could be like the pole-vaulter). In fact, 'innocent' in this context means 'not-an-attacker' in the sense of 'attacker' just elucidated (p. 168).

A surprising consequence of this is that it is a confusion to justify killing enemy soldiers generally in a war *simply* by citing the principle of defense. You need to show, for that justification, not only that the enemies bring your life into danger, but also that you yourself are not causally responsible for that danger. If you provoke or invite an attack by being dangerous to the enemy (and most soldiers are dangerous to their enemies at war[7]) then by Condition (iii) (p. 168) you are not entitled to justify your defense under the principle we have discussed. So the principle of defense cannot ground the moral distinction between soldiers (who may be killed) and civilians (who may not). My argument is thus open to the objection that it undercuts the very moral distinction it seeks to uphold. See the Appendix, 'Self-Defense and the Soldier-Civilian Distinction.'

Now that we know roughly what Miles' principle of defense says, we can turn to the question of whether it warrants his conclusion. Let us consider the three practical questions his argument raised.

a) Does the principle of defense justify killing non-attacking bystanders to repel an attack?

Obviously not. The principle commits Miles to considering attackers in a special light. If he does that, he cannot use the principle to justify killing villagers who attacked no one. (See above, p. 166 and n. 4.) An attack involves action of some kind, and the villagers took no action in connection with the attack on Miles. True, they failed to prevent the attack. But that does not appear to be an action. If they had (contrary to the hypothesis) invited the attackers to work from their village, then *they* would seem to be attackers as well.[8]

---

7 See Appendix, note 13. Genuine cases of self-defense certainly do occur in combat, and justify both carrying weapons and using them. The point is that they are not sufficiently the rule to allow the principle of defense to generate our conventional soldier-civilian distinction.

8 The not-quite-innocent bystander presents us with a practical paradox, however, which cannot be resolved by the principle of defense. See my article, 'The Bystander Paradox,' *Analysis*, **37** (1977) 74-8.

b) Does the principle justify killing persons to deter an attack?

Miles supposes that other villagers will be frightened by the example of the innocents he has killed, and take care in the future that no attacks be made from their village on aircraft such as Miles'. So far, Miles is right. But he tries to justify his killing of innocents on the grounds that he has the right to defend himself against attack by any means necessary, and that deterrence is necessary to his defense.

The principle of defense cannot be stretched so far. It justifies only so much killing *of attackers* as is necessary for survival from *their* attack. But a principle licensing deterrence would justify any amount of killing, and of innocents as well as attackers. So *that* could not be the principle of defense.

c) If one places himself in danger of an attack, by inviting it or provoking it, can he justify killing the attacker by the principle of defense?

Again, the answer is negative. Miles flew an armed aircraft within range of his enemy in order to search them out and kill them. If the enemy responded with a preemptive attack, Miles is responsible for his own plight, and cannot consider the enemy his attacker under the principle of defense. If he really cared to avoid danger he would have refused the mission, or flown at a safe altitude. (See above, p. 168 ff.)

But Miles is not completely in the wrong. Though his plea of self-defense does him no good as such, it points to a sound excuse he may make for himself: that he acted to save his own life. That excuse is really what gave an air of plausibility to his initial plea. We need to explicate the principle of self-preservation to see how much good it does him, and whether it has practical consequences for us.

## 6. Self-Preservation

The desire to go on living is strong in us, so strong that under great pressure we find ourselves trying to survive in ways that are not compatible with the principles we cling to in ordinary circumstances. This is so familiar a fact about human character that the common law counts acts of self-preservation among those natural occurrences that do *not* negative responsibility when they come between another person's act and its consequences.[9] For example, if you put me in a small boat with a

---

9  See Hart and Honoré, 135 and 296, where they classify acts of self-preservation as non-voluntary conduct that does not negative causal connection either in criminal law or in the law of torts.

valuable cargo and cast me adrift in heavy seas, and I must jettison the cargo to survive, you are responsible for the loss of the cargo and I am excused. My action (though voluntary in a sense) does not break the causal chain between you and the loss of the cargo.

It is another matter if you cast me adrift with a third person, and I must jettison her to survive. For me to take a life to save mine is bad and selfish; nevertheless you are responsible for the drowning of whichever of us drowns, and the blame due the survivor is reduced accordingly. (From fear of sanctioning homicide, we hesitate to say how far the survivor's blame is reduced.) This variation in the example illustrates the point that there is a limit to how far an excuse can be stretched. I can expect to be excused for drowning a cargo, and to be partially excused for drowning a person. But if I drown every passenger of the Queen Elizabeth to survive, I must expect to be considered a monster of selfishness. Of course I may undercut the excuse by my own action. If *I* set out in heavy seas with the cargo, and I am forced to jettison it, then I am responsible for its loss. The same goes for the case of the drowned person. I cannot reduce the blame due me for drowning him by causing a situation in which I must drown him to survive.

To see how the principle applies to Miles we must disentangle the web of responsibility for Miles' being in a situation in which he had reason to believe that he had to kill civilians in order to survive. Miles knew that such a situation was likely to occur if he carried out his mission. Yet he did so voluntarily; so it would seem that he has undercut his excuse.

But on this charge Miles can appeal to the further excuse that he was acting under orders which he was bound to obey. We can expect him to refuse to obey direct orders to commit obvious atrocities; but it is not fair to expect him to refuse a legal recon mission. Neither the courts nor the public would accept Miles' plea that the danger to civilians made void his oath to obey. So Miles' excuse passes responsibility for his atrocities on to whoever decided to give him the dangerous mission. Miles' commander bears the blame not because he ordered Miles to kill civilians (he did not) — but because he sent Miles on a mission in which civilian casualties were quite likely to follow from Miles' natural attempts to save his own life.

## 7. Consequences: the Burden of Prevention

If Miles' excuse is sound, then the burden of preventing such incidents would fall on Miles' commander. To see why this is reasonable, imagine that the surviving villagers gather on the morning after the disaster to petition against further destruction of their village. To whom should they go?

To Miles? But surely they cannot expect him to break his oath and ruin his career by not carrying out plainly legal orders for recon missions. Nor can they expect him to give up his life on the chance that there are civilians below him.

To the commander of the troops opposing Miles? If a member of his command had fired at Miles, he must share the blame for the burning of the village. The enemy commander can insure that attacks on aircraft are not made from villages, and he has a responsibility to do so. But the present case could have occurred without enemy action, for we do not know who, if anyone, fired the shot Miles reported. So although it is worthwhile asking the enemy commander, his action alone cannot save the village from people like Miles.

To Miles' commander? That is the best course. He can and should alter Miles' orders in such a way that he will not court attack from populated areas, by cancelling the mission or forbidding Miles to fly below a safe altitude. He should have known the cost of the orders he gave Miles in burnt villages, and so must bear part of the blame, and apparently *keep* it, for none of the excuses we accept from Miles apply to his case. He was not in danger, nor was he acting under direct orders. If he can defend his conduct at all, he must do so by pleading the military utility of Miles' mission. He might make a case that he cannot win the war without such tactics, and argue that what justifies the war justifies whatever must be done to win it. But that sort of argument is incompatible with Miles' absolute position on homicide, and we need not discuss it here.[10]

Our conclusion was that though killing the civilians was wrong (because not a true case of self-defense), Miles was to be excused for doing it, and the blame passed on to his commander. It follows that unless the commander can defend his practice in some way not envisaged, he is morally obliged to stop sending his troops on missions that endanger civilians in the way Miles' reconnaissance did. That is a significant result; if the commander held Miles' mistaken view about self-defense, he would not think the killing was wrong, and consequently could not consider himself responsible for any wrongdoing. If he recognized that the principle of defense did not apply to Miles' sort of case, we can hope he

---

10   Historical note: after a number of actions like Miles' against Chau Doc Province, Vietnam, in 1970, local authorities made representations to both sides. To the credit of all concerned, in one instance the enemy ceased to launch attacks from villages, and in the other the U.S. commander ordered missions such as Miles' to be flown at a higher, safer altitude.

would act differently in future. So although we have found nothing helpful to tell Miles himself, we have identified a mistake about self-defense, a mistake that has no doubt contributed to civilian casualties in war.

## APPENDIX

### Self-Defense and the Soldier-Civilian Distinction

*1. The Principle Fails*

The common morality of warfare allows soldiers to kill enemy soldiers fairly freely in combat, but not to kill civilians (non-combatants). Some recent philosophers have sought a basis for that morality in the principle of defense.[11] But it is difficult, if not impossible, to give a sense of 'innocent' broad enough to include civilians, narrow enough to exclude soldiers, and still morally relevant to the issue at hand.[12] The principle of defense turns out not to help in explaining the common morality of war.

Specifically, the principle is unhelpful within a war because the conditions for its strict application are not regularly met in organized combat. Soldiers on opposite sides are constantly so dangerous *to each other* once a state of war obtains (regardless of who is in a defensive posture) that it is hard to construe action by either side as an attack under the principle of defense. For such an attack must *bring* the life of its intended victim into danger (Condition [iii], p. 168 above), but in organized combat, soldiers *take themselves* (or are led by their officers) into dangerous positions.[13]

---

11  Anscombe, and, most recently, Fullinwider

12  There is an excellent discussion of this problem in Mavrodes, 121 ff.

13  Not all dangers are of this sort. An assault on a soldier who is utterly defenseless, and not acting the part of a soldier at the time (he may be wounded, captured and disarmed, or naked in a brothel, for example) would count as an attack under the principle of defense. Similarly, homicidal attacks by soldiers on non-threatening civilians would justify violent action under the principle of defense. Paradoxically, the principle works best for people who are in no position to defend themselves.

It follows that you cannot justify killing enemy soldiers generally on the simple ground that they pose a threat to you.[14] You must not ask just whether, but *why* they are a threat to you, because if you are responsible, they are not attackers under the principle of defense (by Condition [iii]). So if the principle of defense was what made killing soldiers in combat generally blameless, it would matter which side started the battle and even the war, and we would rightly blame soldiers for fighting on the aggressive side. But in common morality it does not matter which side a soldier is on; we try not to blame him for killing enemy soldiers in combat so long as he follows certain rather minimal rules. That is reflected in the laws of war: military tribunals punish members of governments, not their soldiers, for waging aggressive war. That also has been the basis for our common view that ordinary prisoners of wars ought not to be treated as criminals, whether or not their cause is just. The principle of defense cannot be what warrants our withholding blame from soldiers generally for fighting other soldiers, since we do so for soldiers whether or not they are defenders. Nor can the principle of defense be what warrants our condemning military actions against civilians in particular, since civilians are only a small part of the class of non-attackers under the principle of defense.

There are two ways of modifying the principle to bring it to bear on combat situations, but neither supports the soldier-civilian distinction: (a) The principle is made to govern nations as well as persons, in order to justify any action necessary to the defense of one nation against another. Applied in this way, the principle overrides the distinction between soldiers and civilians, and would appear to justify any homicide deemed necessary. A weaker alternative is to plea self-defense for a nation in killing just those *persons* who are attackers. But the common morality licenses the killing of soldiers who are not (in our technical sense) attackers; so the weaker alternative fails to support the common view.

(b) The principle of defense may be extended in such a way that virtually anyone whose continued existence would be a threat to you would be considered your attacker. With this extension the principle applies readily in combat; but it would justify killing civilians as well as soldiers.[15] Attempts to limit this extended class so as to exclude civilians have excluded some soldiers as well. So with this extension (however limited) the principle apparently fails to underpin the conventional distinction.

---

14  Nagel fosters this confusion by distinguishing combatants from non-combatants morally on the basis of their 'immediate threat or harmfulness' (140).

15  This is the burden of Lawrence Alexander's article. See n. 4.

## 2. An Alternative Basis

Either we have misrepresented the principle of defense, or we should abandon (or perhaps redraw) the conventional soldier-civilian distinction, unless we can support the latter in a new way. In outline, the supporting theory I propose is this: military actions are not in general justifiable in the strict sense; but actions against soldiers are excusable on the grounds that soldiers by being soldiers have accepted the risks of war. That excuse works for soldiers-killing-soldiers but does not work for soldiers-killing-civilians, and so upholds our common-sense distinction. (An additional theoretical advantage is that this account makes coherent the position of those who refuse military service as immoral, but do not want to give up the principle of defense. On the orthodox view that soldiering is justified by the principle of self-defense, such pacifists were faced with a cruel dilemma.)

By the principle of defense, soldiers are usually innocents in our technical sense (not attackers), because even when they attack, they usually attack armed men who are a threat to them. So even to kill an *attacking* soldier is not justified by this principle (unless certain conditions obtain — see note 13). But military actions against military people are excusable on the following grounds: the lives that are taken are taken from soldiers who have chosen to expose themselves to extreme danger — they have taken up arms.[16] Unlike civilians, soldiers go into the danger of war in full knowledge and with the intent to face that danger. Those who bear arms, knowing the consequences, are responsible for what happens to them because they bear arms; and the actual agents of their suffering are thereby excused. Soldiers who kill soldiers may claim that the people they kill are responsible for their own fates, and this (outside of genuine self-defense situations) is a good excuse. That many soldiers take up arms under conscription (which involves a threat) does not undermine the excuse. Even conscripts act, as most civilians do not, to cause danger to themselves in war. And in so far as conscripts are thought automata in the service of their masters, the blame for their deaths must fall on their masters and not their enemy, who must assume

---

16  The principle that excuses a killer when his victim has assumed the relevant risk has a long tradition in law and morals. Athenian law, for example, distinguished between the accidental deaths of athletes and spectators at the games, and this furnishes us a convenient model for the soldier-civilian distinction. War is, after all, very much like a game played by soldiers and watched by civilians. Killing civilians in war would be like tackling spectators at a football game, except that no advantage could be gained by the latter. (See Douglas M. MacDowell, *Athenian Homicide Law in the Age of the Orators* [Manchester: Manchester University Press 1963] 73-4).

Paul Woodruff

that anyone who acts like a soldier may be treated as one. Civilians, by contrast, are rarely responsible for the immediate dangers they face in war. *They* rarely go into battle; battle comes to them. For example, if a farmer is killed in his own field by the crossfire of a battle (whatever his attitude towards the war), that is the fault of the commanders on both sides, for they should have fought elsewhere or cleared the field of civilians. But if a reporter covering the front suffers the same fate, it is his own fault for being there; the soldiers involved are excused. *The responsibility of the victim for his plight* is what differentiates soldiers morally from civilians; it gives the right results even for exceptional cases like that of the reporter. There are other excuses for what soldiers do in combat: the excuses of danger, stress, and fatigue; but these do not make killing civilians a special case.[17]

## Select Bibliography

Anscombe, G.E.M., 'War and Murder,' in *Nuclear Weapons: A Catholic Response*, edited by Walter Stein (New York 1961).

Austin, J.L., 'A Plea for Excuses,' *Proceedings of the Aristotelian Society,* **57** (1956-57) 1-30.

Nagel, Thomas, 'War and Massacre,' *Philosophy and Public Affairs,* **1** (1971-72) 123-44; reprinted in *War and Moral Responsibility,* edited by Marshall cohen, *et al.* (Princeton, NJ 1974).

Wasserstrom, Richard A., 'Conduct and Responsibility in War,' in *Philosophy and Social Issues,* by Richard A. Wasserstrom (South Bend, IN 1980).

Walzer, Michael, *Just and Unjust Wars* (New York 1977).

---

17  I acknowledge with thanks the advice and assistance of Lawrence BonJour, Hardy Jones, and Edmund Pincoffs.

CANADIAN JOURNAL OF PHILOSOPHY
Supplementary Volume VIII, 1982

# The Right To Know In The Workplace*

RUTH R. FADEN and TOM L. BEAUCHAMP,
The Johns Hopkins University and Georgetown University

In recent years, the right of employees to know about health hazards in the workplace has emerged as a major issue in occupational health policy.[1] A general consensus has gradually evolved that there is a right to know, and correlatively that there is a moral obligation to disclose relevant information to workers. For example, the National Institute for Occupational Safety and Health (NIOSH), and several other U.S. federal agencies, informed the U.S. Senate as early as July 1977 that 'workers have the right to know whether or not they are exposed to hazardous

---

* Copyright 1982, Ruth R. Faden and Tom L. Beauchamp. Work on this essay was supported by a grant from the National Library of Medicine. Earlier drafts were read at the Philosophy Department, University of Pittsburgh, at the School of Public Health, University of Minnesota, at the Hastings Center, and at the Philosophy Department, the University of Colorado. We received valuable comments that altered the substance and form of the paper from Stephen Teret and Nancy King. We are also indebted to Alasdair MacIntyre, Terry Pinkard, Ron Giere, Arthur Caplan, Rachel Laudan, Kurt Baier, Nicholas Rescher, David Braybrooke, H. Tristram Engelhardt, Jr., Gilbert Omenn, and Deborah Kohrman for helpful comments and criticism. Small excerpts taken from a much earlier draft of Sections I, III, V, VI and IX were previously published in *Contemporary Issues in Bioethics*, 2nd ed. (Belmont, CA: Wadsworth Publishing Co., 1982). While the bulk of references are to U.S. sources, the issues of policy surpass national boundaries.

1 See Elihu D. Richter, 'The Worker's Right to Know: Obstacles, Ambiguities, and Loopholes,' *Journal of Health Politics, Policy and Law*, **6** (1981) 340; Gail Bronson, 'The Right to Know,' *The Wall Street Journal (Eastern Edition)* July 1, 1977, p. 4 and Editorial, January 1, 1979; George Miller, 'The Asbestos Coverup,' *Congressional Record* (May 17, 1979) E2363-64, and 'Asbestos Health Hazards and Company Morality,' *Congressional Record* (May 24, 1979) E2523-24.

chemical and physical agents regulated by the Federal Government.'[2] In 1980, the Occupational Safety and Health Adminstration (OSHA) promulgated regulations guaranteeing workers access to medical and exposure records.[3] Legislation recently passed in the states of Connecticut and New York and the city of Philadelphia further supports the claim that workers have a right to know. The New York bill, for example, declares that employees and their representatives have a right to 'all information relating to toxic substances' — a right that cannot be 'waived as a condition of employment.'[4]

Although the general belief that worker's have a right to information about health hazards is now well entrenched, there is no clear consensus — and scarcely any commentary — about the nature and extent of an employer obligation to disclose such information. There is also considerable ambiguity about the scope of the right, i.e., which protections and actions the right entails. For example, the 1980 OSHA regulation established a strong worker right of *access* to information. With few exceptions, employers under this regulation are obligated to provide information within 15 days of having received a request for access to records by an employee or an employee's designated representative. On its own initiation, an employer is obligated to inform workers first entering employment (and at least yearly thereafter) about the *existence* of medical and exposure records, about the employee's rights of access to those records, and the person responsible for maintaining the records.[5] However, under the regulation, employers have no affirmative duty to provide the content of these records; only their existence must be disclosed. A direct employee request is necessary for disclosures of content. Also, the day after workers receive exposure records they have requested, an employer could introduce a new toxic substance into the

---

2 NIOSH, *et al.,* 'The Right to Know: Practical Problems and Policy Issues Arising from Exposures to Hazardous Chemical and Physical Agents in the Workplace,' a report prepared at the request of the Subcommittee on Labor and Committee on Human Resources, U.S. Senate (Washington, D.C.: July 1977) 1 and 5

3 Occupational Safety and Health Administration, 'Access to Employee Exposure and Medical Records — Final Rules,' *Federal Register,* May 23, 1980, 35212-77. (Hereafter referred to as OSHA regulations.) Modifications in these regulations are currently under consideration, 'Hazard Communication: Proposed Rules and Public Hearing Announcement,' Federal Register, March 19, 1982, 12092-12124.

4 State of New York, 1979-1980 Regular Sessions, 7103-D, Article 28, para. 880

5 OSHA regulations, Section III, g., 35280

manufacturing process and be under no obligation, pursuant to the regulation, to disclose new information to workers.

Although this workers' right of access to records and to employer analyses of these records is an important component of a general employee right in the United States, it is not solely sufficient to protect workers' interests. As Elihu Richter points out,[6] the difficulty with such access rights is that unless workers request the information, they may not possess even minimal risk information. If the right to know in the workplace is to be adequately protected, there must be an *affirmative duty to disclose* information about health hazards to workers *in addition to a duty to honor worker-initiated* requests for access to records.

This paper focuses on several philosophical and policy-oriented problems about the right to know and correlative duties to disclose. Also addressed are some related rights, such as the right to refuse hazardous work and the right to contribute to the development of safety standards in the workplace. A brief history of the right-to-know problem in federal regulation and the types of risks at issue are presented in sections I-II; legal standards of informed consent and problems with consent requirements in the workplace are treated in sections III, IV, and V; the justification of and problems with certain duties to disclose in the workplace are addressed in sections VI, VII, and VIII; and related employee rights to refuse unsafe work and to participate in regulation of health and safety conditions are discussed in the final sections, IX-X.

**I**

Some elementary background history will help establish the problems that surround these right-to-know issues. By the late 1970s it became apparent that a right-to-know movement had taken hold in the United States, especially in matters of consumer protection. The belief that citizens in general — though not workers in particular — have a right to know about significant risks is reflected in a diverse set of recent laws and federal regulations in the United States. These include The Freedom of Information Act, The Federal Insecticide, Fungicide, and Rodenticide Admendments and Regulations, The Motor Vehicle and School Bus Safety Amendments, The Truth-in-Lending Act, The Pension Reform Act, The Real Estate Settlement Procedures Act, The Federal Food, Drug, and Cosmetic Act, The Consumer Product Safety Act, and The

---

6   Richter, 341

Toxic Substances Control Act. These acts commonly require guidebooks, explanations of products, and warranties; the implicit message is that manufacturing companies and other businesses have a moral (and obviously in some cases an explicit legal) obligation to disclose information without which individuals could not adequately decide about matters of participation, usage, employment, or enrollment.[7]

If the right to know in the workplace parallels these developments in upcoming years, and comes to include a corporate responsibility to provide adequate information to workers about hazards in the workplace, this development could potentially have a pervasive and revolutionary effect on major American corporations. Workers do not now routinely receive such information from their employers, as is evidenced by OSHA's conclusion that, at least prior to the 1980 regulation, *denial* of access to exposure records was a frequent, though not universal, employer practice.[8] More importantly, workers are exposed to many hazards on a wide scale. There are over 30,000 pesticides now in use in the United States. The annual Registry of Toxic Effects of Chemical Substances lists over 25,000 chemicals. An estimated 25 million largely uninformed workers in North America (1 in 4 workers) are exposed to toxic substances regulated by the federal government, and one per cent of the labor force is exposed to known carcinogens. Over 44,000 U.S. workers are exposed *full time* to OSHA-regulated carcinogens.[9] A representative sample of American corporations whose workplaces have encountered controversy in the past about how to control hazards includes Philco, Johns-Manville, General Electric, Kennecott Copper, Union Carbide, RCA Victor, Allied Chemical, Lockheed Aircraft, General Motors, The Raytheon Co., Bell Telephone, American Petroleum Institute (representing virtually all oil companies), Raybestos-Manhattan, and Dow Chemical. In every case unresolved questions remain about the acceptability of known hazards in the workplace.[10]

7  On this point, cf. Harold J. Magnuson, 'The Right to Know,' *Archives of Environmental Health,* **32** (1977) 40-4.

8  OSHA regulations, 35214

9  See NIOSH, *et al., 3, 9.*

10  For a useful public policy perspective, see P. Weiner, 'Testimony to OSHA on Employee Access to Records' (December 5, 1978).

## II

The topic of acceptable risk has received considerable attention in recent years. Literature on criteria of risk, risk/benefit analysis, the regulation of risk, objective evaluation of risks, and fair decisions about the control of risk is growing daily. Moreover, risk assessment is now a prominent factor in decisions about whether to permit substances in a workplace or to produce a new technology.[11] These problems are not the ones addressed here, because our focus is exclusively on questions of risk-related disclosures. However, before we proceed to problems of disclosure, we should be clear about the *concept* of risk and about the *scope* of the risks to be discussed throughout this paper.

*The Concept of Risk.* The term 'risk' is commonly used to refer to a possible future harm; statements of risk are usually probabilistic estimates of such harms. However, the *probability* of a harm's occurrence is only one way of expressing a risk and should be distinguished from the *magnitude* of the possible harm — a second way of expressing risk. When such vague expressions as 'minimal risk' or 'high risk' are used, they commonly refer to an aggregation of the chance of suffering a harm (probability) and the severity of the harm (magnitude) if suffered. Uncertainty may be present in formal assessments of either the probability or the magnitude of harm, and commonly much uncertainty exists in the workplace as to dangers, diagnosis, and prognosis. The probability of exposure to a risk may be known with some precision, while virtually nothing is known about the magnitude of harm; or the magnitude may be precisely expressible, while the probability is too indefinite to be calculated accurately. In many cases 'wild guess' may best describe the accuracy with which risks of physical and chemical hazards may be determined — especially for a worker who constantly changes locations, who works with multiple substances, and whose physical condition is in part attributable to factors independent of the workplace, many of which can magnify the risks of workplace hazards.

There is no general consensus about the relationship between the acceptability of a risk and the ease with which the risk can be eliminated or controlled. There is also no consensus on which levels of probability of serious harm, such as death, constitute sufficiently high risks that steps ought to be taken to reduce or eliminate the risk or to provide information to those affected. However, in an interesting 1976 document

---

11  For a useful essay on contemporary problems of risk and risk assessment, see *'Risks of Risk Decisions,'* by Chauncey Starr and Chris Whipple, *Science* 208 (6 June 1980) 1111-19. See also Baruch Fischhoff, Paul Slovic, and Barry Lichtenstein, *Acceptable Risk* (Cambridge: Cambridge University Press 1982).

*Ruth R. Faden and Tom L. Beauchamp*

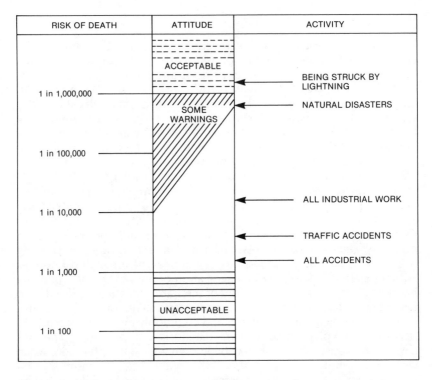

**Figure** *Probability of death for an individual per year of exposure (orders of magnitude).*

prepared in Britain by The Royal Commission on Environmental Pollution[12] – as reflected in the table below – some speculative (perhaps intuitive) guidelines for risks of death were suggested. It was held that risks below 1 in 1 million are Acts of God too infrequent to merit attempts at control, that risks in the vicinity of 1 in 100,000 may be sufficient to justify warnings, that risks of 1 in 10,000 merit public subsidies in an attempt to eliminate or reduce the risk, and that risks of serious harms greater than 1 in 1,000 are unacceptable. As the solid white portion of the attitude column below suggests, some risks greater than 1 in 1,000,000 but less than 1 in 10,000 deserve more than a warning but are not always unacceptable risks. These risks are prime candidates in the

12  *Royal Commission on Environmental Pollution* (1976), 6th Report, Cmnd 6618: HMSO: London

182

range of risks for which a disclosure to workers is appropriate, and 'all industrial work' falls in the middle section of this category.

*The Scope of Risk.* There are so many different kinds of risks in life that attempts to classify them into neat categories may be hopeless. There are risks of psychological harm, physical harm, legal harm, social harm, and economic harm. It is also meaningful to speak of risks of harm to society, to the environment, and even to character formation (in the case of children, for example). However, the risks involved in hazardous work are almost always risks of death, disease, injury, discomfort, and their psychological and economic aftermaths. It is surely reasonable to suggest that workers in *some* cases have a right to know about such risks, and that industry is obligated to provide the information, just as it is meaningful to propose that consumers, clients, the general public and the like commonly need information prior to making important decisions.

At least three types of products and activities found in industrial manufacturing create a general need for risk information. These types and some representative harms they may cause are the following:

I.   *Risks to Consumers* (and their Families)

Tampons (Toxic Shock Syndrome)
Prepared Foods (Cancer caused by Food Additives)
Non-Prescription Drugs (G.I. Bleeding)
Cigarettes (Lung Cancer)
Radiation Therapy (Secondary Cancers)
Children's Clothes (Burns due to Fabric Flammability)
Oral Contraceptives (Pulmonary emboli; Stroke)

II.  *Risks to the Public at Large* (including Environmental Risks)

Coal-Dust Emissions (Respiratory Complications)
Carbon and Other Fuel Emissions (Respiratory Complications)
Recombinant DNA Research (Risks Largely Unknown)
Toxic Chemicals, e.g., Insecticides and Weed Poisons
    (Genetic Defects)
Kepone (Neurological Disorders)
Agent Orange (Birth Defects and Neurologic Damage)
Nuclear Power Plants (Physical and Psychological Injury to the
    Public)

III. *Risks to Workers* (and their Families)

Benzene (Leukemia)

Asbestos (Asbestosis)
Lead (Destruction of Reproductive Capacities)
Microwaves (Cataractogenic Effects, decreased sperm count)
Petrochemicals (Brain Tumors, Sterility)
Machines (Ear Damage from Noises)
Construction (Injury due to Accident)
Cotton Textiles (Byssinosis)
Coal Dust (Black Lung)
Hydrocarbons (Childhood cancer in offspring)

The risks treated here are featured in the third category.

It is assumed in our discussion that at least basic information about the risks of the harms mentioned is now available, even if the risk for any particular worker is impossible to express. This assumption is necessary in order to concentrate on questions of how much information should be disclosed and by whom, whether workers' consent should be solicited, whether worker refusal should be recognized, and how to treat the consequences of worker refusals.

## III

The most developed models of disclosure obligations and the right to know are presently found in the extensive literature on informed consent, which also deals with informed refusal.[13] This literature developed largely from contexts of fiduciary relationships between physicians and patients or investigators and subjects, where there are broadly recognized moral and legal obligations to disclose known risks (and benefits) associated with a proposed treatment or research maneuver. No parallel obligation traditionally has been legally recognized in nonfiduciary relationships, such as that between management and workers. Except for special and limited regulations that require warnings or signs about individual substances or conditions, there is currently no

---

13   The issue of the right to know in the workplace could also be profitably explored through an examination of the literature on the analogous issue of the *patient's right to know*, and in particular, the literature on patient access to medical records. For a discussion of the relationship between this literature and the issue of workers' rights of access to employer records, see the OSHA regulations, particularly pp. 35228-35236. In this paper we draw primarily on the informed consent literature because of our focus on affirmative disclosure standards and the right to refuse hazardous work.

general legal requirement in the U.S. that employers actively warn workers about the above-mentioned hazards in the workplace. There may nonetheless be moral requirements, and the law may need substantial revision. We shall argue for both conclusions.

The recent history of informed consent requirements in fiduciary relationships clearly does provide important and relevant data for discussions of nonfiduciary contexts. It offers a model of disclosure that seems promising for the workplace. However, this model will prove to have only severely limited application in the workplace. In order to see why, a brief synopsis of its history is in order.

Contemporary standards of informed consent gradually developed from two primary sources: standards governing medical therapeutics, as developed in case law, and standards governing biomedical and behavioral research involving human subjects, as developed in such codes as the Nuremberg Code (1949) and the Declaration of Helsinki (1966). In the last decade, government commissions, regulatory agencies, and professional societies have all produced guidelines for obtaining informed consent. However, the standards deriving from malpractice litigation have perhaps had greater impact, both theoretically and practically. Here emphasis has been placed on adequate disclosure of information, in particular the disclosure of information material to a patient's decision. Three influential 1972 cases illustrate the problems involved in developing standards of informed consent — especially as the standards might be used to govern disclosures of risk in the workplace. These cases are *Canterbury v. Spence,*[14] *Cobbs v. Grant,*[15] and *Wilkinson v. Vesey.*[16]

*Canterbury v. Spence* was the first and most influential of the recent landmark informed consent cases. This case involved a laminectomy that led to unexpected paralysis. Judge Spottswood Robinson's opinion focuses on the right to self-determination: 'The root premise is the concept, fundamental in American jurisprudence, that "[e]very human being of adult years and sound mind has a right to determine what shall be done with his own body" ...'[17] True consent is held to be contingent upon the informed exercise of a choice, and thus the physician's

---

14  *Canterbury v. Spence,* 464 F. 2d 772 (1972)

15  *Cobbs v. Grant,* 502 P. 2d 1 (1972)

16  *Wilkinson v. Vesey,* 295 A. 2d 676 (1972)

17  From *Canterbury,* 780 (footnotes omitted), quoting *Schloendorff v. Society of New York Hospitals*

disclosure must provide the patient an opportunity to assess available options and attendant risks. Because the average patient has little understanding of medicine and therefore must rely on a physician, the physician has the duty to convey sufficient information. As to sufficiency of information, the court holds: 'The patient's right of self-decision shapes the boundaries of the duty to reveal. That right can be effectively exercised only if the patient possesses enough information to enable an intelligent choice.'[18] But although possession of information about potential hazards, alternatives, and possible consequences is necessary for an informed consent, actual utilization of the information in reaching a decision is not, because the information is merely a means to afford the opportunity for self-decision.

The two other cases make similar demands. *Cobbs v. Grant,* an ulcer surgery case, requires disclosure of '*all* significant perils pertaining to death or serious harm.' *Cobbs* lays down four postulates: The postulates are: first, patients are generally inferior to physicians in medical knowledge; second, competent adults have the right to control their own bodies, which includes the right to determine to undergo treatment; third, consent must be informed to be effective; and fourth, the patient is dependent on the physician for information.[19] Finally, *Wilkinson v. Vesey,* a radiation therapy case involving radiation burns, rejects the view that decisions whether to proceed with a therapy are *medical* determinations. The court insists that 'all the known material risks peculiar to the proposed procedure' must be divulged, as judged by what 'a reasonable person, in what the physician knows or should know is his patient's position' would want to know. Both 'severity' and 'likelihood' of occurrence are singled out for disclosure. *Wilkinson's* 'keystone' premise is ' "every competent adult's right to forego treatment, or even cure, if it entails what for him are intolerable consequences or risks however unwise his sense of values may be" ...' in the eyes of others.[20]

---

18  *Canterbury,* 786 (footnotes omitted)

19  *Cobbs,* 9

20  *Wilkinson,* 687, 689, quoting Harper & James, *The Law of Torts*

## IV

These three cases reflect the general emphasis in case law on the development of standards for adequate disclosure. Two general standards or rules for defining adequate disclosures are now in competition as a result of these and previous landmark cases: the 'professional practice standard' and the 'reasonable person standard.' In addition, a third alternative legal standard has been proposed, commonly called the 'subjective standard,' or sometimes the 'individual standard.' These standards deserve careful scrutiny.

(1) *The Professional Practice Standard.* This first standard holds that adequate disclosure is determined by the customary rules or traditional practices of a professional community — e.g., a community of physicians or psychologists. The custom in a profession establishes both the topic to be discussed and the amount and kinds of information to be disclosed about each topic. By this standard only expert testimony from members of such professional groups could count as evidence that there has been a violation of a right to information.[21] This standard developed out of deference to the physician's expert knowledge of both treatment risk factors and the psychological effects of disclosure to patients. It goes hand in hand with the adoption of a negligence, as opposed to a battery, theory of liability in informed consent law.[22]

Many problems attend this professional practice standard for disclosure: Do customary standards of disclosure even prevail within the relevant profession — a doubt sure to be registered in the case of industrial management and industrial medicine? How much consensus is necessary to establish that a professional norm exists? Nothing inherent in the professional practice standard suggests criteria for determining either the conditions under which a standard has been established or the reference class constituting the relevant professional group. More significantly, if custom alone is conclusive, then pervasively negligent care can be perpetuated with impunity, for relevant professionals may all offer the same inferior information and precautions.[23]

---

21 See, e.g., *ZeBarth v. Swedish Hospital Medical Center,* 499 P. 2d 1 (1972) 508. This view was pervasive in the early 1970s despite the aforementioned cases. See, e.g., *Shetter v. Rochelle,* 409 P. 2d 74 (1965), *Nishi v. Hartwell,* 473 P. 2d 116 (1970), *Ross v. Hodges,* 234 So. 2d 905 (1970), and *Tatro v. Leuken,* 512 P. 2d 529 (1973).

22 Joseph H. King, Jr., 'In Search of a Standard of Care for the Medical Profession: The "Accepted Practice" Formula,' *Vanderbilt Law Review,* **28** (1975) 1262

23 Jon R. Waltz, 'The Rise and Gradual Fall of the Locality Rule in Malpractice Litigation,' *DePaul Law Review,* **18** (1969) 408

The principal objection to the professional standard, however, is that it undermines individual autonomy, the promotion of which many hold to be the primary justification of informed consent requirements. The individual's right to determine what is done with his or her body and the right to information necessary to that determination generally have been given moral and legal priority over any privilege to withhold information.

(2) *The Reasonable Person Standard.* In the aftermath of *Canterbury,* the reasonable person standard emerged as the prevailing legal criterion in only 25% of the legal jurisdictions in the United States. According to this standard, the amount and types of information to be disclosed are determined by reference to a hypothetical reasonable person: 'Materiality may be said to be the significance a reasonable person, in what the physician knows or should know is his patient's position, would attach to the disclosed risk or risks in deciding whether to submit or not to submit to surgery or treatment.'[24] The reasonable person standard thus centers inquiry on the information the person needs in order to exercise the right to make an autonomous decision. The principal argument for this standard is therefore based on considerations of autonomy: Proponents of the reasonable person standard believe that considerations of autonomy generally outweigh those of beneficence and that, on balance, the reasonable person standard better serves the individual than does the professional practice standard. The purest autonomy-based argument holds that risk evaluation always belongs to the individual affected, not to the professional(s) involved, regardless of the latter's expert knowledge and ability to protect the individual from harm.

Unfortunately, the reasonable person standard also harbors conceptual and practical difficulties. The concept of materiality is only ambiguously defined, and the central concept of the reasonable person goes altogether undefined in the aforementioned cases. The courts have not attended to these conceptual problems, and Prosser's definition of the reasonable person – which predates the cases – seems still to be the operative interpretation:

> This mythical person ... is not to be identified with any ordinary individual, who might occasionally do unreasonable things; he is a prudent and careful man who is always up to standard. Nor is it proper to identify him even with any member of the very jury who are to apply the standard; he is rather a per-

---

24   *Wilkinson v. Vesey,* 295 A. 2d 676 (1972) 689, quoting Waltz and Scheuneman, 'Informed Consent to Therapy,' *Northwestern University Law Review,* **64** (1970) 64

sonification of the community ideal of reasonable behavior, determined by the jury's social judgment.[25]

Because application of the abstract reasonable person standard to a concrete case would require the incorporation of specific facts of the case, a pressing question is what the reasonable person would do 'under the same or similar circumstances.' A critical issue is thus how broadly 'the patient's circumstances or position' should be construed? In *Cobbs* it is said that 'the scope of the physician's communications to the patient ... must be measured by the patient's need, and that need is *whatever* information is material to the decision.'[26] But what is the 'whatever' in this formulation? Depending on how ambiguous elements of the reasonable person standard are interpreted, this standard can be taken as requiring a severely limited or a generously broad disclosure.

(3) *The Subjective Standard.* In the reasonable person model employed in contemporary law, sufficiency of information is to be judged by reference to the informational needs of the so-called 'objective' reasonable person, and *not* by reference to the specific informational needs of the individual subject − as proposed by the third or *subjective* standard. Yet individual informational needs can differ, because the subject may have highly personal or unorthodox beliefs, unusual health problems, or unique family histories that require a different informational base than that required by most persons. For example, a female employee with a family history of reproductive problems might need information no other person needs to obtain before becoming involved in research on sexual and familial relations or accepting employment in some industries.

If a physician knows or has reason to believe that a person needs special information, then withholding it may deprive the patient of the opportunity to make an informed choice, and thus may undermine autonomy. The issue here is the extent to which the reasonable person standard should be tailored to the individual patient (i.e., made 'subjective'). There is clearly a continuum of possible interpretations: At the conservative end, the phrase 'in the patient's position' could be taken to include only the person's medical condition and related physical characteristics. Under this interpretation, the physician would be obligated to disclose in light of the informational needs of the mythical reasonable patient imbued only with these limited characteristics. The language used by courts has generally been ambiguous with respect to

---

25  W.L. Prosser, *Torts,* 4th Edition (St. Paul: West Publishing Co. 1971) 151

26  *Cobbs,* 11 (italics added)

this issue.[27] At the liberal end of the continuum, the patient's position could be construed to include any factor particular to the patient's desire for information which a physician could reasonably be expected to know. Under this construal, the reasonable person standard perhaps collapses into the subjective standard. The physician is obligated to disclose the information that a particular patient wants or needs to know, so long as there is a reasonable connection between these informational needs and what the physician should know about the patient's position.

It remains undecided in the contemporary literature whether, from a moral point of view, the more narrow objective reasonable person standard or the subjective standard will emerge as the favored standard — or whether they should somehow be combined to include an objective reasonable person requirement for relevant information together with a subjective requirement that individuals be given an opportunity to ask pertinent questions and be given special information that a physician knows or ought to know to be considered relevant by the individuals. There has been little analysis of points on the continuum between these two extremes, and both *Canterbury* and *Wilkinson* ultimately leave determination of materiality to the jury. The jury is asked to interpret for itself whether a reasonable person in the patient's situation would have 'attached significance' to the fact or cluster of facts in question in order to make an informed decision.

This construal suggests that the *moral* question is not whether the information necessarily, probably, or possibly would have led the patient to forego therapy — the critical *legal* question — but rather whether the information was necessary for an informed decision *regardless* of the outcome. Despite the ambiguities attached to a more subjective reasonable person standard, this criterion does seem a proper standard of disclosure from a moral point of view — based, as any standard must be, on respect for autonomy.

# V

Let us now return to issues specifically surrounding the workplace. According to *Canterbury*, 'the physician's duty to disclose is governed by the *same legal principles applicable to others in comparable situations,*

---

27 See, for example, Alexander Morgan Capron, 'Informed Consent in Catastrophic Disease Research and Treatment,' *University of Pennsylvania Law Review,* (1974) 407 note 161

with modifications only to the extent that medical judgment enters the picture.'[28] Assuming the correctness of this generalization, what can be learned from the above history? Specifically, do the principles involved apply to disclosure, consent, and refusal in the workplace?

These consent cases indicate that a fiduciary relationship such as the one between a patient and a physician includes a duty to disclose — a duty ubiquitously recognized in the common law tradition.[29] Disclosure requirements imposed on the fiduciary are measured by the informational needs of the person whose trust has been placed in the fiduciary, and these needs include disclosure of all significant risks and hazards. Failures to disclose may result in a negligence or a battery action. It is arguably the case that there is therefore a fiduciary relationship between an employer-provided physician and an employee-patient.[30] However, we must acknowledge from the outset that there is *no reasonable analogy drawn in contemporary law between a traditional fiduciary relationship and the employer-employee relationship.* Nor can any direct analogy be made to the union-employee relationship, for unions too are not fiduciaries in the eyes of the law. Consequently neither employers nor unions have a fiduciary obligation in law to warn of risk or to obtain an informed consent. Employers can be sued for fraudulent misrepresentation of the risks of a job, but not for failure to disclose risk. These are the main lines of the common law tradition.

The nonfiduciary nature of the relationship between employers and employees certainly provides one sound reason for skepticism about applying an informed consent model to risk in the workplace. There are other reasons as well. There is currently no pervesive legal duty of disclosure in the workplace because risks in this environment have thus far been handled by workmen's compensation laws. These laws were

---

28  *Canterbury,* 785 (italics added)

29  Our approach to consent in the workplace is modelled on developments in *case law.* For an approach based on developments in biomedical *research,* see Deborah Johnson, 'Individual Consent and Toxic Substances,' Technical Information Project, *Toxic Substances and Trade Secrecy* (Washington: Technical Information Project 1977), esp. pp. 6, 12.

30  Although traditionally courts have not recognized a physician-patient relationship between company doctors and workers, according to OSHA the current judicial trend favors the finding of a fully developed physician-patient relationship in the occupational setting. This trend is in line with the position of the American Occupational Medical Association, which maintains in its code of ethics that the occupational physician's first obligation is to the employee-patient and that the occupational physician is bound by ordinary professional obligations. See OSHA regulations, p. 35231.

originally designed for problems of accident in instances of immediately assessible damage. Duties to warn or to disclose are formally pointless under the no-fault conception operative in workmen's compensation, and there is no functional equivalent of the concept of an explicit voluntary assumption of a risk. To be compensated for an injury, a worker must show only that an injury occurred; there is no need to show that someone was responsible, and therefore no reason to show that there should have been a warning or a valid consent. The problem is one of legal causation: a physician may be sued by causing an injury through nondisclosure or underdisclosure; management may not, unless fraudulent misrepresentation is involved.

Reasons traditionally invoked for establishing such starkly different arrangements of responsibility, causation, and compensation for medicine and for industry are now crumbling. It has been relatively easy in the past to disassociate disclosure of information from causation of industrial 'accidents' and from problems of compensation; but the fact that asbestos or cotton fibers, for example, present serious long-term risks of injury, disease, and death is different from the fact that radial saws and pathways along steel girders lead to similarly serious accidents. Every worker on the job already knows of the existence of the latter dangers — though not of the magnitude of those risks; e.g., plant injury rates are seldom known. (Moreover, as *Canterbury* and other cases make clear, there is no duty even in fiduciary contexts to disclose what a reasonable person in the situation would *already* know.) Recently discovered risks to health in the workplace thus carry with them a *greater need* for information on the basis of which a person may wish to take one or several actions, including choosing to forego employment completely, to refuse certain work environments within a place of employment, to wear protective devices, or to agitate for higher minumum exposure standards.

While relatively little is known at present about the knowledge and comprehension of workers, there is evidence that in at least some industries ignorance is a causal factor in occupational illness or injury. A recent blistering and remarkably detailed report on The Hurley Reduction Works — a smelter owned by Kennecott Copper — concludes that 'the smelter's work force has little or no understanding of occupational health hazards, their evaluation, or prevention.'[31] Much of this report probes the implications of this ignorance for workers in the smelter who are exposed to airborne arsenic, sulfur dioxide, and copper dust — all of

---

31  Manuel Gomez, Richard Duffy, and Vincent Trivelli, 'Kennercott/Hurley,' in *At Work in Copper: Occupational Health and Safety in Copper Smelting*, Vol. 3 (New York: Inform Inc. 1979) 123

which appear in high to very high levels in the reverberatory furnace and converter areas. The exposure levels of more than one-third of the work force must be classified as 'unknown', because no specific data have yet been gathered. OSHA has characterized the exposures in the plant as high to very high, and the aforementioned report rates as 'very poor' both the industrial hygiene program and the information provided about health and safety. At the time of the report, union representatives (United Steelworkers) had no access to company reports about safety and health conditions.

The implications of worker ignorance about similar health hazards in many industries were given compelling expression in recent testimony before an OSHA hearing by a worker exposed to the toxic agent dibromochloropropane (DBCP):

> We had no warning that DBCP exposure might cause sterility, testicular atrophy, and perhaps cancer. If we had known that these fumes could possibly cause the damage that we have found out it probably does cause, we would have worn equipment to protect ourselves. As it was, we didn't have enough knowledge to give us the proper respect for DBCP. Had we been warned of these dangers, some may not have accepted employment in the first place, and others, myself included, would certainly have handled this material more carefully.[32]

We are presently unprepared by our legal tradition to deal with these questions about the worker's need for information. Clearly the informed consent model cannot simply be transplanted to the workplace. We are therefore ripe for a discussion of the responsibility of employers — and perhaps other parties — to make disclosures about risks quite independently of current law. However, this discussion will be enhanced by reference to the informed consent model, for there is potentially a great deal to be extracted about obligations of disclosure from landmark cases of informed consent. Both the right to know and the right to refuse exposure to risks in the workplace may be enlightened by reference to these cases, as we shall now see.

## VI

Unlike physician-patient relationships, employee-employer relationships invite disclosure requirements for risk information *because* no fiduciary relationship or common goal exists between the parties — the

---

32   OSHA regulations, 35222

relationship often being confrontational, with few interests and goals shared in common, and therefore increased risks presented to workers.[33] The greater likelihood of harm to employees, and even their relative powerlessness in the employer-employee relationship, may not be sufficient to justify employer disclosure obligations in all cases, but placing relevant information in the hands of workers surely seems appropriate in at least some cases. By what criteria, then, shall such disclosure obligations be determined to begin and end, and how is negligence to be determined?

It will not do to argue that workmen's compensation relieves employers of responsibility and makes the issue moot. This response is appropriate only from a narrow legal perspective, as the law's focus on causation carries a certain blindness to broader moral issues. The moral point of view is more prospective than retrospective; its focus is not on obligations in the event of injury, but on obligations to promote autonomy and to prevent injury. Whereas case law necessarily asks whether respect for autonomy *was* violated, morality places a premium on the communication needed to ensure that autonomy *will* be respected and injury prevented.

Let us return to the earlier discussion of disclosure standards and the accompanying argument that the withholding of relevant information (by a fiduciary, in the earlier discussion) unduly deprives individuals of opportunities to know and refuse, thus undermining autonomy. We may now ask whether an employer's withholding of vital information — in those cases where employers are the relevant sources of information — similarly deprives individuals of the opportunity to know and refuse, and thus similarly undermines autonomy.

We must again resist all temptation to squeeze the analogy to medicine dry, for it is implausible to suppose that employers can be reconceived as fiduciaries. As customarily conceived, both government and unions have a relationship to employees more closely approximating to a fiduciary relationship than do employers. This only indicates, however, that in some contexts the government or a union leader is a more likely candidate to be held culpable for not providing information than an employer.[34] The question still must be faced whether an

---

33 However, we hasten to add that assertions of industry's reluctance to provide information and disclose risks may often be unduly exaggerated by critics. It is frequently in industry's long-term interest to report hazards and restructure environments.

34 There may of course be circumstances in which employers or other parties will *justifiably* withhold information from employees, just as the government or physicians will sometimes justifiably withhold information.

employer or any other party must be bound to the requirements of either the objective standard or the subjective standard, both of which, but particularly the latter, industry may view as unreasonably demanding. Does the moral point of view provide an adequate argument for the acceptance of a particular standard of disclosure in the workplace?

One plausible argument is the following: Because large employers, unions, and government agencies must deal with multiple employees and complicated causal conditions, no standard *more* demanding than the objective reasonable person standard is appropriate for general industry disclosures. That is, no party is to be held responsible for disclosing information beyond that needed to make an informed choice about the adequacy of safety precautions, industrial hygiene, long-term hazards, and the like, as determined by what the reasonable person would judge to be the worker's need for information material to a decision about employment or working conditions. It does not follow, however, that this general standard of disclosure — which would in practice be used for disclosures to unions who represent employees (or to groups of employees) — is adequate for all individual disclosures. At least in the case of extremely serious hazards — such as those involved in short-term, but concentrated doses of radiation — the subjective standard may be more appropriate.[35]

Accordingly, in cases where disclosures to *individual* workers may be expected to have significant subjective impact and variance, the reasonable person standard should perhaps be supplemented by a subjective standard that takes account of independent informational needs. An alternative that might be viable would be to include the following as a component of all general disclosures under the reasonable person standard: 'If you are concerned about the possible effect of hazards on your individual health, and you seek clarification or personal information, a company physician may be consulted by making an appointment.' An entirely subjective standard would be inappropriate, because workers will rarely know what information would be relevant for their deliberations and underdisclosures would therefore regularly occur. Perhaps the most satisfactory solution is a compromise standard: whatever a reasonable person would judge material to the decision-making process should be disclosed, and in addition any remaining in-

---

35 The special needs of *unrepresented* workers would also have to be considered in electing any general standard(s). For an account that in effect demands a subjective standard for carcinogens, see Andrea Hricko, 'The Right to Know,' in Thomas P. Vogl, ed., *Public Information in the Prevention of Occupational Cancer: Proceedings of a Symposium,* December 2-3, 1976, (Washington: National Academy of Sciences 1977), esp. p. 72.

formation material to an individual worker should be provided through a process of asking what he or she is concerned about as a special problem.[36]

However, acceptance of this standard for risk disclosure in the workplace would skim only the surface of many related issues that also deserve attention. Such a general standard would only bring to greater prominence the question of to whom the risk must be acceptable and under what conditions workers should be allowed to accept particular risks that others (including federal officers) consider unacceptable. For example, special attention would have to be paid to various programs by industry and unions to bar fertile women from workplaces that might affect reproductive capacities or the health of offspring. For example, at Du Pont some women of childbearing age have chosen sterilization rather than forfeiture of their jobs. (Actually mutagens are capable of altering genetic information in either sperm or eggs, which raises another touchy issue of sexual discrimination.[37]) General Motors (Delco-Remy), Allied Chemical, and The Lead Industries Association have all recommended or established policies barring women from accepting reproductive risks and dismissing presently employed women who seek to accept the risk and retain their positions. An informed consent or informed refusal model could easily be fashioned to challenge such company policies.

## VII

A presupposition of the analysis thus far is that respect for the autonomy of workers is a directly relevant and overriding moral consideration. It may not be. It is reasonable to ask whether there are sufficient moral grounds to show that workers ought to be respected through

36 As more and more data are gathered regarding the effects of workplace hazards on particular predisposing conditions, the need for disclosure of such information can be identified through preemployment physical examinations without the worker's needing to ask questions. Thus, in addition to reasonable worker disclosure, which will be a very broad-based, public risk standard, worker disclosure (by categories such as asthmatic worker, pregnant worker, worker with a cardiac pacemaker) can accomplish many of the ends sought by the subjectively interested individual worker.

37 A 1977 American Cynamid Co. literature search revealed more than 30 chemicals that could adversely affect fetuses. See the article by G. Bronson, *The Wall Street Journal* CXCIII: (Feb. 9, 1979).

mechanisms which expand their information base and their options rather than through mechanisms which afford increased health and safety protections. This question suggests a need to analyze the function or goal of risk disclosures. It asks for a general justification of the right to know and of correlative disclosure requirements in the workplace.

The problem is the following: The main goal of regulatory actions in the workplace has always been and probably always will be to ban or limit conditions that negatively affect worker health and safety. At present the government establishes safety standards and controls enforcement; if these regulatory initiatives were sufficiently thorough, there might seem to be no need for disclosure requirements, and therefore no justification for their introduction. They would simply be gratuitous, as indeed would the right to know.

Suppose workers' safety and health could be maximally protected — i.e., morbidity and mortality statistics could be kept at their lowest levels — if and only if precise health and safety standards were vigorously enforced and no disclosures to workers and no decisions by workers were permitted. Under these conditions, would it nonetheless be justified to introduce disclosure requirements? The reason for an affirmative answer to this question, we contend, is uncomplicated, though profoundly controversial: The broad purpose of disclosure requirements is to protect and enhance autonomous decision making; and the demands of *autonomy* should not be confused with the demands of *beneficence,* which justify regulation and enforcement provisions intended to assist or protect workers. As the workers' testimony quoted above indicates, choosing to risk testicular atrophy requires a worker's choice. It *cannot* be fully decided by any health and safety standards. Moreover, it deserves notice that morbidity and mortality statistics are aggregate outcomes. Exposure standards that bring about the lowest levels of morbidity and mortality in a population of workers nevertheless may be inadequate to protect the interests of any *particular* worker — for example, the worker who is hypersusceptible to a particular toxic agent. Both autonomous choice and personal health will be adequately protected for such workers only if there exists a vigorously enforced right to know in the workplace.

It is generally agreed that the larger purpose of gaining information about risks in the workplace is to facilitate intelligent decision-making about proper standards of safety and health. These decisions, as traditionally conceived, are essentially *regulatory* decisions made in various branches of the government, whose function is to protect the safety and health of the labor force. It is generally presupposed that, once obtained, the information will dictate safety standards. However, we are now beginning to appreciate that information gathered about risks to safety and health commonly does *not* determine which set of regulatory alternatives should be accepted. Usually a situation of substantial ambiguity prevails, where the risks are uncertain by the assessment of the most informed expert, and the dose levels at which there is concern for health and safety can be made no clearer.[38] Often epidemiology offers the only method of discovering occupational health risks. Unfortunately, these epidemiological studies may deliver conflicting conclusions. For example, there is disagreement about whether there is *any* increased risk of brain cancer from routine work in petrochemical plants. Moreover, the tradeoffs involved — as between control of health hazards and increased production costs or between cessation of production and negative employment effects — are differently assessed by different parties. Worker representatives and management generally disagree about acceptable levels of risk, appropriate epidemiological evidence, and acceptable increases in corporate costs to control or eliminate risk. Workers' assessments can also differ markedly from those of government, even assuming that government is operating from benevolent motives.

This particular feature of the relationship between government and workers is analogous to that between physicians and patients. Physicians, like agents at the Department of Labor or OSHA, have expert technical information and expert skill in evaluating risks and alternatives. But — as *Canterbury* and other cases make clear — it does not follow that physicians should interpret what is best for their patients merely because of their expertise. Such judgments are non-medical, even if they require medical information. Patients are sometimes unwilling to assume risks that their physicians think are eminently reasonable — the psychological risks of mastectomy being a prime example. Patients are also, on occasion, willing to assume what physicians view as unreasonable risks to their health. They value other goods more — as indicated by obese people or cardiac patients who refuse recommended diets. Presumably such differences in perception and evaluation exist between workers and government officials, as well as between doctors and patients.

It follows that it is morally insufficient to protect workers' rights by health and safety standards alone. These protections may satisfy the demands of beneficence, but not of autonomy. In the case of controversies about information and its use, the demands of autonomy are different from those of beneficence. In cases of conflict, it remains an open question which principle should take precedence.

---

38  See, e.g., Barry Bloom, 'News about Carcinogens: What's Fit to Print?' *The Hastings Center Report,* 9 (August 1979) 5-7, with a response by Arthur C. Upton, 'Carcinogen Testing and Public Information,' *The Hastings Center Report,* 10 (February 1980) 9-10.

Although the principles of autonomy and beneficence can conflict in the workplace, respecting the autonomy of workers by disclosure duties is generally compatible with obligations to protect workers from harm that are grounded in beneficence. The obvious link between the two principles is the presumption that because workers place a high premium on maintaining a safe working environment, they will seek to use information about health hazards to control or minimize risks in the workplace. This position has been argued in the public policy arena before OSHA by Chief Counsel Weiner of the California Department of Industrial Relations, who grounds the right to know in a principle very close, and perhaps identical, to the principle of respect for autonomy:

> The right to know is ... an integral part of the right of people in a free society to have information in order to be able to determine for themselves what their actions will be. It is a personal right, and one with special relevance to the workplace. No right is more basic than the right to protect oneself from life-threatening harm. And it is only when one is armed with a basic knowledge of workplace hazards and how one's own medical record reflects one's reaction to that environment, that one can evaluate risks and act responsibly to protect oneself from those hazards.[39]

The position that respecting the worker's right to know generally results in a safer workplace underlies the 1980 OSHA regulation on the right of access to employer records. According to OSHA, the most immediate purpose of the regulation is to enable workers to play a central role in resolving health and safety issues in the workplace, on the theory that no other party can be expected to pursue the goal of workers' health with the same commitment as the workers themselves.[40]

## VIII

Despite the direction of the arguments thus far, there are reasons why it will prove far more difficult in practice to honor the right to know for workers than corresponding rights for patients. There are, for example, more complicated questions about the kinds of information to be disclosed, as well as by whom, to whom, and under what conditions it ought to be released. There is also the problem of what to do if workers

---

39   OSHA regulations, 35232

40   OSHA regulations, 35213

themselves are inhibited from reacting to information as they would otherwise act because of economic or other constraints — e.g., industries where ten persons stand in line for every available position. The intractability of these questions is magnified in the workplace by the massive numbers of persons directly affected and by the legitimate interest of third parties — in this case the federal government and the public whose cost concerns it represents.

One weighty concern is how workers and their representatives may use information about health hazards. Mary Melville has pointed out that labor unions often seek to include in their contracts an employer obligation to disclose information about hazards in the workplace. For example, in their 1980 contract negotiations, the United Steelworkers sought to secure the right of workers to know about the kinds of toxic substances to which they would be exposed.[41] It is likely that the primary motivation behind union attempts to secure a worker's right to know is a desire to increase the ability of workers to protect themselves against health risks. However, it is at least theoretically possible that unions may seek out information about occupational risks for use as a chip at the bargaining table. Bargaining agents know that work-related harms, being but 'statistical risks,' are remote for any given worker; but they also know that the specter of harm carries powerful emotive value. A strategy under these conditions could be to bargain away better working conditions that would minimize risks in order to negotiate higher wages or more favorable contracts — in effect trading risks to health for economic benefits. The most immediate concern is whether unions adopting this tradeoff strategy are faithfully representing the informed preferences of their workers for higher salaries over safer working environments (especially over the long term), and not simply settling for options that enhance union power and resources (in the short term). If unions do not represent the informed wishes of workers (an empirical matter), then perhaps bargaining away safety and health considerations ought not to be permitted — a requirement which might prove impossible to institutionalize and enforce, even if it were desirable.

Let us suppose, however, that union tradeoffs do accurately represent workers' priorities and values. There remains the question of who under such circumstances bears the *responsibility* for any subsequent harm caused to workers by conditions that might have been eliminated. Ex hypothesi, the sole reason that installable protective (risk-reductive) measures are not in place is that they were intentionally bargained

---

41  Mary Melville, 'Risks on the Job: The Worker's Right to Know,' *Environment*, **23** (1981) 13.

away. If workers or their representatives agree to such an absence of protective measures in the employment arrangement, then the workers themselves assume responsibility for negative outcomes of the arrangement. If worker safety was treated as negotiable, then management can perhaps evade what would otherwise be taken to be its direct and perhaps sole responsibility. Just as a physician's responsibility for various precautions ceases when a patient voluntarily assumes the risk of not taking those precautions, so industry's responsibility would cease when workers waive their 'right' to the precaution.[42]

More importantly, to the extent that public monies are necessary to assist workers and their families after an injury or illness — through such programs as workmen's compensation or some form of federally subsidized health care — society may justifiably refuse unions (and individual workers) the 'freedom' to choose against maximally safe working conditions. Alternatively, numerous strategies could be adopted which provide strong incentives to workers not to bargain away their protections — e.g., a requirement that workers pay higher premiums to public insurance schemes in order to compensate for their acceptance of a higher risk. Effectively this strategy would penalize workers for accepting work-related hazards entailing correlative risks to public monies and health. However, the practical and equity problems that confront such strategies are formidable.

It is also arguably the case that workers have a right to a safe working environment independent of pay scales or bargaining situations, and that superordinate wages should be allowed only as compensation for uncontrollably unsafe occupations — that is, for occupations where it is not possible to reduce significant risks to a more acceptable level. According to this argument, only a morally unsatisfactory *system* of employment and governance would provide workers or their representatives with a strong incentive to bargain away health for economic gain. The system itself, that is, deprives them of their just due — which is adequate safety protection. This reasoning attempts to show that irrespective of their own objectives, individual workers or their representatives

---

42 A central issue turns on what it means to say that a patient or a worker *voluntarily* assumes a risk. In a recent California case a doctor had suggested that a patient have a pap test, but the patient consistently refused. The patient subsequently died of cervical cancer. The California Supreme Court held that the doctor's mere recommendation of the test was insufficient; he should have pointed out to the patient the *risks* associated with the patient's refusing to have the test: *Truman v. Thomas*, 27 Cal. 3d 285, 611 P. 2d 902 (1980). Without such disclosure from the physician, it might be argued that the patient had not *voluntarily* assumed *the risk,* despite the patient's autonomous refusal of the pap test.

should not be allowed to assume significant risks in the workplace if such risks are manageable or reducible. Thus there can be an 'informed consent' only to a predetermined threshold level of acceptable risk. A problem with even this limited role for informed consent in the workplace is that in the end it may be impossible to develop sufficient consensus about levels of acceptable risk, particularly agreement between workers and management.

This argument conceals still another mammoth difficulty. Many problems of health and safety in the workplace involve employer negligence in providing a safe working environment; we therefore should be cautious about endorsing any scheme of disclosure that allows employers to abrogate their responsibility to provide workers with a safe environment merely by informing them that the environment is hazardous. An employer should be required both to *inform about risks* and to *perform in eliminating risks* in accordance with applicable health and safety standards. Thus government regulations should require *both* safety standards *and* disclosure requirements. To allow employers to fulfil their duty of actively eliminating risks by merely providing information would be analogous to permitting a physician to escape responsibility for iatrogenic problems by informing patients that serious mistakes of practice sometimes do occur.

One possible solution is the following: there is no role at all for informed *consent* in the workplace, because consent is a way of transferring responsibility and will be exploited by industry to precisely this end. Therefore, all efforts should be aimed at obtaining protections for workers on the one hand, and at disclosures of hazards on the other hand. Disclosure is necessary, according to this argument, not to assure that workers knowledgably consent to risks, but to give workers a meaningful opportunity to protect their own interests through such alternative actions as bargaining for higher safety and exposure standards, refusing assignments to hazardous jobs, wearing protective clothing and devices, requesting OSHA investigations, and having extra medical examinations. This forces consideration of whether addressing issues of 'the right to know' through issues of worker consent addresses the wrong problem. Workers need to know only in order to do as much as possible to improve their situation — not in order to *consent* to exposure to risk. Thus, it appears that a strategy of informed consent has a starkly limited application in the workplace, while the right to know and correlative requirements of disclosure have pervasive application.

These issues also raise questions about the nature of management's and government's precise obligations to disclose information to workers. For example, we are increasingly in the situation of deciding whether to inform workers that they have been or are being exposed to a suspected carcinogen — but without being able to provide them with an estimate of the personal risk of cancer they might bear as a result of exposure. Often, we can suggest only that there may be an increased risk of cancer and that the extent of the increased risk, if it exists, is dependent not only on the level of exposure to the suspected carcinogen but also on complex interactions between such factors as personal habits and history, genetic structure, and stress. In most cases of cancer, long-term effects alone are in question, where disabilities are not expected for a considerable period of time — possibly 20 to 30 years. Not infrequently there is little of medical value (beyond epidemiological and related risk information) that can be offered to these workers. No reliable early detection yet exists, and prognosis is as risky as the risk it attempts to express.

Despite these vagaries of the medical situation, it also has been argued that these same workers are inappropriately funnelled into a medical system of recurrent and often invasive diagnostic examinations — most of them of questionable value, if not inconsiderable costs, and sometimes with risks attached to the examination (e.g., risks of over-radiation). That such useless and possibly harmful examinations may result in part from duties to warn illustrates one significant and compelling part of the dilemma of what is owed workers exposed to hazards. But this is scarcely the end of the factors creating the dilemma. It has not yet been established, for example, how information about risks affects workers and their families psychologically. It seems likely that significant emotional stress and fears do result, particularly when there is nothing that the worker can do to reduce a suspected risk once informed of its presence.

Additionally, there are problems about the extent to which individuals can meaningfully evaluate remote probabilities of serious harm, even when relevant information is provided. A recent study by Baruch Fischhoff suggests that temporary workers (and potential workers) in facilities handling nuclear materials may have erroneous presuppositions about risks that significantly affect cognitive processing of risk information. Their opinions, he argues, are often impervious to contradictory information; and even when preconceptions do not distort their processing of the information, they may not be able meaningfully to comprehend the information when uncertainties are disclosed. They tend to dismiss many qualifications that surround risk information, as if the qualifications had not been introduced at all. Fischoff's study also indicates that these workers rate their own understanding of the risks involved as better than that of the scientists who make assessments of the risk and that only about one-half of these workers believe the government should establish safety standards for radiation exposure.[43]

On the other hand, one of the more interesting features of Fischoff's study is the virtually unanimous view expressed among these workers (and potential workers) that informational pamphlets expressing known risks should be distributed as early as possible in the employment process. Currently in the nuclear industry, as well as in other industries, it is not general practice to inform prospective employees of occupational health hazards prior to employment.[44] However, Fischhoff did distribute informational pamphlets to his subjects and as a result about 50% said that they would not accept the position under any circumstances at current levels of risk *now that they know the risks.* Additionally, less than 10% said they would accept the job at $50/day — probably an unrealistically high wage for such workers at the time, though almost all those polled would accept the job if the risks were substantially reduced.[45]

There is, however, a problem with both this approach and the current OSHA regulations mentioned earlier when applied to industries where pay and unemployment are both high. Physicians who work in occupational medicine have noted a pattern of worker reluctance to ask about health risks in such industries; workers forthrightly say they do not want to know the risk *because* they cannot afford not to continue in or to accept the job.[46] In such situations, it may be of greatest urgency to inform workers of alternative actions that they can take to reduce risks even if they are not free to eliminate the risks altogether by changing jobs. However, this information is obviously no substitute for information about the nature and consequences of the health risks themselves.

These are but a few of the reasons why *in practice* it will prove extremely difficult to honor and institutionalize any broad and detailed right to know in the workplace.

---

43 Baruch Fischhoff, 'Informed Consent for Transient Nuclear Workers,' in R. Kasperson and R. Kates, eds., *Equity Issues in Radioactive Waste Management* (Cambridge, MA: Oelgeschlager, Gunn, and Hair, Inc. 1983)

44 Melville, 14

45 Baruch Fischhoff, 'Informed Consent for Transient Nuclear Workers.'

46 See Irving R. Tabershaw, 'How is the Acceptability of Risks to the Health of the Workers to be Determined?', *Journal of Occupational Medicine,* **18** (1976) 675. For a radically opposed position, see Aaron Wildovsky, 'No Risk is the Highest Risk of All,' *American Scientist,* **67** (1979) 32-7.

**IX**

The right of workers to know about health hazards is an important autonomy right, but it clearly is not the only autonomy right needed to protect workers' interests. To make the right to know truly meaningful and functional in the workplace context, other worker rights must be secured.[47] These will include (1) the right to participate in regulatory mechanisms for controlling health hazards in the workplace and (2) the right to refuse unsafe work. Deep complications surround both of these rights, but we will focus in this paper only on the second.

Several important issues turn on the options available to informed workers to reduce or remove personal risks. In a limited range of cases, it is possible for informed workers to reject employment because health and safety conditions are regarded as unacceptable. This decision is most likely to be reached in a job market where workers have alternative employment opportunities or where a worker is being offered a new assignment with the option of remaining in his or her current job. More commonly, however, workers are not in a position to respond to information about health hazards by seeking employment elsewhere. For the information to be useful, it must be possible for the worker to effect change while staying on the job.

The United States Occupational Safety and Health Act of 1970 (OSH Act)[48] confers a series of rights on employees which appear to give increased significance to the duty to disclose hazards in the workplace. Specifically, the OSH Act grants workers the right to request an OSHA inspection if they believe an OSHA standard has been violated or an imminent hazard exists. Under the Act, employees also have the right to participate in OSHA inspections of the worksite and to consult freely with the inspection officer. Perhaps most importantly, employees requesting an inspection or otherwise exercising their rights under the

---

47    OSHA has argued that the right of access to exposure and medical information is necessary to facilitate the effectiveness of at least six employee rights established by the Occupational Safety and Health Act. These six rights are (1) the right to complain to OSHA about perceived safety and health problems and to obtain prompt OSHA inspections, (2) the right to accompany OSHA officials during plant inspections, (3) the right to contest the reasonableness of OSHA-proposed abatement periods, (4) the right to participate in relevant adjudicatory proceedings, (5) the right of workers to request a NIOSH workplace Health Hazard Evaluation (HHE), and (6) the right to employee training and education funded by OSHA. See OSHA regulations, pp. 35213, 35222-35223.

48    29 U.S.C. § 651-78 (1970)

OSH Act are explicitly protected in the Act from dischargement and from any form of discrimination by current or future employees.

While these worker rights under the OSH Act are important, it can be argued that they do not go far enough in ensuring that workers have effective mechanisms for initiating inspections of suspected health hazards. It should be noted that federal, state, and municipal employees are not covered by the OSH Act and that unions are not afforded the same protections against discrimination as individual employees. There are also serious questions about the ability of the Occupational Safety and Health Adminstration to enforce provisions of the OSH Act. If workers are to make effective use of disclosed information about health hazards, they must have unimpeded access to an effective and efficient regulatory system.

It is also essential that workers have an adequately protected right to refuse unsafe work. It is difficult to determine the extent to which this right is legally protected at the present time. Although the OSH Act does not grant a general right to refuse unsafe work,[49] provisions to this effect exist in some state occupational safety laws. In addition, the Secretary of Labor has issued a regulation that interprets the OSH Act as including a limited right to refuse unsafe work, a right which was upheld by the U.S. Supreme Court in 1980.[50] A limited right of refusal is also protected explicitly in the Labor-Management Relations Act (LMRA) and implicitly in the National Labor Relations Act (NLRA).[51]

Unfortunately, these statutory protections vary significantly in the conditions under which they grant a right to refuse and the consequences which they permit to follow from such refusals. For example, the OSHA regulation allows workers to walk off the job where there is a 'real danger of death or serious injury,' while the LMRA permits refusals only under 'abnormally dangerous conditions.'[52] Thus, under the LMRA, the nature of the occupation determines the extent of danger justifying refusal, while under OSHA the character of the threat is determinative. By contrast, under the NLRA a walkout may be justified for even minimal safety problems, so long as the action can be construed as a

---

49  Susan Preston, 'A Right Under OSHA to Refuse Unsafe Work or A Hobson's Choice of Safety or Job?', *University of Baltimore Law Review,* **8** (1979) 519-50

50  The Secretary's interpretation of the OSH Act was upheld by the Supreme Court on February 26, 1980, see *Law Week,* 48:33, 4189-95, for Feb. 26, 1980, and *The New York Times* (February 27, 1980) 15.

51  Preston, 519-50

52  29 U.S.C. §143 (1976), and 29 CFR §1977.12 (1978)

concerted activity for mutual aid and protection and there does not exist a no-strike clause in any collective bargaining agreements.[53] While the NLRA would appear to provide the broadest protection to workers, employees refusing to work under the NLRA may lose the right to be reinstated in their positions if permanent replacements can be found.[54]

The relative merits of the different statutes are further confused by questions of overlapping authority. It is not always clear (1) when a worker is eligible to claim protection under each law, (2) which law affords a worker maximum protection in a particular circumstance, and (3) whether or under what conditions a worker can seek relief through more than one law or directly through the courts.

The overall legal situation concerning the right to refuse hazardous work in the United States is far too complicated to be adequately treated here. Any definitive treatment of the problem will need to consider not only narrow legal questions of jurisdiction and remedy but also important policy and moral questions raised by the conflicting interests of employees and employers. Unfortunately, these questions have not received much attention outside limited legal circles. Consider, for example, whether a meaningful right to refuse hazardous work entails an obligation to continue to pay nonworking employees, or to award the employees back-pay if the issue is resolved in their favor. It could be argued that workers without union strike benefits or other income protections are unable to exercise their right to refuse unsafe work because of undue economic pressures. On the other hand, it could be argued that to permit such workers to draw a paycheck is to legitimate strike with pay, a practice generally considered unacceptable by management and by Congress.

Also unresolved is whether the right to refuse unsafe work should be restricted to cases of obvious, imminent, and serious risks to health or life (the current OSHA and LMRA position) or expanded to include lesser risks and also uncertain risks — e.g., as discussed centrally in this paper, exposure to suspected toxic or carcinogenic substances. Certainly, if 'the right to know' is to lead to meaningful worker action, workers must be able to remove themselves from exposure to *suspected* hazards, as well as *obvious* or *known* hazards.

Related to this issue is the question of the *proper standard* for determining whether a safety walkout is justified. At least three different stan-

---

53  Nicholas Ashford and Judith P. Katz, 'Unsafe Working Conditions: Employee Rights Under the Labor Management Relations Act and the Occupational Safety and Health Act,' *Notre Dame Lawyer,* **52** (1977) 802-37

54  Preston, 543

dards have been proposed (and even imposed): a good-faith standard, which requires only a determination that the worker honestly (subjectively) believes that the health hazard exists; a reasonable person standard which requires that the belief be reasonable under the circumstances, as well as sincerely held; and an objective standard which requires evidence, generally established by expert witnesses, that the threat actually exists.[55] (The similarities between these three standards and the three standards for the duty to disclose discussed in Section IV are obvious and pertinent.) Although the possibility of worker abuse of the right to refuse has been a major factor in a current trend to reject the good faith standard, recent commentary has argued that this trend raises serious equity issues in the proper balancing of this concern with the needs of workers confronted with basic self-preservation issues.[56]

Still another related issue is whether the right to refuse hazardous work should be protected only until a review is initiated (at which time the worker must return to the job) or whether the walk-out should be permitted until the alleged hazard is at least temporarily removed. So long as the hazards covered under a right to refuse are restricted to those risks which are obvious in the environment and which are easily established as health hazards, this issue is relatively easy to resolve. However, if the nature of the risk is less apparent — as in the case of the risks treated in this paper — major functions of the right to refuse will be to call attention to an alleged hazard and to compel regulatory action. If this chain of events is set in motion, requiring workers to continue to be exposed while OSHA or the NLRB conduct investigations may be unacceptable to workers and certainly will be unacceptable if the magnitude of potential harm is perceived as great. On the other hand, compelling employers to remove suspected hazards during the evaluation period may result in intolerable economic burdens. We therefore need a delineation of the conditions under which workers may be compelled to return to work while an alleged hazard is being evaluated and the conditions under which employers must be compelled to remove alleged hazards. This problem is a special case of the aforementioned issue of setting standards for acceptable risks in the workplace.

---

55  Nancy K. Frank, 'A Question of Equity: Workers' "Right to Refuse" Under OSHA Compared to the Criminal Necessity Defense,' *Labor Law Journal*, **31** (1980) 617-26

56  Ibid.

## X

We have argued in this paper for a worker's right to know and for such related worker rights as the right to participate in the establishment and regulation of safety standards and the right to refuse hazardous work. A thorough analysis of the legal status of these rights has not been attempted. However, were such an analysis conducted, current legal protections in these three areas would surely be found inadequate from a moral perspective. In addition to the need to improve statutory protections, at least one final issue deserves mention. Legal rights will be of no practical consequence if workers remain ignorant of their options.[57] It is doubtful that many workers, particularly non-union workers, are even aware that they have a legally protected right to refuse hazardous work, let alone that there are at least three statutory provisions protecting that right. Even if workers were aware of such a right, it is unlikely that they could weave their way through the maze of legal options unaided. If there is to be a meaningful right to know in the workplace, there will also have to be an adequate program to educate workers about their rights and how to exercise them, as well as adequate legal protection of this and related worker rights.

### Select Bibliography

Ashford, Nicholas, and Judith P. Katz, 'Unsafe Working Conditions: Employee Rights Under the Labor Management Relations Act and the Occupational Safety and Health Act,' *Notre Dame Lawyer,* **52** (1977) 802-37.

Bloom, Barry, 'News About Carcinogens: What's Fit to Print?' *The Hastings Center Report,* 9 (August, 1979) 5-7, with a response by Arthur C. Upton, 'Carcinogen Testing and Public Information,' *The Hastings Center Report,* 10 (February, 1980) 9-10.

Fischhoff, Baruch, 'Informed Consent for Transient Nuclear Workers,' in *Equity Issues in Radioactive Waste Management,* edited by R. Kasperson and R. Kates (Cambridge, MA: Oelgeschlager, Gunn, and Hair, Inc. 1983).

---

57 As noted previously, the OSHA regulation guaranteeing workers' rights of access to medical and exposure records specifically requires employers to inform workers of these rights and to make readily available to workers copies of the regulation. See p. 35280. The extent to which workers are now aware of their access rights is unknown.

Frank, Nancy K., 'A Question of Equity: Workers' "Right to Refuse" Under OSHA Compared to the Criminal Necessity Defense,' *Labor Law Journal,* **31** (1980) 617-26.

Johnson, Deborah, 'Individual Consent and Toxic Substances,' in *Toxic Substances and Trade Secrecy,* Technical Information Project (Washington: Technical Information Project 1977).

Melville, Mary, 'Risks on the Job: The Worker's Right to Know,' *Environment,* **23** (1981).

Occupational Safety and Health Administration, 'Access to Employee Exposure and Medical Records — Final Rules,' *Federal Register,* May 23, 1980, 35212-77.

Preston, Susan, 'A Right Under OSHA to Refuse Unsafe Work or A Hobson's Choice of Safety or Job?,' *University of Baltimore Law Review,* **8** (1979) 519-50.

Richter, Elihu D., 'The Worker's Right to Know: Obstacles, Ambiguities, and Loopholes,' *Journal of Health Politics, Policy and Law,* **6** (1981).

Vogl, P. (editor), *Public Information in the Prevention of Occupational Cancer: Proceedings of a Symposium,* December 2-3, 1976 (Washington: National Academy of Sciences, 1977).

CANADIAN JOURNAL OF PHILOSOPHY
Supplementary Volume VIII, 1982

# Commerce and Selfishness

RICHARD J. ARNESON, University of California at San Diego

Does the existence of a capitalist market economy foster the character trait of selfishness? Does a market[1] elicit narrowly self-interested conduct? Many great minds have advanced notably weak arguments to support affirmative answers to these questions. In section I, I canvass several unsuccessful attempts by Karl Marx to demonstrate that market economies are causally implicated in the production of undesirable character traits. Sections II and III venture a suggestion that partially vindicates Marx's hunch. The suggestion I develop relies on the truth of an empirical hypothesis regarding the effect on the disposition to altruism

---

1 By *exchange relations* I understand the voluntary trading of goods among individuals who are the owners of those goods. With respect to some good, a *market* exists to the degree that production and distribution of the good are organized through exchange relations. A *market economy* is one in which exchange relations predominate. A *capitalist* market economy is one marked by substantial inequality in the ownership of property, so that some persons, to make a living, must sell their labor to others.

of activity by public authority that is perceived by those affected to be fair. In conclusion I discuss a study by Richard Titmuss that offers an attempt at confirmation of this hypothesis, along with a lively polemic against the commercialization of medical care that is flawed by failures of analysis reminiscent of Marx's broadside arguments.

# I

In some of his early writings Marx's rejection of market relations is especially pure, thoroughgoing, and unequivocal. Marx's most thorough, though still sketchy, treatment of this topic occurs in the section of the *1844 Manuscripts* entitled 'Geld.'[2] Although Marx's examples focus specifically on monetary exchange, the arguments he develops by means of these examples would appear to apply to any economy organized around exchanges of goods among individual owners, even in the absence of any agreed-upon medium of exchange. (A medium of exchange facilitates trade and so presumably exacerbates whatever problems of trade are associated with an expansion of its volume.) Marx makes three allegations regarding the tendency of exchange: (1) it threatens individuality, (2) it corrupts nonexchange standards of value, and (3) it lessens care for other persons. I take up each of these charges briefly, in turn.

*Threat to Individuality.* Marx laments the circumstance that market exchange permits an individual to attach qualities to himself artificially, through purchase, that he could not otherwise secure for himself. This is the gist of the literary quotations Marx adduces. In his own voice he writes:

> That which is for me through the medium of *money* — that for which I can pay (i.e. which money can buy) — that am I *myself*, the possessor of the money. The extent of the power of money is the extent of my power. Money's properties are my — the possessor's — properties and essential powers. Thus, what I *am* and am *capable of* is by no means determined by my individuality. I am ugly, but I can buy for myself the *most beautiful* of women. Therefore I am not *ugly*, for the effect of *ugliness* — its deterrent power — is nullified by money. (324-5; 565-6)

---

2 Karl Marx and Frederick Engels, *Collected Works,* vol. 3 (New York: International Publishers 1975) 322-6. Page references in the text are to this work, followed by a reference to the parallel passage in the *Marx-Engels Werke,* Ergänzungsband (Berlin: Dietz Verlag 1968).

Marx's prostitution example introduces a complicating factor, namely that with money people may attempt to purchase intangible items such as affection or reciprocal attraction that by definition are unpurchaseable.[3] Simplifying the example by eliminating this complication, let us suppose that I am ugly, but with the purchase of cosmetics I can render myself somewhat more appealing visually. In this manner I can offset the effects of accidents of birth. However, I can think of no principle that should appeal to Marx (or to us), from which it would follow that taking advantage of the opportunities of exchange to improve on one's stock of individual traits is in any respect morally unfortunate or problematic. The inequality that obtains between the ugly and the handsome is for the most part due to genetic accidents that are as arbitrary from a Marxian moral point of view as are inequalities due to inheritance of property. Tinkering with such inequalities in the manner proposed undermines nothing that ought to be sacrosanct.

One feature of his style of argument that prevents Marx from acknowledging this point is that his examples typically conflate the distinct effects of market exchange and of unequal distribution of the means of exchange. A concern for distribution is evident when Marx distinguishes between demand in the sense of need or desire from the effective demand of somebody who besides desiring X also controls exchangeable goods wanted by some current possessor of X. Pressing the same point, Marx observes, 'I, according to my individual characteristics, am *lame,* but money furnishes me with twenty-four feet. Therefore I am not lame' (324; 565). This example conjures up the image of a wealthy man who commands the labor of twelve servants who wait on him hand and foot. No doubt it is bad that the twelve should abjectly serve the one. But the example is not squarely aligned with Marx's target. The example suggests some bad consequences of maldistribution of market resources, not of market relations per se. If we excise the confusion from Marx's discussion, his underlying objection would appear to be to relations of lordship and servitude, and to market relations only insofar as the latter issues in the former.[4] (Consider a feudal lord whom fixed custom assigns the power to command the labor of serfs and retainers, so that if he is lame they must carry him about at his

---

3  I discuss this complicating factor under the 'Corruption of Non-market Values' section below.

4  Lest it be thought that the market and market inequality are indissolubly linked, consider a Rousseauian economy in which property rights are limited by the proviso that people may trade as they like so long as no individual accumulates an amount of wealth more than ____% above the average.

whim.) Amending the example to exclude these features of maldistribution, we can imagine a poor lame urchin who pays some pennies to a carpenter, in exchange for crutches. Money enables the urchin to benefit from the talents of others and to avoid the misery that would otherwise befall him in consequence of his incapacities. No doubt it would be nicer if the carpenter were willing to fashion a pair of crutches for the youth without market compensation, but his lack of generosity does not by itself introduce an ethically unsavory element into the imaginary exchange. The price is not excessive; the carpenter does not gouge his customer. Marx says that 'money is thus the general distorting of *individualities* which turns them into their opposite and confers contradictory attributes upon their attributes' (325, 566), but notice that such distortion of individualities is not peculiar to exchange but likewise characterizes gift relationships: a free gift of crutches will transform a child who is lame into one who is effectively non-lame. Once again it is unclear on what ground Marx could find any feature of the imagined situation objectionable.

*Corruption of Non-market Values.* In some passages Marx's complaint against market relations is that they swallow up non-market relations. All are reduced to a cash nexus. Consider this line of argument:

> If *money* is the bond binding me to *human* life, binding society to me, connecting me with nature and man, is not money the bond of all *bonds*? Can it not dissolve and bind all ties? ... Money, then, appears as this *distorting* power both against the individual and against the bonds of society, etc., which claim to be *entities* in themselves. It transforms fidelity into infidelity, love into hate, hate into love, virtue into vice, vice into virtue, servant into master, master into servant, idiocy into intelligence, and intelligence into idiocy ... He who can buy bravery is brave, though he be a coward. As money is not exchanged for any one specific quality, for any one specific thing, or for any particular human essential power, but for the entire objective world of man and nature, from the standpoint of its possessor it therefore serves to exchange every quality for every other, even contradictory, quality and object: it is the fraternization of impossibilities. It makes contradictions embrace. Assume *man* to be *man* and his relationship to the world to be a human one: then you can exchange love only for love, trust for trust, etc. (324-6; 565-6)

I have spliced this quotation from separated passages. It gathers various threads. Part of what Marx is saying is that as market relations come to predominate in the economic arena, considerations drawn from non-market norms lose their power to convince and to motivate the individual. According to Marx market relations exhibit a 'distorting' power which causes people to become cynical in relation to traditional values, to call virtue 'vice' and vice 'virtue' whenever this suits their economic convenience. There are two claims here: (1) the development of the market causes belief in traditional codes and values to disappear, and

(2) in the minds of most market agents, naked egoism comes to replace adherence to traditional conceptions. Market relations are taken to be abrasive, scouring the human mind until traditional morality and religion are rubbed away. Enormous efficacy is here ascribed to the market in its assumed role as ideological scouring pad. Even if one accepts this causal claim, it is still the case that in order to arrive at an overall assessment of the effects of the market on human character one needs to assess the traditions that are eroded as the market develops, and one needs also to assess the modern forms of belief that have arisen in response to the development of the market. Pending this overall assessment, it would be misleading to describe the abrasive tendency of the market as a tendency to corrupt individual motivation. Whether (1) leads to corruption depends in part on whether (2) is true. Hence Marx's complaints against the market on this score reduce to the complaint to be discussed below, that the market fosters egoism. It should be noted that although Marx here appears to affirm (some of) the values that the market erodes, at times he affirms the erosion. For example, the *Communist Manifesto* is almost jaunty in tone in a passage that praises the market's supposed elimination of ersatz community relations, pseudo-morality, and religious superstition.[5] The polemical rhetoric of the *Manifesto* here suggests agreement with the *1844 Manuscripts'* claim that the market brings about the disappearance of all morality, but other writings of Marx change 'all' to a more sensible 'some.'

Moreover, in other writings Marx shows himself cognizant of the fact that market relations do not carry egoism alone in their train.[6] There are market norms which are functional to the system and in relation to which individual economic agents are not at all encouraged to be cynical or subversive. One thinks of the norm of honesty in the keeping of contracts, or prohibitions against fraud. In his later work, Marx presumes that individuals in their economic activity are often motivated by a sense of class solidarity, and whether the spirit of class solidarity is applauded or deplored, it certainly is not reducible to 'naked egoism' or narrow self-interest. The *Manuscripts* commentary here reproduced is sentimental in sidestepping these complex issues with the simple claim that the market corrupts the virtuous, transforms fidelity into infidelity, love into hate, hate into love, etc.

---

5 Karl Marx and Frederick Engels, 'Manifesto of the Communist Party,' in *Collected Works*, vol. 6, 486-7

6 For evidence that Marx observes that capitalism tends to erode some but not all traditional moral conceptions, see *Capital*, vol. 1, tr. by Samuel Moore and Edward Aveling (Modern Library Edition) 91-2. See also the 'Manifesto,' 504.

Richard J. Arneson

A related thread in Marx's discussion appears to be a confusion. Marx claims, 'By possessing the property of buying everything, by possessing the property of appropriating all objects, money is thus the object of eminent possession. The universality of its property is the omnipotence of its being' (323; 563). Although I hesitate to force a determinate interpretation on this passage, it does seem that Marx is confusing the idea that money serves as a universal medium of exchange with the very different idea that money comes to be desired by everybody more than any other value.

A third strand distinguishable in the passage quoted three paragraphs back is the thought that market relations increase the motivation of individuals to purchase the semblance of emotions, virtues, character traits, and other items which are as a matter of logic unpurchaseable. I cannot purchase bravery because possession of this virtue requires performance of brave acts. I cannot pay someone to have affection for me because if affection is not forthcoming in the absence of money payment, whatever is tendered in view of the prospect of money gain cannot count as affection. What is Marx thinking of when he refers contemptuously to the purchase of bravery? He may have in mind a scenario in which I am cowardly but shield myself from the effects of cowardice by hiring brave soldiers to fight in my stead. The example then makes the same points, and is subject to the same criticisms, as the lameness example discussed above under 'Individuality.' It would be a mistake for me to pride myself on my bravery in virtue of the valor exhibited by substitutes I have hired, but this mistake can hardly be ascribed to the influence of market relations. (Compare a lord who preens himself on the exploits of his knights.)Perhaps Marx has in mind a false pretense. Imagine that bravery medals are awarded to those judged especially deserving, and I surreptitiously purchase a bravery medal from a recipient and parade it as my own. The evil here would seem to be dissembling, and what makes it possible is not the development of complex market relations but the presence of conventional external marks of virtue (or vice – a person who felt burdened by chastity could induce Hester Prynne to relinquish her scarlet letter in trade). A market form of society perhaps offers more opportunities for this sort of dissembling than earlier forms of society, though this might be doubted, but if so this is probably due to the enlarged scale of social relations rather than to their market character. Perhaps it is easier to lie successfully about one's accomplishments in a city than in a small village where one's life history is common knowledge. None of these elaborations of Marx's comment gives an initially plausible construction of his meaning.

Perhaps it is worth mentioning that it is not obvious that, for example, monetary compensation schemes erode the capacity for discrimination of non-market values. The thief who proposes to make restitution to his victim need not be under the illusion that he is transforming crime into non-crime. (By calling his compensation 'restitution' he affirms a moral judgment on his thieving activity.)

*Lessening of Care for Others.* With characteristic energy of assertion Marx comments, 'Money is the *procurer* between man's need and the object, between his life and his means of life. But *that which* mediates *my* life for me, also *mediates* the existence of other people for me. For me it is the *other* person' (323; 563). Here there is a suggestion that money is distracting in human relationships: a person comes to concentrate his attention not on his fellow trader but on the dollar gain he hopes to realize from the transaction. Of course trade will not occur if one party has an altruistic concern for the other party to the trade; the one will simply give to the other.[7] The occurrence of trade does not, however, preclude that the traders are altruistically motivated; each might be seeking the good of some person or cause not involved in the trade. A society that tolerates exchange relations tolerates the possibility that the parties to any given exchange will be motivated solely by narrow self-interest. Some of Marx's broadside attacks on property attack this toleration.[8] Whatever quantum of selfishness exists at a particular moment of time, allowing exchange relations permits this selfishness to show itself in behavior. Some passages, including that quoted in this paragraph, raise the more interesting issue whether in time the social toleration of trade will cause an increase in the extent and intensity of selfishness. This way of putting the question suggests that the baseline for comparison is whatever degree of selfishness accompanies pre-market institutions of varying kinds, but one could also ask whether market institutions raise the level of human selfishness above what it would be in some feasible set of ideal institutions, a cooperative commonwealth, or whatnot.

Given the great difficulty of gaining direct empirical evidence that has a clear bearing on these comparisons, we are in need of some relatively a priori argument: that is, an argument that locates a feature of market institutions that, in the light of our general knowledge, we can

---

7  That is, except in special circumstances, as when one judges that a gift here and now will not conduce to the long-run well-being of the recipient. On the slack between profits and selfish conduct, see Antony Flew, 'The Profit Motive,' *Ethics,* **86** (1975-76).

8  The clearest expression of this broadside attack occurs in 'On the Jewish Question.' Cf. John Plamenatz, *Karl Marx's Philosophy of Man* (Oxford: Clarendon Press 1975) 120-2.

reasonably judge to be likely to give rise to a tendency to promote the disposition to selfish conduct. In the *Manuscripts,* at any rate, I do not see that Marx has identified any such argument, that goes beyond the bare claim, variously reiterated, that the market does indeed have this unfortunate tendency. Still, there may be an argument Marx failed to notice.

## II

Against the image of a market economy as an engine of selfishness, we must set the picture of the market mechanism as a neutral transmission belt for whatever nonaggressive demands people want to make of one another.[9]

Consider the market in child-care services.[10] Assume that parents prefer to hire as babysitters persons who are genuinely affectionate toward children. Babysitters anxious to maximize their wages cannot by a single act of will produce affectionate dispositions upon demand. If we further assume — as is realistic — that the opportunities for feigning a liking for children are so slight that they can be ignored, the situation then is that babysitters affectionately disposed toward children will tend to do better on the child-care market than their less kindly competitors. Now consider the rational strategy for a pre-teenager calculating how best to maximize his income from babysitting over the term of his adolescence, given market conditions. Assuming that one can choose to act so as to alter one's disposition over a period of time, and assuming that this disposition-altering behavior is not costly in comparison with its expected gain, we can predict that the pre-teenager's best strategy is to work to change his disposition so that he becomes, at the least, less irritable and nasty in the presence of children. (Once he succeeds in this endeavor, he will no longer be a profit-maximizing egoist, if he was that initially.) In this example the tendency of market relations is to motivate persons to develop unselfish dispositions, in order to succeed as market

---

9 'Compare the manner in which the market is neutral among persons' desires, as it reflects and transmits widely scattered information via prices, and coordinates persons' activities.' Robert Nozick, *Anarchy, State, and Utopia* (New York: Basic Books 1974) 164-5

10 This example is borrowed from Thomas Nagel, 'Comment,' in *Altruism, Morality, and Economic Theory,* ed. by E.S. Phelps (New York: Russell Sage Foundation 1975) 66.

competitors. As Thomas Nagel observes, 'It seems likely that some motive broader than strict self-interest is part of what is being paid for when someone is hired to perform almost any service or task — not only the tasks which consist primarily of taking care of people.'[11]

Perhaps it is fanciful to imagine the pre-teenager self-consciously choosing a strategy to guide him through several years, but the point holds without the fancy: without conscious deliberation people can induce character changes in themselves that are in fact strategic and can be rationalized as such. It is broadly true that people display some tendency to shape themselves into character types that are appropriate to the social roles they have selected. The ubiquitous role of market agent consists in ministering to the desires of other market agents, including their desires regarding the character types they prefer to encounter in their trading.

Beyond babysitting, one could easily construct parallel examples more directly germane to Marx's worries. The point of the examples would be to rebut Marx's claim that inherent in the market mechanism is a tendency to foster unattractive character traits, especially selfishness. If we stipulate the truth of empirical assumptions that do not affect the defining or essential features of a market, we can show instances in which the market will have a propensity to foster attractive character traits. Of course there are countertendencies. Babysitters who are fiercely aggressive self-promoters will also succeed on the child-care market, ceteris paribus. Business agents who nurture in themselves a capacity to notice spectacularly lucrative opportunities and to do whatever is necessary — however morally odious — to make best use of those opportunities will succeed in market competition, ceteris paribus. But now the consequences of the market on character formation can be seen to depend not on its supposed inherent or essential dynamic but on various contingencies crucial among which are the expectations and desires of those with whom one engages in market activity. The picture of the market as a neutral mechanism would appear to be vindicated.

## III

The appearance of market neutrality in relation to human desires is illusory across a certain range of desires. Consider the desire, shared by many people, that Lake Superior be kept free of pollutants. Suppose

---

11   Ibid.

that at present three taconite plants line the shores of the lake and dump pollutants into it. It is technically feasible to screen pollutants from the waste discharge, but the screen costs money. Other things equal, if one taconite plant screens its discharge while its competitors do not, it must sell its ore at a higher price and can be expected to go under in competition. — As so far presented, the example abstracts from the desires of taconite industry stockholders, employees, and customers to keep Lake Superior free of pollution. If these desires are sufficiently strong, people will modify their trading behavior to favor non-polluting firms. Once again the market appears to be neutral — a transparent medium that takes its coloration from the desires of people in contact with it.

However, the desire that Lake Superior be pollution-free is a public good with respect to the people who share this desire. With respect to a given group of persons, a good is *public* to the degree that it is characterized by jointness of supply, i.e. one person's consumption of the good does not leave any the less available for others, and non-excludability, i.e. it is unfeasible to exclude any person from consuming the good if others are consuming it. With respect to the children attending a birthday party, the quality of the singing of the 'Happy Birthday' anthem can serve as an example of a public good, while the birthday cake is paradigmatically a private or nonpublic good. A clean Lake Superior is more akin to the singing than to the cake. Cooperation among many persons, each interested in a clean Lake Superior, must occur if boycott activities are to succeed. These persons all have other interests some of which suffer the more the Lake Superior interest is pursued. Each person in the multitude of potential boycotters can reasonably surmise that his participation in the boycott is extremely unlikely to make the difference between its success or failure. The boycott will succeed or fail, each correctly thinks, depending on what others do. In this situation, under familiar assumptions, familiar reasoning[12] leads to the conclusion that voluntary schemes of cooperation to supply the public good in question will be highly fragile, liable to collapse. This resistance of public goods to voluntary or market supply generates an argument for coercive provision of the good and compulsory exaction of dues from all beneficiaries to pay for this provision.

So much is agreed. But one might wonder what any of this has to do with character formation. After all, governments routinely enforce schemes for supplying valued public goods from national defense to

---

12 See Mancur Olson, *The Logic of Collective Action* (Cambridge: Harvard University Press 1961) ch. I. See also my 'The Principle of Fairness and Free Rider Problems,' *Ethics*, **92** (1982) 616-33.

lighthouses to lampposts to elementary education to mosquito control.[13] It is on the face of it doubtful that these quotidian government activities do much to improve the moral character of the citizens who benefit from these state activities. Why should we expect that an institutional arrangement that requires individuals to pay dues to finance some public goods should have any discernible effect at all on people's underlying dispositions? Why is it not simply a matter of people seeking their own good (which need not be fixated narrowly on the self) as best they can under changing circumstances?

Some things we desire as means to satisfy further desires, and some things we desire for their own sakes. Very roughly overlapping this distinction is another: between desires that change quickly with changing circumstances and desires that in the short run are stable in the face of changing circumstances. We are wondering if state activity to secure public goods can be expected to alter non-instrumental, relatively fixed long-term desires.

One can be overly hasty in dismissing the possible good effects on character of the perception that public goods that are important to our well-being are being provided in a manner that is judged to be equitable and efficient. A respectable administration of routine may have subterranean and diffuse effects in increasing citizens' propensity to subordinate private interest to the common good in humble matters. But for the sake of argument we concede that no very dramatic steps toward human perfection are likely to be taken in this way.

To cut closer to the matter at issue, let us distinguish between egoistic and altruistic public goods, as follows: a purely egoistic public good is one that is desired by an individual only in virtue of the gain to himself that he expects from provision of the public good. A purely altruistic public good is one that is desired by an individual only in virtue of the gain to persons other than himself that he expects will follow upon provision of the good. National defense is an egoistic public good for an individual who cares only about the security of his own life and property; altruistic for an individual who cares only for the lives and property of others. A given public good can be egoistic for some persons and altruistic for others, and for a single individual mixed motives are pretty clearly possible. With this background we can state an empirical hypothesis: the provision of altruistic public goods by means of schemes that are judged reasonably fair and efficient by those affected, will tend to foster altruism within the group. Further: when failure to institute a

---

13   The last three items on this list are only partially public goods. Spraying insecticide to control mosquitoes in a given neighborhood, for example, will also diminish, to some degree, the mosquito population in adjoining neighborhoods.

Richard J. Arneson

plan for securing some valued altruistic public good results in its non-availability, altruism within the affected group will tend to diminish.

The idea here is quite simply that the satisfaction of a desire prompts its continuance and the proliferation of allied desires, while repeated frustration of a desire over time will motivate an individual to relinquish the desire if he can.[14] Supply affects demand. The fable of the fox and the grapes illustrates the point. Being unable to get the grapes he wants, the fox would prefer not to want the grapes, and his 'sour grapes' mutterings are a reasonable first step toward divesting himself of the unwanted desire. If the market offers a set of levers that work well to satisfy some desires but not others, the market nurtures the desires it fulfills and dampens the desires it frustrates. The stereotype of the market as a neutral transmission belt is inaccurate, as well as hackneyed.


## IV


The argument above presumes that provision of altruistic public goods will foster altruism. Is there any factual warrant for this claim?

Something akin to this empirical hypothesis seems to be entertained by the late Richard Titmuss in *The Gift Relationship,* a study of the supply of blood for transfusions in Britain and the U.S. In that work Titmuss asserts that the existence in Britain of a National Health Service, funded by compulsory taxation, and supplying free health care to all Britons without discriminating on any basis except need for health care, fosters a sense of community solidarity and a disposition to altruism as manifested in the success of the voluntary blood donation program that is administered in conjunction with the National Health Service. Titmuss's argument is complicated by his insistence on another claim, also pertinent to the broad issue of the influence of the market on human character formation. Titmuss asserts that the existence of a market in blood reduces the propensity of potential blood suppliers to donate blood voluntarily and freely, from altruistic motives. More generally, Titmuss seems to suspect that the intrusion of commercial relations into any part of the medical care system will reduce the incidence of altruistic conduct in this domain. As he says, 'Altruistic donors cannot be

---

14 See Gilbert Harman, 'Practical Reasoning,' *The Review of Metaphysics,* **29** (1975-76) 460-3.

expected to give their blood to profit-making hospitals.'[15] More specifically, Titmuss states that in comparing commercial provision of blood for medical use with reliance on the altruism of voluntary unpaid donors, commercial supply does badly on four testable criteria: (1) the cost per unit of blood delivered to the patient is five to fifteen times as high when commercially supplied blood is used than in the English voluntary system, (2) commercial blood is 'administratively inefficient,' (3) wastage of blood and erratic matching of supply and demand afflict commercial supply, and (4) most spectacularly, the quality of blood commercially supplied, as measured by the risk of post-transfusion hepatitis, is much worse that the quality of blood supplied through voluntary unpaid donation.

Since Titmuss's study was prepared, based mainly on fragmentary data gathered in the 1960's, the application of advances in medical technology has made possible some lessening of the risk of contracting disease through blood transfusion, but to date the residue of problems is formidable.[16] Hence another look at Titmuss's reasoning seems warranted. Our discussion of Titmuss will attempt to show that while his study promises some confirmation of Marx's glowering suspicion of commerce, it actually shows how difficult and tricky is the task of establishing cause-and-effect relationships in this area. Further, Titmuss's study provides some confirmation of the claim that the conflations and errors that plagued Marx's discussion still crop up in contemporary debate on this topic.

As a preliminary it will be helpful to sketch Titmuss's strong prima facie case against commercially marketed blood. In England and Wales, according to evidence assembled by Titmuss, virtually all blood for transfusion is obtained from voluntary unpaid donors and is distributed by the National Health Service at no charge, according to patients' needs. In the U.S.A., by contrast, Titmuss calculates that in the 1960's only about nine per cent of blood donations were voluntary and unpaid, roughly a third was supplied by donors who were paid for their contribution, and most of the remainder was given on a quid pro quo or barter basis.[17] A serious and debilitating disease, hepatitis, in its more

---

15 Richard M. Titmuss, *The Gift Relationship — From Human Blood to Social Policy* (New York: Pantheon Books 1971) 151. (The four numbered points below are taken from p. 246.)

16 See Raymond S. Koff, *Viral Hepatitis* (New York: John Wiley and Sons 1978) chs. 1-4, 8, 9.

17 Titmuss, chs. 6 and 7. These figures refer only to donation of whole blood and do not include donation of blood components.

virulent form is spread largely from transfusion of blood contaminated with hepatitis virus. While in England and Wales less than one per cent of units of blood for transfusion prove to be hepatitis carriers, (and one study shows an almost-nil incidence of post-transfusion hepatitis), in the U.S.A. three or four per cent of the units of blood supplied during the term of Titmuss's study were hepatitis carriers. There is clear evidence that commercially supplied blood, drawn from Skid Row and derelict populations, together with blood obtained from prison inmates in exchange for implicit assurances of early parole, is responsible for the increased risk of hepatitis (and other diseases of lesser incidence) that is borne by American consumers of blood.[18] Since there is no completely reliable and efficient test for checking blood to determine the presence of hepatitis, blood-gathering agencies must rely on the truthfulness of donors in reporting their medical histories, and paid donors have an incentive to conceal their medical history that is lacking in voluntary unpaid donors.

Titmuss asserts that the cause of these observable and terrible disparities between the English and American blood supply systems is the circumstance that in England blood is supplied only by voluntary unpaid donors while the U.S. permits a commercial traffic in blood. Or rather, in Titmuss's view the cause is this circumstance coupled with the fact that in England blood donations are distributed through the socialized National Health Service, while in the U.S. medical-care system commercial relations are increasingly prevalent.

From comparisons like those Titmuss adduces it would be hard to establish anything very definitive about causal relations. A striking contrast is observed between two countries that differ in myriad respects that could explain the contrast. One tells a story in which one of these differences is singled out as the cause of the contrast, but other stories can be told.[19] Let us concentrate on the two claims: (a) that the ongoing operation of a workable scheme for supplying all Britons equal access to medical care fosters altruism in those affected by the scheme, and (b)

18  Titmuss, 146-9. See also T.C. Chalmers, 'Carrier Blood Donors,' in *Hepatitis and Blood Transfusion*, ed. by Girish Vyas, Herbert Perkins, and Rudi Schmid (New York and London: Grune and Stratton 1972) 277 ff. For qualifications and hedges see ch. 2 of *Hepatitis from Blood Transfusions: Evaluation of Methods to Reduce the Problem, Report to the Congress* by the Comptroller General of the United States, 1976.

19  This point is made by Kenneth Arrow, 'Gifts and Exchanges,' *Philosophy and Public Affairs*, **1** (1971-72), reprinted in *Altruism, Morality, and Economic Theory*, 13-28. Further references are to the reprinted paper. Also, Robert M. Solow, 'Blood and Thunder,' *Yale Law Journal*, **80** (1970-71) 1704-5.

that the existence of a commerical market in blood lessens altruism among potential blood donors.

Some untangling is necessary prior to assessing (a). Although Titmuss does not talk in terms of altruistic public goods, he does not mention any other link between public policy and individual motivation, so I think his proposal can be elaborated in my terminology. An initial difficulty then is to ascertain whether the British National Health Service qualifies as an altruistic or predominantly altruistic public good. The official government rationale for a policy need not correspond closely with individual citizen desires regarding it. Some might favor socialized medicine after calculating that this program best advances their personal advantage. Some citizens might be hostile to socialized medicine. Obviously desires are disparate and any simple assumption will involve some regimenting of the variety of individual response. Clearly, however, the provision of medical care to all citizens is a public good for all who desire that medical care be available to all. It is not implausible to suppose that a large element of impersonal caring for others enters into such a desire. One further possibility is worth mention: supplying a good of a certain type may eventually bring it about that the person to whom the good is supplied develops a desire for a good of that type. This suggests another version of the fox-and-grapes fable: some forest deity arranges matters so that grapes can always be had without fuss, and although initially the fox has no taste for grapes, their availability induces him to sample and eventually to like them.

Setting aside doubt, let us assume that the National Health Service does supply an altruistic public good to all Britons. What evidence would show that this situation promotes altruism? One bit of evidence would be the greater willingness of citizens living under socialized medicine to make voluntary unpaid donations of blood, compared with the willingness to give of citizens living under commercial medicine. Titmuss's figures do indicate that in proportion to population, more English make voluntary unpaid contributions of blood than do Americans. But this is hardly probative, given that (to name one alternative explanation) socialized medicine in England might be the effect rather than the cause of the disposition to share. A related claim urged by Titmuss is that in England voluntary unpaid donations of blood keep pace with demand, whereas in the U.S. the supply of blood from commercial and noncommercial sources lags behind demand.[20] How this claim is supposed to implicate the market as cause of the lag, is not clear. In any case, the claim itself seems to emerge from a misreading of what is known about

---

20   Titmuss, ch. 4. See comments by Arrow, 23-4.

the comparative demand for blood, according to one commentator: 'Titmuss seems to have missed a fundamental difference between British and American medical practise. In England, an order by a physician for a blood transfusion is usually conditional on the availability of the blood; In the United States, this is not so...'[21]

Although the evidence one way or another is scanty, let us suppose it is true as well as plausible that the provision of the altruistic public good of free medical care for all fosters altruism. So far as I can see, this supplies no grounds at all for claim (b), that the spread of market or commercial relations in medicine diminishes altruism. Titmuss's discussion tend to merge these claims, but their distinctness is evident when one thinks of non-medical examples: one might believe an equitable and efficient provision of national defense will enhance community solidarity while denying that the existence of markets supplying private items of security such as locks and bolts will tend to diminish community solidarity. Outlawing a market in locks and bolts will likely increase people's jitteriness, not their communitarian feelings.

Titmuss draws a broad distinction between 'universalist' bureaucratically administered public service and the market, and roundly declares the superiority of the former in terms of promoting justice and welfare. Titmuss is quite emphatic in his insistence that an all-or-nothing choice must be made for socialized or commercial medicine. This emphasis is reminiscent of Marx's insistence that what might seem to be distinguishable effects of distinguishable elements in a market system are really parts of one all-embracing social phenomenon, a totality that demands acceptance or rejection as a whole. I'm not sure why Titmuss does not go whole hog here, with Marx. Titmuss evidently believes that one can create an altruistic mentality in the field of medical care while the rest of the economy is organized on a profit basis. But if a commercial blood bank will taint the disposition to altruistic conduct on which voluntary blood banks rely, why won't avaricious traffic in beans or beefsteak have a similar contaminating effect? Or to put it another way, if one believes an altruistic sector of the economy can be insulated from the commercial remainder, why not believe a commercial sub-sector of this sector can exist without draining away the altruism from the rest of the sector?[22]

---

21  D. MacN. Surgenor, 'Human Blood and the Renewal of Altruism,' *International Journal of Health Services*, **2** (1972) 444

22  Some passages in Titmuss (pp. 13, 198, 213, 223) suggest another construal of his argument, namely, that if a market in blood is allowed there will be no sanctuary anywhere for non-commercial relations. See also Solow, p. 1703, especially the footnote.

Titmuss does suggest a hypothesis that if true would seem straightforwardly to confirm the view that permitting a market in blood services diminishes the disposition to altruism. The hypothesis is that if a commercial system of blood-gathering exists alongside the voluntary unpaid system, fewer voluntary unpaid donations will be forthcoming than would be the case if the voluntary system stood alone. Supposing for the sake of argument that this hypothesis proves true, we note that this fact would admit of various elaborations and interpretations:

(1) Some of the persons who gave freely under the voluntary-only system would have preferred to sell their blood had that been permitted. When this option is made available, they exercise it. Here it looks as though the addition of a commercial system does not alter people's motivations but simply allows some to satisfy a first preference hitherto beyond reach. On this interpretation, no support is given to the thesis that suppression of market relations improves people's character. Moreover, the argument against commerce in blood will now hinge entirely on the allegedly bad consequences of commerce other than its allegedly bad impact on character.

The idea that permitting market relations enables existing preferences to express themselves and does not alter what is expressed is susceptible to challenge. In the long run, one might argue, allowing or disallowing a person's first preference to be satisfied may be expected to influence preference. Satisfied preferences will sustain themselves; frustrated preferences will wither.

Quite obviously it must be only within a sharply limited range that human desires are malleable in this fashion, or sumptuary legislation would never collapse against stable decadent wants. I propose a very simple distinction between two kind of situations in which individuals are denied the freedom to do what they want. In the first case, we restrict A's freedom to satisfy a given desire for what are recognized by A to be independent and compelling reasons that have nothing to do with any project of improving A's desires (which project might arouse A's suspicion). In the second case, we restrict A's freedom to satisfy a given desire precisely in order to effect a decrease in that desire. Directly coercive attempts to alter a person's desires are much more likely to encounter resistance and give rise to unpredictable effects. We anticipate that A will bridle at direct attempts to manipulate the formation of his desires.

(2) When the commercial system opens and some persons make use of the new opportunity to profit from the sale of their blood, some of those who have been voluntary unpaid donors may now feel themselves to be 'suckers.' Why should they give for free while others are making money? If this question continues to nag, a person may stop his charitable contributions.

_Richard J. Arneson_

However, recall that under the supplanted voluntary-only system, only a minority of those eligible to donate do donate. The person who gives blood can compare his situation with that of any eligible counterpart who devotes the time he could have spent giving blood to personal enjoyment or profit-making instead. In the English system, both giver and non-giver are equally eligible to receive blood transfusions. The voluntary unpaid donor who feels himself a sucker later, in relation to paid donors, by parity of reasoning ought to experience himself as sucker earlier, in relation to those who could give but do not and still enjoy the benefits of a free blood supply. Given that people think through the situation in full clarity, it is hard to see why — apart from an ideological or superstitious aversion to commerce in blood as such — someone who is willing freely to give his blood when the majority of his fellow citizens are unwilling, will become resentful and unwilling to give after a commercial blood-gathering system is opened and some persons make money from the sale of their own blood.

Kenneth Arrow mentions a consideration that is pertinent here, and strengthens the above line of thought. Commercial donors according to report are clustered at the bottom end of the income distribution scale. Why should an affluent voluntary donor of blood resent the fact that a poorer person who needs the money more than he is being paid for the same contribution of blood?

(3) Peter Singer tells another story designed to explain how the addition of the opportunity to sell blood could decrease people's disposition to give freely.[23] Quoting from questionnaires distributed by Titmuss and his associates that asked blood donors why they choose to give, Singer stresses the sense of interdependence that is generated by an all-voluntary system. Since under such a system no amount of money enables a person to purchase blood, those who need blood must rely on the charity of others. Blood will be available only if sufficient numbers of people are steadily generous. Whereas if commercial blood is available for sale, it no longer is true that we are dependent on one another's charity. Singer concludes, 'So commerce replaces fellow feeling.'[24] (Interestingly, to support this conclusion he cites passages from Marx, including some I have examined.)

The line of reasoning here ascribed to blood donors strikes me as odd or mysterious. Suppose that a previously all-voluntary system is altered by the addition of a commercial supply of blood and by the pro-

23 Peter Singer, 'Altruism and Commerce,' _Philosophy and Public Affairs_, **2** (1972-73) 315-18

24 Singer, 316

228

viso that blood will now be available gratis only to those who cannot afford payment. Or perhaps a sliding scale of payment according to means is adopted. Or perhaps the free blood program and the commercial system operate side-by-side, with no restrictions as to eligibility for the available free blood, but it is generally known that poor people must have cheap blood freely donated if they are to have any. In any of these circumstances the poor at least are still dependent on charity. How are we supposed to construe the motivation of those who were willing to give under an all-voluntary system, but are unwilling to give now on the ground that it is no longer the case that each person is dependent upon the altruism of others? How is the circumstance that the affluent are no longer so dependent on the good will of others supposed to operate as a dampener of altruism? The only answer I can think of, that preserves the coherence of Singer's supposition, is that individuals whose willingness to give now lessens were motivated by a sense of gratitude to the affluent, a need for community with the rich, or perhaps the desire to give a gift to the 'man who has everything.' These motives strike me as unintuitively odd — and empirically doubtful.

The argument above depends on the prevalence of substantial inequalities in the distribution of wealth. In still another respect Singer's 'interdependence' surmise seems odd. This oddity does not depend on any assumptions about the distribution of wealth or income. We can distinguish between two sorts of interdependence: natural and artificial. Natural interdependence is brought about by natural forces that are beyond human power to control, as when a sudden storm causes an airliner to crash in the mountains and all must cooperate under harsh conditions if anybody is to have a chance of survival. Certain man-made catastrophes can create situations akin to natural interdependence, as long as there is an identifiable group of people affected by the catastrophe and bearing no responsibility for its occurrence. It is a plausible surmise that natural interdependence engenders a blurring of the line between care for self and care for others and a consequent expansion of care for others. In contrast, artificial interdependence is deliberately created by human agents that are felt to be in some sense responsible to those who are rendered interdependent. Where some individuals are creating interdependence among others, it is naive to expect that individuals placed in this predicament will treat their placing as beyond critical scrutiny, like the action of a hurricane. Artificial interdependence fostered by government in many situations will promote not a spirit of *Gemeinschaft* but popular resentment of government artifice. The blood-supply situation that Singer and Titmuss depict is one of artificial interdependence in the sense just noted.

I have given reasons to doubt that initiating a commercial system of blood-gathering alongside an established system of voluntary unpaid

Richard J. Arneson

donations would decrease people's motivation to give even if an initial drop in the number of unpaid contributions was observed. The view that the commercial spirit once unleashed will drive out altruism upon examination relies on one or another ascription of empirically unfounded and bizarre motives to blood donors.

Beyond the squelching of altruism, Titmuss ascribes assorted other evils to the spread of commerce in the field of medical care. Of these the most spectacular, and the most intimately linked to worries about character formation, is the finding that blood drawn from commercial sources, rather than from voluntary unpaid donors, is much more likely to carry the disease of hepatitis to the recipients of blood transfusions. From this startling fact Titmuss infers that 'Freedom from disability is inseparable from altruism.'[25] More careful reasoning would conclude that freedom from disability is correlated with socio-economic status. Titmuss's indictment of rampant commercialism in medicine recalls Marx's failure clearly to distinguish between the effects of market relations and the effects of inequality in the distribution of market resources. Although commercial blood is more likely to be contaminated than voluntary unpaid blood, some commercial blood is of better quality than some non-commercial blood. For years the Mayo Clinic achieved low rates of post-transfusion hepatitis by drawing the bulk of its blood for transfusion from paid donors dwelling in rural Minnesota where hepatitis rates are low.[26] Studies have shown that the factor that correlates most reliably with risk of post-transfusion hepatitis is low socio-economic status of the blood donor. Hepatitis rates are high in conditions of poverty and urban squalor, and particularly among children many cases are thought to be sub-clinical — that is, suffered without a visit to the doctor that identifies the malady for the patient. Having had hepatitis, one can become a chronic lifelong carrier.[27] So blood drawn from poor people is likely to be poor blood quite apart from any consideration that the incentive of cash payment induces potential donors to conceal a history of hepatitis. Moreover, narcotics usage involving unsterilized needles makes one an extremely risky blood donor.[28]

25 Titmuss, 246

26 Reuben A. Kessel, 'Transfused Blood, Serum Hepatitis, and the Coase Theorem,' *The Journal of Law and Economics*, **17** (1974) 272-3 and the references cited there.

27 Yvonne E. Cossart, *Viral Hepatitis and its Control* (London: Baillière Tindall 1977) ch. 9. See also *Report to the Congress*, 18-20.

28 Koff, 112-15; Cossart, ch. 20; *Report to the Congress*, 20-1

Within the Skid Row and prison populations that supply the overwhelming bulk of dangerous, low-quality blood, it may be that a Skid Row desperation about life's prospects contributes to a mentality that is willing to impose serious risk of grievous harm on others in order to gain for oneself a modest cash payment. Such desperado reasoning is the product of a culture of extreme poverty, and it is misleading to the point of absurdity to identify this phenomenon, as Titmuss does, with a generalized culture of commerce or with the 'laws of the marketplace.' One way of putting the point is to note that no studies of the etiology of hepatitis give any reason to suspect that in a market economy with redistribution programs operating effectively to maintain equality of income and wealth, and with slums eliminated, there would be any reason to fear blood drawn from persons who are paid some compensation for this service.

Moreover to speak at the present time of a market in blood services is something of a misnomer, given the fact that people facing blood transfusion have little choice as to the quality of blood they will receive. It has been noted that hospital patients 'are more likely to be offered choices in room accommodations than in the quality of blood transfused.'[29] If consumer sovereignty reigned here, and if knowledge of the cost of hepatitis and of the increased risk from low-quality blood were prevalent, consumers would eschew Skid Row blood and pay higher prices for better blood. In this regard the problem would appear to be too little commercialization rather than too much.

The prospect of a fully articulated market in blood services has called to at least one observer's mind the grisly spectacle of affluent people purchasing the best-quality blood for transfusion while low-income persons must make do with such low-quality blood as they can afford.[30] This spectacle is genuinely unsettling. However, I suggest that the aspect of the matter that is troubling is not that people buy and sell human blood, nor that some people decide to buy better blood than others, but rather that poverty or unequal distribution of resources forces some persons to accept inferior goods that they would avoid if they could. Sermons against commerce, whether preached by Marx or Titmuss, fail to articulate just what features of market society are objectionable.

---

29  Kessel, 272. See also pp. 284-85.

30  Solow, 1706-7

*Richard J. Arneson*

## Select Bibliography

Arneson, Richard J., 'The Principle of Fairness and Free-Rider Problems,' *Ethics,* **92** (1982) 616-33.

Arneson, Richard J., 'Prospects for Community in a Market Economy,' *Political Theory,* **9** (1981) 207-27.

Cohen, G.A., 'Capitalism, Freedom, and the Proletariat,' in *The Idea of Freedom,* edited by Alan Ryan (Oxford: Oxford University Press 1979).

Hampshire, Stuart (editor), *Public and Private Morality* (Cambridge: Cambridge University Press 1978).

McConnell, Terrance C., 'Moral Blackmail,' *Ethics,* **91** (1981) 544-67.

Moore, Stanley, *Marx on the Choice Between Socialism and Communism* (Cambridge MA: Harvard University Press 1980).

Parfit, Derek, 'Later Selves and Moral Principles,' in *Philosophy and Personal Relations,* edited by Alan Montefiore (London 1973)

Schick, Frederic, 'Toward a Logic of Liberalism,' *Journal of Philosophy,* **77** (1980) 80-98.

Sen, Amartya, 'Liberty, Unanimity and Rights,' *Economica,* **43** (1976) 217-45, and the literature on 'Sen's Paradox' therein cited.

Sen, Amartya, 'Rights and Agency,' *Philosophy and Public Affairs,* **11** (1981-82) 3-39.

Stretton, Hugh, *Capitalism, Socialism, and the Environment* (Cambridge: Cambridge University Press 1976).

# NOTES ON CONTRIBUTORS

**Richard J. Arneson** is Associate Professor of Philosophy, University of California at San Diego. He has published recently in *Ethics, Political Theory,* and the *Journal of the History of Philosophy.* His article on 'Mill's Doubts About Freedom Under Socialism' appeared in the *Canadian Journal of Philosophy,* Supp. Vol. V, *New Essays on John Stuart Mill and Utilitarianism,* co-edited by Wesley E. Cooper, Kai Nielsen and Steven C. Patten (Guelph 1979).

**Tom L. Beauchamp** teaches in the Department of Philosophy and at the Kennedy Institute of Ethics, Georgetown University. He is author of *Philosophical Ethics* and co-author of *Hume and the Problem of Causation* and *Principles of Biomedical Ethics.* He previously served as consulting philosopher in ethics for the National Commission for the Protection of Human Subjects of Biomedical and Behavioral Research.

**Arthur L. Caplan** is Associate for the Humanities at the Hastings Center, Institute of Society, Ethics and the Life Sciences. He received his Ph.D. in philosophy from Columbia University. He is the editor of *The Sociobiology Debate* (Harper & Row 1978), and the co-editor of *Concepts of Health and Disease* (Addison-Wesley 1981) and *Ethics in Hard Times* (Plenum 1981). He has written numerous articles on applied ethics and the philosophy of science which have appeared in such journals as *Philosophy of Science, Erkenntnis, Studies in the History and Philosophy of Science, The Hastings Center Report,* and *Ethics.*

**Ruth R. Faden** teaches health services administration, behavioral sciences, and population dynamics in the School of Hygiene and Public Health, and psychology in the Graduate School at The Johns Hopkins University. She is also a Senior Research Scholar at the Kennedy Institute of Ethics, Georgetown University. She is co-editor of *Ethical Issues in Social Science Research.* Professor Faden has published numerous articles on biomedical ethics and has served as consultant to several federal agencies on problems in health care.

**John Kleinig** is Senior Lecturer in Philosophy at Macquarie University, New South Wales, Australia. He has held visiting appointments at The Australian National University (1981) and The University of Arizona (1982). He is the author of *Punishment and Desert* (1973) and *Philosophical Issues in Education* (1982), and is at present completing a book on paternalism.

**Judith Lichtenberg** is Research Associate at the Center for Philosophy and Public Policy, University of Maryland at College Park. She has contributed to *Boundaries: National Autonomy and Its Limits,* edited by Peter G. Brown and Henry Shue.

**A.T. Nuyen** received his M.A. from The University of Queensland (Australia) where he is now Lecturer. His articles on ethics have appeared in *Idealistic Studies, The Journal of Value Inquiry,* and *The Southern Journal of Philosophy.*

**Laurence Thomas,** who is primarily interested in the relevance of psychology to moral theory, is Associate Professor of Philosophy at The University of North Carolina at Chapel Hill. For the 1982-83 academic year, he was awarded a fellowship at the National Humanities Center to begin a book entitled 'A Theory of Moral Character'.

**Mark T. Thornton** is Associate Professor, Department of Philosophy, Victoria College, University of Toronto. Recent publications include 'Making Sense of *Majewski*,' *Criminal Law Quarterly,* 1982. He has also contributed to *Analysis, Dialogue, The Monist,* and *Philosophical Quarterly.*

**Paul Woodruff** is Associate Professor of Philosophy at The University of Texas at Austin. He has published articles in *Analysis, Phronesis, Philosophy and Literature,* and the *Canadian Journal of Philosophy.* He is the author of *Plato: Hippias Major* (1982). His duties as a captain in the U.S. Army in Vietnam included the occasional command of helicopter missions.

**James Woodward** is Assistant Professor of Philosophy at Memphis State University. His interests include ethics and philosophy of science. Recent publications have appeared in *The British Journal for the Philosophy of Science, Philosophy of Science,* and *Philosophical Studies.*

**Robert Young** is a Reader in Philosophy at La Trobe University, Victoria, Australia. He is the author of *Freedom, Responsibility and God* as well as various papers in ethics, social and political philosophy, metaphysics and the philosophy of religion.

# PREVIOUS SUPPLEMENTARY VOLUMES
## Issued By
# THE CANADIAN JOURNAL OF PHILOSOPHY

| Supplementary Volume | Canada* | Outside Canada* |
|---|---|---|
| Vol. I (1975) | | |
| New Essays in the History of Philosophy (107 pp) | CDN 10.00 | US 10.00 |
| New Essays in the Philosophy of Mind (128 pp) | CDN 10.00 | US 10.00 |
| Vol. II (1976) | | |
| New Essays in Plato and the Pre-Socratics (180 pp) | CDN 13.00 | US 13.00 |
| Vol. III (1977) | | |
| New Essays in Contract Theory (178 pp) | CDN 13.00 | US 13.00 |
| Vol. IV (1978) | | |
| New Essays in Rationalism and Empiricism (218 pp) | CDN 13.00 | US 13.00 |
| Vol. V (1979) | | |
| New Essays on Mill and Utilitarianism (249 pp) | CDN 13.00 | US 13.00 |
| Vol. VI (1980) | | |
| New Essays in Philosophy of Language (223 pp) | CDN 13.00 | US 13.00 |
| Vol. VII (1981) | | |
| Marx and Morality (379 pp) | CDN 15.00 | US 15.00 |
| Vol. VIII (1982) | | |
| New Essays in Ethics and Public Policy (233 pp) | CDN 14.00 | US 13.00 |

*(prices include postage)

------------------------------------------------------------

## ORDER FORM

NAME _____

ADDRESS _____

CITY _____ PROVINCE/STATE _____

POSTAL/ZIP CODE _____

SUBSCRIPTION _____ $           .

SUPPLEMENTARY VOLUMES _____ $           .

_____ $           .

TOTAL           _____

$           .

Orders may be addressed to The University of Calgary Press, The University of Calgary, 2500 University Drive N.W., Calgary, Alberta, Canada, T2N 1N4. Payment by cheque or money order, payable to THE UNIVERSITY OF CALGARY PRESS.

Prices are as of November 1982 and are subject to change without notice.

PREVIOUS SUPPLEMENTARY VOLUMES

Issued by

THE CANADIAN JOURNAL OF PHILOSOPHY